GERMAN INFANTRYMAN

The German soldier 1939–45

COVER IMAGE: The German infantry squad was built around the machine gun. Here, an NCO (at left carrying an MP38/40 (note his magazine pouches, binoculars and Tresse on collar) is seen with his squad in June 1941 a few days before the opening of Operation Barbarossa: the invasion of Russia. Next to him the machine gunner carries an MG34 over his shoulder (note the rectangular accessories pouch on his belt) and the two other men carry boxes of ammunition. A rectangular gas cape pouch hangs round the neck of all four men. *(Bundesarchiv bild 146-1991-077-20)*

First published in September 2018

A catalogue record for this book is available from the British Library.

ISBN 978 1 78521 168 3

Library of Congress control no. 2018935489

Published by Haynes Publishing,
Sparkford, Yeovil,
Somerset BA22 7JJ, UK.
Tel: 01963 440635
Int. tel: +44 1963 440635
Website: www.haynes.com

Haynes North America Inc.,
859 Lawrence Drive, Newbury Park,
California 91320, USA.

Printed in Malaysia.

Senior Commissioning Editor: Jonathan Falconer
Copy editor: Michelle Tilling
Proof reader: Penny Housden
Indexer: Peter Nicholson
Page design: James Robertson

GERMAN INFANTRYMAN

The German soldier 1939–45

Operations Manual

An insight into the uniform, equipment, weaponry and lifestyle of the German Second World War soldier

Simon Forty

INFANTERIE

ÜBER ALLEM STEHT DIE DEUTSCHE INFANTERIE

DER MARSCH

Der Marsch der Infanterie bestimmt das Tempo der Schlacht

DIE ABWEHR

Der Feindangriff zerbricht an der zähen Abwehr der Infanterie

DER ANGRIFF

Im Schwerpunkt der Schlacht stürmt unwiderstehlich die Infanterie

DER SIEG

Des harten infanteristischen Kampfes stolze Krone ist der Sieg

Contents

6 Acknowledgements

7 Introduction

12 Militarism and education under the Nazis

- *Hitlerjugend* (Hitler Youth) 15
- Special schools 16
- Women 18
- The *Reichsarbeitsdienst* (Reich Labour Service) 19

24 The growth of the army and its organisation under the Nazis

- Getting round the Treaty of Versailles 26
- The growth of the army under the Nazis 28
- The organisation of the army 32
- The divisions 36

42 The soldier

- Conscription 44
- Training 47
- Personal documentation 50
- Life in the field 52

56 Uniform and equipment

- Introduction 58
- Rank and insignia 58
- Medals, badges and cuff titles 65
- Uniform and equipment 69

92 Weapons

- Introduction 94
- Pistols 94
- Rifles 95
- Sub-machine guns 102
- Machine guns 105
- Hand grenades 108
- Mortars 111
- Mines 114
- Anti-tank guns 115
- Flamethrowers 125
- Flak 126
- Infantry guns and howitzers 128
- Ammunition 132

134 Transportation, bridging and communications

- Transportation 136
- Cars 138
- Halftracks and armoured cars 140
- Motorcycles 141
- Lorries 143
- Bridging 144
- Communications 145

150 Medical services

- The infantryman 152
- Battalion 152
- Division 153
- Motorised ambulance trains 154
- Corps 156
- Army 156
- System of aid to/evacuation of casualties 156
- German war graves 158

160 Tactics

- Introduction 162
- In the attack 162
- *Gefechtsaufklärung* (battle reconnaissance) 165
- The squad in combat 166
- Infantry in the defence 168
- Sniping 172

174 Appendices

- Abbreviations, German words and designations 174
- Comparative ranks 176

177 Bibliography and sources

178 Index

OPPOSITE ***'Über allem steht die deutsche Infanterie'*** **(Above all stands the German infantry) – *der Marsch* (the advance), *die Abwehr* (the defence), *der Angriff* (the attack), *der Sieg* (the Victory). This set of contemporary postcards used as a slogan a quotation from a speech made by Hitler on 3 October 1941.** *(via Hennepin County Library, Minnesota, Digital Collections)*

Acknowledgements

I have been helped considerably in the preparation of this book. Thanks in particular must go to Patrick Hook for material assistance with the sections on uniforms and equipment and transport; to Richard Charlton-Taylor for his photos, his work – especially on the weapons and tactics chapters – and his help with captioning; and to Sandra for scanning and proof reading. Thanks, too, to Jonathan Falconer at Haynes and Michelle Tilling for her editorial work.

The photographs have come from a number of sources: Battlefield Historian, Richard Charlton-Taylor and Tanis have provided some great material, as has the WikiCommons online facility. All uncredited photos come from my late father's collection or were taken during photo shoots at which the following were generous with their time and facilities: Preston and Tim Isaac of the Cobbaton Combat Collection, an unrivalled arsenal of military equipment from tanks to tommy guns, who allowed a weekend's photography; Tony Helm, the font of all knowledge when it comes to radios, for access to his assortment of equipment; Ken Adams for allowing photography of his excellent collection; and the 304th Panzergrenadiers, in particular Sam Cureton for organising the photo shoots and Tanis Harkonnen for access to his wonderful albums of Second World War photos.

Finally, I wish to acknowledge the material sourced from research at the following online facilities: the US Army Medical Department Office of Medical History (http://history.amedd.army.mil/booksdocs/wwii/MedSvcsinMedtrnMnrThrtrs/appendices/appd.htm); the paraphernalia carried by German troops (http://www.dererstezug.com/german_pocket_litter.htm); the MG42 quote in Chapter 5 was paraphrased from the contributor Mark V (https://forum.axishistory.com/viewtopic.php?t=12041&start=45); additional information on radios (http://www.lexikon-der-wehrmacht.de/Waffen/Funkgeraete.htm); bridging equipment information (https://forum.axishistory.com//viewtopic.php?t=21636); and finally, information on wartime Feldpost numbers (http://www.axishistory.com/axis-nations/383- germany-military-other/feldpost/8994-feldpost-numbers).

RIGHT The 304th Panzergrenadiers Reenactment Group. Back row, left to right: Val Czerny, Sam Cureton, Preston Isaac. Front row, left to right: Alistair Davies, Tanis Harkonnen, Ryan Pearson, Aaron Medlin. Not present: Tim Isaac, Thomas Driscoll and Ash Hale.

Introduction

At the end of the First World War, as the Allies chased the German Army back towards its home borders, few could have foreseen that in 20 years the roles would be reversed and that Germany would once again invade its neighbours and start a world conflict. Over the 1914–18 period the Germans lost 1.8 million soldiers from the 11 million who served; the Austro-Hungarians around 900,000 from 7.8 million.

The figures for the Second World War are surprisingly similar. (Second World War casualty statistics are notoriously unreliable and debated. The figures used here are from Rüdiger Overmans' 2000 study.) Between 1939 and 1945 close to 13 million men served in das Heer: the German Army. The bulk of these were infantrymen, who slogged their way, mostly on foot, from Finisterre to Moscow, Kirkenes to Tripoli. They swore unlimited obedience to Adolf Hitler and were ready to stake their lives for this oath: as a consequence over 4 million men of das Heer were killed during the war – the figure rises to 5 million when Waffen-SS and other arms are included.

Just as they had done in 1914, the German Army took Europe by storm in 1939–40. Well trained and motivated, with an effective air force, nothing could stand in its way in the early years. The results of the invasion of Russia in summer 1941 changed all that and highlighted the army's main problem: their supreme leader, Hitler himself. His position allowed him to exert a level of control over the armed forces that tolerated no dissent. He lacked the strategic acumen of his idol, Frederick the Great, and his increasingly authoritarian regime saw the dismissal of many able senior officers – such as von Manstein in spring 1944 – for daring to debate with the Führer. Supreme Commander of the Wehrmacht from 1938, in December 1941 Hitler took over as OKH at that time (*Oberkommando des Heeres* – Supreme Commander of the Army) and all major military decisions from then on went through him.

LEFT A patrol returns. Between 1933 and 1939 Germany built up its armed forces and trained for war, at first in secret and then, after repudiating the restrictions of the Treaty of Versailles in 1935, in the open through general compulsory service. By 1939 its infantry could draw on a large pool of trained men. *(via RCT)*

LEFT The German infantry squad was the building block of the Third Reich's army; in turn, it was built around the machine-gun team. The MG34 could be used as a LMG from its bipod or an HMG from its tripod. *(via RCT)*

ABOVE German troops at the captured Palace of Versailles near Paris, June 1940. Louis XIV's palace was a symbol of French power and, more importantly, was where the hated treaty was signed in 1919. *(via Tanis)*

In summer 1941, the army was ill prepared for a long campaign. The optimism engendered by early successes led the Germans to believe their own propaganda: as the Russian armies crumbled in front of them and they advanced deeper into the country, they assumed that the Soviet regime would fall and that they would be quickly victorious. It was an easy mistake to make after Poland, the Low Countries, France and Norway had fallen so rapidly, and when the reality hit home, it provided harsh lessons.The consequence of this lack of preparation was the breakdown of the supply system and the shortage of adequate clothing during the winter of 1941/42. Hitler had planned for a short campaign of between 9 and 15 weeks with two bounds of around 200 miles. He thought that his forces would defeat the Red Army before it could fall back behind the Dnieper River and – after the collapse of the Soviet state that this defeat would force – his troops could be sent forward on captured railway trains, just as in 1918.

BELOW The Winter War of 1939–40 pitted Finland against its mighty Russian neighbour. The Soviet army struggled to defeat the Finns – something that contributed to Hitler's negative assessment of Russian fighting ability. The Finns fought alongside Germany from 1941 (the Continuation War), but signed an armistice on 4 September 1944. In 1944–5 they fought the Lapland War against their former allies. From Kurt Kranz's *Winteralltag im Urwald Lapplands* (Winter Life in the Lapland Forest). *(via RCT)*

When this didn't happen, the Germans were left with extended supply lines that made Eisenhower's problems in France and the Low Countries seem minor – Leningrad was over 500 miles from the border; it was more than 750 miles to Moscow and more than 1,000 to Stalingrad. By September 1941 General Fritz Halder, then head of the OKH, was complaining that the three Russian fronts would get only 26 trains of fuel daily against requirements for 30; and that tank numbers were down 40%, cars and trucks 22% and other vehicles over 30%.

The German Army – always touted as the best-equipped of the Second World War – was only partially motorised. In fact it used more horses in the Second World War than it had done in the First – 2.7 million as against 1.4 million. Blitzkrieg always has the connotations of speed, mechanisation, modern state-of-the-art warfare, but most of the infantrymen who reached the outskirts of Moscow did much of the hard graft on foot – so no better than Napoleon's army in the 18th century.

Conditions in Russia were much tougher than the soldiers were used to. Before the war it was joked that German Army horses couldn't survive a night in the open. For all the harshness of the Nazis' brutal educational regime, the soldiers had also become accustomed to centrally heated barracks with running water. Adjusting to the primitive conditions in Russia was far from easy. Standards had to be revised for replacements: the average age was lowered and the physical fitness requirements were raised. Soldiers also had to adjust to the cold, the brutality and the opposition: the Russians fought without let-up throughout the biting cold winter, causing innumerable German casualties and thereby shook the confidence and morale of the troops.

The German Army lost the cream of its troops – its young savvy combat veterans – in the bitter winters of 1941 and 1942, as Hitler learnt what Napoleon had discovered a century before: Russia is vast and its winters are extremely cold. That the German Army was able to hold out for so long after the reverses at Stalingrad and in North Africa, particularly after the Allies invaded first Italy and then France, was a reflection on its training, indoctrination, unrivalled defensive abilities and sheer bravery.

Of the 7,361 men awarded the initial grade of the highest German combat honour of the Second World War, the Knights Cross, 4,777 were from the Heer, making up 65% of the total awarded. But however brave its soldiers, the German Army had lost more than men in the war with Russia. It lost its honour and its moral compass. Charged to cooperate with the *SS-Einsatzgruppen* (the mobile death squads responsible for the murder of those the Nazis thought were undesirable), it was, therefore, complicit with the brutality of the ethnic cleansing and partisan warfare of the Eastern Front where over 2 million civilians were killed. In spite of post-war obfuscation there is no denying this link – albeit forced – that ranged from the supply of logistical support to actual participation.

In the West we tend, understandably, to focus on the theatres in which the Western Allies fought the German Army: France and the Low Countries; Norway; North Africa, Sicily and Italy; and north-west Europe after D-Day. However, most historians would identify the Eastern Front as the graveyard of Nazism. There were more German divisions involved in the east – although their quality is often overstated (those in the west were often better equipped). There were more casualties in the east: Overmans lists the German losses

ABOVE The strategy behind Hitler's invasion of Russia was simple: he planned to advance quickly enough to destroy their army and force Stalin to sue for peace. By October 1941 he was well on the way to achieving that aim: 3 million Soviet troops were POWs; Stalin was teetering on the edge considering both flight and a peace treaty. *(via Tanis)*

LEFT The heady days of 1941 were the high-water mark of German aggression. The wave broke on the outskirts of Moscow as the year ended. Up until then little had been able to deflect the German infantrymen. They would make more gains in early 1942 but their chance to topple Stalin had gone.

on the Eastern Front as some 4 million dead and subsequently nearly a million while held as Soviet captives. The battlefield was larger – probably the largest in human history – and the battles were immense and ferocious. While the 'what ifs' of history are impossible to define categorically, it is difficult to see the Western Allies defeating Nazi Germany by 1945 without Soviet Russia's involvement, assisted as it was by United States and British Lend-Lease and the bombing operations of the Western Allies.

By the time of D-Day there's no doubt that elements of the German Army were not as effective as they had been in 1940, but they certainly couldn't be taken lightly, not even the static coastal defence divisions who gave a good account of themselves on D-Day or the 'sickness' divisions such as the *Magen* (Stomach) Division on Walcheren in 1944. There's an old saying 'If you haven't fought the Germans you don't know real war.' There are few who took part in the battles of the Second World War who would disagree. In 1944, in retreat on every front, the German Army was still a formidable force as anyone who fought in Italy, the Netherlands, the Ardennes or the Reichswald would attest. What made the German soldier so tough and why did they keep fighting so tenaciously when defeat seemed obvious and inevitable?

There are many reasons: first, propaganda – many German soldiers still utterly believed in ultimate victory. They had grown up in a Nazi regime and accepted the propaganda. New super-weapons played an important role in fostering this delusion. They had been comprehensively indoctrinated to believe in their Führer, their race and their cause.

Second, education: the cornerstone for the German Army's success and fighting capacity was the rigour with which it selected and educated its officers and non-commissioned officers (NCOs). The ability shown by NCOs after their officers were killed and the flexibility and resolve exhibited by small ad hoc units was remarkable – look no further than the response to the Arnhem landings and the blocking forces that stopped the British Paras from reinforcing the small number who reached Arnhem Bridge. As long as a reasonable number of the officers or NCOs remained to instruct the replacements, they were seemingly able to perform miracles of training and leadership. Once pulled out of the line, German units demonstrated an astonishing ability to rebuild very quickly from shattering casualties – as was shown by those who escaped from the Falaise Pocket.

Third, honour and duty: even against the sternest odds, officers and men felt – as did their opponents – that they couldn't let their mates down. They endured day to day and fought for each other.

Fourth, and some would say the biggest difference between the Western Allies and their Axis opponents, was the summary justice meted out to those who would not fight. The Western Allies executed only one person for desertion – American Eddie Slovik. The German Army saw over 15,000 executed – some put the figure as high as 50,000, although many of these executions were for reasons other than desertion. One captain said, '... this must be crystal clear to you, [if I disobeyed orders] I would have been put against the wall and executed. No single doubt about that. Already many men had undergone the same fate and were hung from a rope in Germany.'

Fighting over such a period of time and in

RIGHT Georg Sluyterman von Langeweyde (1902–78) joined the NSDAP in 1928, putting his graphic art education to use designing party posters and other images for *Die Neue Front*, the weekly newspaper of the Düsseldorf Gau. This image was inspired by Albrecht Dürer's 1513 engraving, *The Knight, Death and the Devil*. The epithet below reads 'Victory or defeat lies in our Lord's hand, but we alone are lord and master of our own honour.' Typical of Nazi propaganda, it promoted an image of chivalry and honour.

LEFT The Russian armies fought doggedly to hold up the German attack. Like Napoleon's invasion that started at the same time of year – 24 June, two days later than Hitler's – the campaign became bogged down as early and unseasonal snow melted and brought the *rasputitsa*, the literal translation of which is 'unmade road season'. *(via Tanis)*

so many different locations – from the Arctic Circle to the Western Desert, the coasts of Brittany to the Russian steppes – the German infantryman is certainly difficult to categorise. Six years of fighting makes the cadre of men who went to war in 1939 very different to those fighting in 1945. The formations in which they fought, the weapons they used and the uniforms they wore all varied over the period as needs and resources changed. In particular, the standards and quality levels were dependent on the availability of manufacturing plants and raw materials, something that led to differences especially towards the end as so much of the Reich fell to the Allies.

This book surveys the range of soldiers who fought as infantrymen for the Germans in the Second World War. It mentions briefly the Waffen-SS, includes the Fallschirmjäger and other Luftwaffe and Kriegsmarine units who fought as infantry, but it concentrates on the infantry of the German Army *Landser* (common soldier) – the Grenadier, Panzergrenadier, Gebirgsjäger and Volksgrenadier – giving details of their organisation, weapons and uniforms and how they waged war.

WHAT'S IN A NAME?

The German infantryman in the Second World War was nicknamed the *Landser* – a name that derives from *Landsmann*, used in the late 19th century by Saxon soldiers to differentiate their mates from soldiers from other states. The *Landser* usually referred to an enlisted soldier of some experience: *ie* not recruits and not officers.

During the war infantrymen and the units they served with went through a number of changes of nomenclature. These will be discussed in more detail in the appropriate place, but a quick outline identifies:

- at the start of the war infantrymen served in infantry regiments
- after 1942, with overtones of Hitler's idol Frederick the Great of Prussia, infantry regiments became Grenadier Regiments and privates – *Schütze* – became grenadiers – *Grenadiere*
- some infantrymen were called *Jäger* (hunters) – such as the mountain troops – *Gebirgsjäger* – or ski troops who were called *Skijäger*
- light divisions, raised in late 1941, were made up of *Jäger* regiments. In 1942, all light divisions were renamed *Jäger* divisions
- anti-tank troops after 1940 became *Panzerjäger* (tank hunters)
- infantry in Panzer divisions started out in *Schützen* regiments. When the general infantry became Grenadiers, the Schützen regiments (and the men within them) became *Panzergrenadier*
- some infantry in the *Großdeutschland* Division were also termed *Fusilier*, others *Musketier*.

Chapter One

Militarism and education under the Nazis

In most countries – now as then – education and schooling of young people is seen as an essential part of growing up, a time when both boys and girls are instructed in their behaviour as citizens and are developed to enable them to improve society and themselves, to ensure their own personal growth and happiness. Education is available to all and while it seeks to ensure that talent is promoted, it is essential that everyone is educated. This was not the case in Nazi Germany.

OPPOSITE **Hitler was always happy to be photographed with children – but in his view education was to prepare boys to become soldiers; girls were destined for home and child-raising and required less education.**

Education was straightforward for Hitler: first, it was to emphasise the sense of race and to revile any – particularly the Jews – who were not Aryan. Second, it was to knock away all weakness to ensure that young people were hardened physically and mentally, with strong self-command and virility. Third, it was to prepare for war and victory, instilling patriotism and devotion to the National Socialist cause. Finally, it was to relegate women to the home: any education outside that needed for motherhood – especially further education – was unnecessary.

This quote from *Mein Kampf* (translated into English by James Murphy; a Project Gutenberg of Australia book), sums up his views:

> *The deliberate training of fine and noble traits of character in our schools today is almost negative. In the future much more emphasis will have to be laid on this side of our educational work. Loyalty, self-sacrifice and discretion are virtues, which a great nation must possess. And the teaching and development of these in the school is a more important matter than many other things now included in the curriculum. To make the children give up habits of complaining and whining and howling when they are hurt, etc., also belongs to this part of their training. If the educational system fails to teach the child at an early age to endure pain and injury without complaining we cannot be surprised if at a later age, when the boy has grown to be the man and is, for example, in the trenches, the postal service is used for nothing else than to send home letters of weeping and complaint. If our youths, during their years in the primary schools, had had their minds crammed with a little less knowledge, and if instead they had been better taught how to be masters of themselves, it would have served us well during the years 1914–1918. ... The young boy or girl who is of German nationality and is a subject of the German State is bound to complete the period of school education which is obligatory for every German.*
>
> *Thereby he submits to the system of training which will make him conscious of his race and a member of the folk-community. Then he has to fulfil all those requirements laid down by the State in regard to physical training after he has left school; and finally he enters the army. The training in the army is of a general kind. It must be given to each individual German and will render him competent to fulfil the physical and mental requirements of military service. The rights of citizenship shall be conferred on every young man whose health and character have been certified as good, after having completed his period of military service.*

All children had to stay at school until they were 14, after which education was optional. Universities were frowned upon and attendance dropped from 127,830 in 1933 to 58,325 in 1939, by which time the teaching staff had also been cut – losing liberals, Social Democrats and, of course, Jews. They were replaced by younger, inexperienced men whose Nazi credentials were unimpeachable, but whose lack of ability saw a huge erosion in German education standards.

A side effect of this treatment of educationalists was to drive many overseas – over 2,600 in 1933 – and the educational establishments of many countries outside Germany, particularly the United States and Great Britain, benefited. Take Göttingen University, a world leader in all physics, especially quantum physics, where Robert Oppenheimer, later of the atomic bomb project, had spent some time: only 11 of 33 staff of the physics and mathematics institutes stayed. Those who left included James Franck, head of the Second Physical Institute, Max Born, director of the Institute for Theoretical Physics and Richard Courant, director of the Mathematical Institute. All were Jews. *Hitler's Gift* quotes a story:

> *After the exodus the great mathematician David Hilbert was asked by a government minister, 'and how is mathematics in Göttingen now that it is free of Jews?' 'Mathematics in Göttingen?' Hilbert repeated, 'There is really none any more.'*

The most famous of all theoretical physicists, possibly the most famous scientist in the world at the time, Albert Einstein, was also a

Jew and also a casualty. He left Germany for, eventually, Princeton.

The expulsion of teachers and lecturers – initially simply by depriving them of jobs and a livelihood and, later, by more intrusive methods – was made easier by the fact that the new educational order was centrally controlled by the Minister of Science, Education and National Culture (*Reichsminister für Wissenschaft, Erziehung und Volksbildung*), Bernhard Rust, from 1 May 1934. Teachers were enrolled in the NSLB (*Nationalsozialistische Lehrerbund* – National Socialist Teachers League) and indoctrinated in special training camps. By 1936 over 32% of teachers were members of the Nazi Party. This was a much higher figure than for other professions. Teachers who were members wore their uniforms in the classroom.

By 1938 two-thirds of all elementary school teachers were being indoctrinated at special camps in a compulsory one-month training course of lectures. Schools brought in a Nazi curriculum – strong on PE, boxing was compulsory; weak on religion. The subjects, *Der Angriff* outlined:

> *German Language, History, Geography, Chemistry and Mathematics must concentrate on military subjects – the glorification of military service and of German heroes and leaders and the strength of a regenerated Germany. Chemistry will inculcate a knowledge of chemical warfare, explosives, etc., while Mathematics will help the young to understand artillery calculations, ballistics etc.*

Hitlerjugend (Hitler Youth)

Outside school, all young men were expected to join the Hitler Youth (HJ), under Baldur von Schirach. Set up in 1923, by 1930 it had 26,000 members; by the beginning of 1933 107,956. By the end of that year, after the Nazis came to power, 2.3 million had joined, some voluntarily, others were forced – like the Lutheran *Evangelische Jugend* (Evangelical Youth) whose 600,000 members were incorporated into the Hitlerjugend in 1934, the year all youth movements other than the HJ were declared illegal. Parents could not refuse their children and after December 1936 joining was a legal requirement for all Aryans. That year the HJ took over all youth sports facilities.

One teacher wrote:

> *In the schools it is not the teacher but the pupils, who exercise authority. Party functionaries train their children to be spies and agents provocateur. The youth organizations, particularly the Hitler Youth, have been accorded powers of control which enable every boy and girl to exercise authority backed up by threats. Children have been deliberately taken away from parents who refused to acknowledge their belief in National Socialism. The refusal of parents to 'allow their children to join the youth organization' is regarded as an adequate reason for taking the children away.*

ABOVE Every Hitlerjugend unit had a drum and bugle corps and they were used to great effect at parades and pageants all over Germany. Promoting the youth organisations helped advance Nazism: HJ membership rose steadily from 2.3 million in 1933 to 7.3 million in 1939 when it became compulsory.

LEFT **Give me a child and I will give you the man. Hitler understood the importance of catching them young and indoctrinating them: the fanaticism of many of the young defenders of Germany in 1945 was fostered by membership of the Hitlerjugend.**

LEFT **There's nothing like a good badge to motivate children – as Scouts have discovered the world over. Instituted in 1934 in three classes, the silver version was 'For Proficiency in the HJ' (*Für Leistungen in der HJ*) for boys over 17 who had passed a four-part test proving physical, military and political proficiency.**

When war began the Hitlerjugend had 8 million members, many of them fanatically imbued with National Socialist principles. After von Schirach was superseded by Artur Axmann, the Hitlerjugend took on war duties: helping fire brigades, the Reich postal service and railroad services, other government offices, the army and AA crews. Soon, as the adult casualty figures rose, so the Hitlerjugend duties became more overtly military. The boys of the HJ were advanced into the ranks of the army earlier and earlier. The culmination of this process was the creation of the 12th SS-Panzer Division Hitlerjugend in 1944. It proved to be exactly what Hitler had wanted when the Nazis rearranged the education system: fanatical, ferocious, the Allies were amazed at their youth – and their fighting ability.

Elsewhere, HJ members joined the national militia, the *Volkssturm*, and by 1945 Berlin was defended by boys as young as 12, all tutored by the HJ.

Special schools

As was typical of the Nazi regime, they planned special schools to train the elite: the children of the upper echelons and best of the rest. First, there were the 10 *Adolf-Hitler-Schulen* (there would eventually be 12) – the Führer allowed his name to be used from January 1937. These covered the elementary grades providing a strongly militaristic and physical education, which concentrated on the squad rather than the individual. The end

LEFT **Baldur von Shirach (1907–74) – seen behind Hitler – was *Reichsjugendführer* from 1929 to 1940. His position was undermined by Martin Bormann and others and he was replaced by Artur Axmann, who went on to suggest the formation of the Hitlerjugend Division.**

RIGHT Planned for construction in 1938–40, the foundation stone for what would have been an Adolf Hitler school at Hesselberg was laid on 15 January 1938 by Julius Streicher. It was never finished. *(WikiCommons)*

product was an 18-year-old who could either go to university or – as most chose – enter the military.

Alongside these Adolf Hitler schools were the *Nationalpolitische Erziehungsanstalten* – usually called Napolas after the *Nationalpolitische Lehranstalt* (National Political Institution of Teaching) – boarding schools for secondary students. The Napolas prepared entry into the Wehrmacht and Waffen-SS. The first three were founded in 1933 by Bernhard Rust in Plön, Potsdam and Köslin; by war's end there were 43 of them (three for girls) and 13% of their students entered the ranks of the SS. Their religion was *Endsieg* – final victory – and they would die in the last months of the war fighting as infantry for their cause.

After school, there were the *NS-Ordensburgen* for post-high school students who had completed their time at the Adolf Hitler schools, undergone their six months of compulsory labour service training and two years in the army and had chosen their professions.

On 24 April 1936 three Ordensburgen were formally handed over to Adolf Hitler, and the first 500 cadets – *Ordenjunkers* – all in their mid-20s, moved in. There was Ordensburg Vogelsang in the Eifel, Ordensburg Krössinsee in Pomerania and Ordensburg Sonthofen in Allgäu. A fourth was planned in Prussia, Ordensburg Marienburg, based on the historic castle of the Teutonic Knights (today in Malbork, Poland).

The NS-Ordensburgen provided four years of training – much of it military with live ammunition – and more racial prejudice. At the

ABOVE The *Reichsführerschulen* (Reichs Leadership schools) were training centres at which four-week residential courses for leaders within Nazism – the SA, SS and HJ – took place. This one, at Bernau near Berlin, was set up as a *Reichsführerschule* for the NSDAP and German Labour Service (DAP) in 1933 by appropriating an existing AGDB (German Trades Union) school. The Bauhaus architecture of the building complex earned it UNESCO World Heritage Site status in 2017.

RIGHT The foundation stone for the Napola at Ballenstadt was laid in 1936 but it wasn't until October 1942 that the school opened. There were some 6,000 students in Napolas by 1941. Life in the schools was tough and around 20% dropped out. *(Wolkenkratzer/WikiCommons (CC BY-SA 3.0))*

ABOVE **The first 500 cadets entered NS-Ordensburg Vogelsang in spring 1936 but left when war began. For the next six years it was used by the Hitlerjugend, the Adolf Hitler schools and to billet troops preparatory to attacks on the West in 1940 and the Ardennes Offensive in 1944.** *(VoWo/ WikiCommons (CC BY-SA 3.0))*

BELOW **A column of girls of the *Bund Deutscher Mädel*. With three age-group sections, the BDM involved girls from the ages of 10 to 17. In spite of the Nazis' belief that women should spend their lives at home, many of the BDM girls would end up as part of the war effort.** *(WikiCommons)*

end, the cadets who left the schools were more remarkable for their arrogance and ignorance than anything else. Disliked in the main even by the party faithful, most ended up in the military rather than taking party positions.

The SS founded its own pair of leadership schools – Bad Tölz in 1934 and Braunschweig in 1935 – known from 1937 as *Junkerschulen*. Three more followed: at Klagenfurt and Posen-Treskau in 1943, and Prague in 1944. They provided ideological training for the SS and the various police organs of the Nazi state.

Women

The Third Reich did not believe in the education of women and actively promoted the reduction of numbers in higher education. On 12 January 1934, Reichsminister of the Interior Wilhelm Frick cut the number of girls who were allowed to go to university to no more than 10% of the number of boys. Of the 10,000 girls who passed the *Abitur* entry exam that year, only 1,500 went to university. In 1932 there were over 18,000 women students in German universities. By 1939 there were 5,447. In 1937 the Nazis abolished grammar-school education for girls and banned them from learning Latin (a requirement for university entrance).

Women, the Nazis said, shouldn't work or seek employment outside the so-called three Ks

– *Kinder* (children), *Kirche* (church) and *Küche* (kitchen). They were not supposed to wear make-up, colour or perm their hair, although – as Propaganda Minister Joseph Goebbels pointed out in a speech in 1934, 'Women have the task of being beautiful and bringing children into the world.'

Girls were expected to join the female equivalent of the Hitlerjugend, the *Bund Deutscher Mädl* (BDM), which had a subdivision – the *Jungmädel* (Young Girls) section – for 10–14-year-olds.

In 1938, another section was introduced for older girls, the *BDM-Werk, Glaube und Schönheit* (Work, Faith and Beauty Society), to promote physical wellness and the preparation for maternal life.

In reality, of course, the need for men in the Wehrmacht ensured that German women were forced to enter the workplace: some even served as AA guncrew. The various societies in the end educated girls to help the Red Cross, to work in hospitals and to bring in the harvest.

ABOVE Northern European countries had their share of Fascist organisations and the Netherlands was no exception. The Dutch Nazi Party (*Nationaal-Socialistische Beweging in Nederland*) had a youth movement similar to the Hitlerjugend: the *Nationale Jeugdstorm*. Membership during the war reached only 12,000. At age 18 they had to choose between the Waffen-SS and the *Nederlandse Arbeidsdienst.* *(WikiCommons/W.F.M. Mol (Stapf Bilderdienst))*

The *Reichsarbeitsdienst*

The 1920s and 1930s were difficult times for world economies. In Germany, the post-First World War years saw unemployment, economic stagnation and hyperinflation. The Great Depression led to massive unemployment: in the UK this peaked at more than 22% of the workforce in 1932; in the same year, in Germany it reached nearly 25%.

One thing governments could do was help with national relief schemes. In the USA, the Works Progress Administration ran from 1935 to 1943, just after America joined the

RAD DISTRICTS (ARBEITSGAUE) AND WORKING GROUPS (ARBEITSGRUPPEN)

Number	Name of Arbeitsgau	Arbeitsgruppen
I	Ostpreußen	10–17, 19
II	Danzig-Westpreußen	20, 20A, 21–29
III	Wartheland	30–39
IV	Pommern-Ost	40–47
V	Pommern-West	50–55
VI	Mecklenburg	60–64, 67
VII	Schleswig-Holstein	70, 71, 73–77
VIII	Brandenburg-Ost	80–87
IX	Brandenburg-West	90–96
X	Niederschlesien	100–107
XI	Mittelschlesien	110–116, 119
XII	Oberschlesien	120–127
XIII	Magdeburg-Anhalt	130–138
XIV	Halle-Merseburg	140–145
XV	Sachsen	150–157
XVI	Westfalen-Nord	160–165
XVII	Niedersachsen-Mitte	170–177
XVIII	Niedersachsen-Ost	180–188

Number	Name of Arbeitsgau	Arbeitsgruppen
XIX	Niedersachsen-West	190–198
XX	Westfalen-Süd	200–209
XXI	Neiderrhein	210–217
XXII	Hessen-Nord	220–227
XXIII	Thüringen	230–238
XXIV	Moselland (until 1941 Mittelrhein)	240–249
XXV	Hessen-Süd	250–258
XXVI	Württemberg	260–267
XXVII	Baden	270–279
XXVIII	Franken	280–288
XXIX	Bayern-Ostmark	290–298
XXX	Bayern-Hochland	300–306
XXXI	Köln-Aachen	310–319
XXXII	Westmark	320–329
XXXIII	Alpenland	330–335
XXXIV	Oberdonau	340–348
XXXV	Niederdonau	350–356
XXXVI	Südmark	360–368
XXXVII	Sudetenland-West	370–376
XXXVIII	Böhmen-Mähren (until 1941 Sudetenland-Ost)	380–386
XXXIX	Süd Ostpreußen	390–393
XL	Wartheland-Ost	400–405, 408, 500, 501

BELOW Sankt Oswald ob Eibiswald is in the Deutschlandsberg district of Austria. It was the location for an RAD camp built in 1938 to help improve roads and transport links in the area. The RAD men from the camp ended the war fighting partisans. *(WikiCommons)*

war. More than 3 million unemployed young men were put into more than 2,500 Civilian Conservation Corps work camps; the Civil Works Administration created manual labour jobs for millions of unemployed workers during the winter of 1933/34. The Public Works Administration lasted longer, building bridges, airports, dams … even the Lincoln Tunnel in New York City.

In Germany there had been similar attempts and similar work camps culminating in 1931 with the creation of the FAD – *Freiwilliger Arbeitsdienst* (Voluntary Labour Service) – under Konstantin Hierl. This welded together the many disparate work camps and provided the Nazis with a ready-made organisation. Initially renamed the *Nationalsozialistischer-Arbeitsdienst*, or NSAD (National Socialist Labour Service), on 26 June 1935 the *Gesetz für den Reichsarbeitsdienst* (RAD Act) was passed creating the RAD and making service in it compulsory. Hierl continued in command with Ministry of Interior taking overall responsibility.

Young men would join the RAD after a stint in the Hitlerjugend and provide 'honorary service to the German people'. Access was denied to Jews and criminals. In effect, while not being part of the Wehrmacht, the RAD provided young men with six-months of drill, training and hardening-up before they started their time in the armed forces. All RAD training was conducted away from home; personnel lived in barracks and, from 1934, wore a uniform, working up to 76 hours a week. RAD workers were used on the land draining boglands, cultivating new farmland, tree removal, road construction and harvest work. The RAD *Dienststellenabzeichen* arm badge – a downward-pointing shovel blade on the upper left shoulder of their uniforms and greatcoats – spoke directly of the duties expected. After the war began, however, they were increasingly employed in work related to the armed forces supporting them as *Wehrmachtsgefolge* (armed forces auxiliary).

The RAD had separate sections for men and for women: *RAD Männer* (RAD/M) and *RAD der weibliche Jugend* (RAD/wJ) respectively. The RAD/M was organised into *Arbeitsgaue* (*Arbeitsgau* working district; pl: *Arbeitsgaue*) from I to XL.

LEFT AND BELOW
The arm badges of the Reichsarbeitsdienst identified detachment and work group. 141/6 was from Bad Liebenwerda in the Arbeitsgau of Halle-Merseburg and 76/4 from Schleswig-Holstein. *(LutzBruno/WikiCommons) (CC BY-SA 3.0))*

An Arbeitsgau was headed by an officer with an HQ staff and a *Wachabteilung* (Guard Company) numbered according to the Arbeitsgau in which it was located. Each Arbeitsgau also included between six and eight battalion-sized units – *Arbeitsgruppen* – assembling some 1,200 to 1,800 men into six company-sized *Abteilungen*. The Arbeitsgruppen could also be formed into a *Bereich* (region) – a regimental-sized unit.

The Abteilung was the cornerstone of the RAD, based at a location where the men would train. These locations and their Abteilung were given a number designation displayed together with the Arbeitsgau number on the RAD arm badge. An RAD Abteilung had 214 men grouped into a six-man staff and four *Züge* (platoons) of 69 men. Each *Zug* had three *Truppen* each of 17 men with bicycle transport.

From the Anschluß onwards the RAD supported the Wehrmacht during its major operations – such as the occupation of the Sudetenland and Czechoslovakia. From 1938 until September 1939, RAD units helped build the Westwall along Germany's border with France and the Low Countries, while in the east, another 100 RAD units aided in the

RIGHT Arbeitsgau XIV was based in Halle-Merseburg, north-west of Leipzig. Bad Liebenwerda, east of Leipzig, was close to Torgau – the location made famous by the meeting of American and Soviet troops on the banks of the Elbe in 1945. *(LutzBruno/WikiCommons)*

construction of the Ostwall fortification line along the eastern German border.

On 26 August 1939 general mobilisation was declared in Germany and over a thousand RAD units were transferred to the Heer to form the *Bautruppen* (construction troops). In the German Army *Pioniere* – engineers – were mainly tasked with combat missions such as water crossings and (as *Truppenführung* puts it), 'Engineers support the supporting infantry by removing blockades, by overcoming hindrances and

BELOW Among other things, the RAD workforce was involved – along with the civilian Organisation Todt – with the construction of Atlantic Wall coastal fortifications. They laid minefields, helped guard locations and prisoners, and performed combat support functions. *(WikiCommons)*

LEFT The motto of the RAD was *Arbeit adelt* – work ennobles. In fact it gave the Third Reich an unpaid, militarised cadre of fit young men ready for conscription into the armed forces or to help frontline troops by supplying food and ammunition, repairing damaged roads and working on airstrips. *(via RCT)*

by attacks upon fortified strongpoints. As for the rest, they can give essential battle service by preparing the terrain for the supply columns in rear of the troops.' The Bautruppen were units whose mission was to perform non-combat engineering tasks, such as trench-building, road, bridge, railway and fortress construction.

The RAD Abteilungen were expanded to 401 men by adding older untrained army reservists. Four of these new larger Abteilungen formed a *Bau-Bataillon*; in turn, four Bau-Bataillone (numbered in the 1 to 335 series) formed an *Abschnittsbaustab* (pl: *Abschnittsbaustäbe*) of which there were initially 55 numbered in the 1 to 111 series.

Thirty motorised road construction battalions were also formed from the RAD units transferred to the Wehrmacht; indeed, 60% of the Bautruppen during the Polish Campaign cleared roads to the front. After the campaign ended, the Bautruppen units stayed in the Wehrmacht and 900 new RAD Abteilungen were created.

For the rest of the war the RAD continued this dual arrangement. On the one hand it trained young men before they joined the Wehrmacht – the period of training getting shorter and shorter until in February 1945 it was only six to eight weeks. However, additionally the RAD took on more directly supportive duties. In the campaigns of 1940, RAD units repaired roads, built and repaired airstrips, processed supplies and ammunition, laid minefields, performed guard duties at key locations and even guarded prisoners.

There were over 400 RAD units serving on the Eastern Front and the lines between combat and non-combat duties blurred. This was particularly true of those who served in the Luftwaffe in RAD Flak batteries, the *Luftwaffe-Flakhelfer*, of which there were at least 60,000 in October 1944.

At the very end of the war the RAD could not avoid conscription into the front lines. Six front-line RAD divisions were formed and half of them saw action. Indeed, RAD men helped retake Arnhem Bridge from the British Paras.

RAD divisions in the Heer

- RAD-Division zbV 1 Infanterie-Division Albert Leo Schlageter
- RAD-Division zbV 2 Infanterie-Division Friedrich Ludwig Jahn
- RAD-Division zbV 3 Infanterie-Division Theodor Körner
- RAD-Division zbV 4 Infanterie-Division Güstrow
- Gebirgsjäger-Brigade Steiermark
- Gebirgsjäger-Brigade Enns.

Chapter Two

The growth of the army and its organisation under the Nazis

The German Army was defeated in 1918 but the Armistice saved it both from annihilation and, more importantly, from defeat on German soil. This let senior German military leaders spread the 'stab in the back' conspiracy theory. The underlying resentment – hardened by war reparations, territorial losses and Allied occupation – and the febrile political situation were the spawning ground of Nazism. And once in power, Nazism required a powerful army to right the wrongs of 1918.

OPPOSITE In 1933 the German Army, under the Treaty of Versailles, was 100,000 strong. By the start of the war in 1939 that figure had reached 3.7 million.

Getting round the Treaty of Versailles

Signed on 28 June 1919, the military section of the Treaty of Versailles was designed to ensure Germany would not be able to start another major war. The overall terms of the treaty were contentious at the time and are still argued over to this day: was the treaty, as John Maynard Keynes had it, a 'Carthaginian peace designed to destroy Germany'? The Germans thought so and this enabled the Nazis to build on the nation's discontent and aided their rise to power. The Americans, too, polarised by internal politics and with sizeable anti-British and pro-German factions, were against it. It was never ratified by the United States, which helped Germany with loans in the 1920s. On the other hand, the reparations never came close enough to make up for the depredations of war in France or Belgium; they were nowhere near as harsh as those visited on Russia by Germany at Brest-Litovsk. Many people – including those liberated from German rule in Poland and Czechoslovakia – were delighted to see German power curbed.

RESTRICTIONS ON THE GERMAN ARMY IMPOSED BY THE TREATY OF VERSAILLES

Articles 160–163 restricted the German Army to fewer than 100,000 effectives in no more than seven divisions of infantry and three divisions of cavalry. There was a specific restriction on the number of officers allowed – 4,000 – the size of HQ staff, the number and strengths of the units of infantry, artillery, engineers, technical services and troops. The Great German General Staff and all similar organisations were to be dissolved.

Articles 164–170 limited the amount of armaments the German Army could possess.

Material	Max arms	Max rounds
Rifles	84,000	40,800,000
Carbines	18,000	
HMGs	792	15,408,000
LMGs	1,134	
Med trench mortars	63	25,200
Lt trench mortars	189	151,200
Field artillery		
7.7cm guns	204	204,000
10.5cm howitzers	84	67,200

Limited armament building was allowed; imports were banned.

RIGHT Propaganda poster for the Reichswehr, the army of the Weimar Republic. Limited by the Versailles treaty to 100,000 men, its commanders ensured that it was officer-light and that each of the soldiers was trained to pass on his knowledge when the time came.

Articles 173–179 abolished universal compulsory military service and outlined periods of enlistment – the latter to ensure that frequent changes of personnel couldn't sidestep the intention of the restriction. Other ranks had to serve for 12 consecutive years with restrictions on discharges; officers had to serve to the age of 45 years at least; new entrants for 25 consecutive years at least, with restrictions on discharges.

Military schools were cut to one school per arm with the number of students admitted to be directly in proportion to the vacancies. All other military academies or similar institutions were to be abolished.

Training was restricted – military exercises could only involve serving personnel and other establishments and societies were forbidden from occupying themselves with any military matters, or instructing or exercising the profession or use of arms.

These military restrictions, on the face of it, cut deeply into the German war machine, in particular those for the army, slashing its numbers. But, as we all know, these restrictions didn't work. On the contrary, 20 years after Versailles, Germany invaded Poland and a second war began with the German Army making mincemeat of the Polish, Belgian, French and British forces it attacked between September 1939 and June 1940. Part of the reason for these victories is the way in which the German High Command reacted to the Versailles restrictions.

It is, perhaps, simplistic to say that the winners of the First World War were left with outmoded weapons, outmoded tactical ideas and an outmoded leadership, whereas the Germans, starting from scratch, were able to rip up the established rulebook and end up with a shiny new modern army – but there is a kernel of truth here. To begin with, the Imperial German Army's General Staff didn't disappear, it went underground and became the *Truppenamt* under Generalmajor Hans von Seeckt, who had been FM August von Mackensen's chief of staff during the First World War. Von Seeckt immediately set up committees to examine the lessons of the recent war, ensuring debate by junior officers who would go on to develop the tactics of Blitzkrieg. The result was the two-part *Führung und Gefecht der verbundenen Waffen* (Command and Battle of the Combined Arms) that appeared in 1921 and 1923. The tactics outlined were the basis for Blitzkrieg.

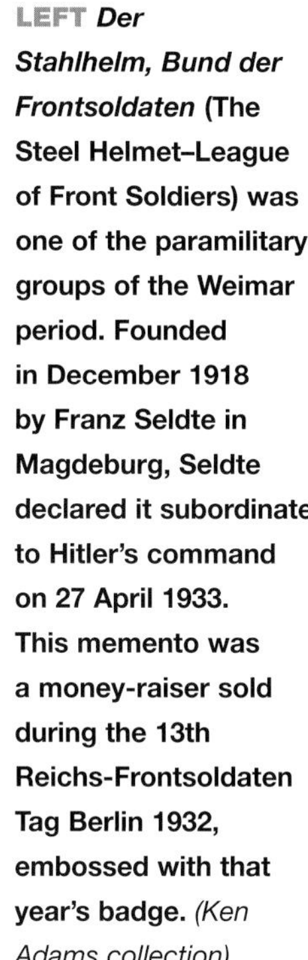
LEFT *Der Stahlhelm, Bund der Frontsoldaten* (The Steel Helmet–League of Front Soldiers) was one of the paramilitary groups of the Weimar period. Founded in December 1918 by Franz Seldte in Magdeburg, Seldte declared it subordinate to Hitler's command on 27 April 1933. This memento was a money-raiser sold during the 13th Reichs-Frontsoldaten Tag Berlin 1932, embossed with that year's badge. *(Ken Adams collection)*

Von Seeckt became head of the Weimar Republic's army in 1921. He met Hitler in 1923 and later said, 'We were one in our aim; only our paths were different.' He also said in 1925, 'We must become powerful, and as soon as we have power, we will naturally take back everything we have lost.' To ensure this happened, he was prepared to make a pact with the devil. All those who were surprised by the Molotov-Ribbentrop Pact of 1939 must have been unaware of the treaties in the 1920s – Rapallo (1923) where Germany and Russia renounced territorial and financial claims against each other and Berlin (1926) where they pledged neutrality if either were attacked.

These treaties also had secret clauses, which allowed the Germans, clandestinely, to train soldiers, particularly Panzer crew and airmen, in Russia, and also to build weapons there. To

LEFT The architect of the Wehrmacht, 'Hans' von Seeckt (1866–1936) learnt his trade under August von Mackensen. His post-First World War position as nominal – if not titular – head of the army, ensured that it was his vision that prepared the Reichswehr for mobile operations with a strong air component. *(Bundesarchiv, Bild 146-2005-0163/Tellgmann, Oscar/CC-BY-SA)*

THE BLACK REICHSWEHR

Evading the strictures of the Versailles treaty under the noses of the Governments of the Principal Allied and Associated Powers – the military commission set up to ensure Germany kept to its treaty obligations – started immediately. Von Seeckt and the Defence Minister, Otto Gessler, used a number of stratagems from deceit to outright lies to ensure that Germany maintained not only the forces it was allowed but trained new ones, manufactured weapons and trained with new tactics and new machines both inside and outside Germany. Part of this deception was the so-called Black Reichswehr, those organisations – often paramilitary – that were nominally outside Reichswehr control. They included *Arbeitskommandos* – labour battalions – raised from Freikorps units and numbering as many as 50–80,000 men by September 1923. They were commanded by Major Bruno Buchrucker under the Reichswehr aegis of Oberstleutnant Fedor von Bock (who would go on to command Hitler's Heeresgruppe 3 and lead troops into Vienna in 1938). The Black Reichswehr was responsible for as many as 350 murders – the so-called Feme murders – of 'informants' to the military commission and for acts of sabotage in the Ruhr. The Arbeitskommandos proved unsuccessful, however, as Buchrucker attempted a coup using them and his force was disbanded.

BELOW The repudiation of the Treaty of Versailles led to recruiting for the Wehrmacht. Here recruits are sworn in at the Odeonsplatz in front of the *Feldherrnhalle* (Field Commander's Hall), Munich, on 7 November 1935 – some 12 years after it had been the backdrop to the failure of the Beer Hall Putsch, the Nazi attempt to take over Bavaria.

control this, von Seeckt set up *Sondergruppe R* (for *Rußland* = Russia) under Kurt von Schleicher (who would go on to be the last Weimar Republic chancellor and die during the Night of the Long Knives). Other members were Schleicher's adjutant Eugen Ott, future CiC of the Reichswehr Kurt von Hammerstein-Equord, Fedor von Bock and, in the Russian office, Oskar von Niedermayer.

Von Seeckt's new tactical systems led to intensive training. As there was such a small officer base, this training concentrated on the NCOs, ensuring not only that each could do his own job but that of the next level above him. The army was, in effect, a training cadre that would be able to expand quickly and train new recruits. Von Seeckt also kept the air forces alive by ensuring men with air combat knowledge and skills were part of the 100,000.

The growth of the army under the Nazis

By the time Hitler gained power, he took control of armed forces that were more numerous and much better trained than his European rivals realised. The organisation of these forces was in embryonic form, and under Hitler it immediately began to grow. By 1935 he felt strong enough to repudiate the Treaty of Versailles, outlining plans to substantially increase the armed forces through conscription into the newly named Wehrmacht. The progression of the army's numbers shows how adaptable a nucleus von Seeckt's 100,000 proved:

1933 Army size nominally the **100,000** men allowed by Versailles, but the actual number is larger when *Sturmabteilung* (SA) and paramilitaries are taken into account.

1935 Conscription brought in. The army almost immediately reaches at least **300,000** men.

1938 The army has 36 infantry divisions and over **600,000** men.

1939 When the war starts, there are **3,737,000** men in the army (not all have been trained) and 35,000 in the SS-VT (*SS-Verfügungstruppen* – the combat arm of the SS that formed the basis for the Waffen-SS). This includes 1,050 RAD Abteilungen that were incorporated into the army as *Abschnittsbaustäbe* and increased in size by adding reservists.

1940 Army numbers have risen to **4,550,000** men and 50,000 SS.

1941 Army size **5 million** men and 150,000 SS.

1942 Army size **5,800,000** men and 230,000 SS. Growth is hampered by heavy casualties. The *Statistisches Jahrbuch für die Bundesrepublik Deutschland 1960* gives figures of 443,300 dead and 94,600 missing or POW.

1943 The army reaches its peak size with **6,550,000** men and 450,000 SS in spite of massive casualty figures: 448,600 dead and 343,600 missing or POW.

1944 The army size is **5,100,000** men and 600,000 SS. Incomplete figures give at least 458,000 dead and over a million missing or POW.

1945 Army size **5,300,000** men and 830,000 SS. At the end of the war there were around 11 million German POWs – around 3.6 million in US hands; 3 million in British; 3 million in Russia and a million in France.

These figures – as Bernhard Buckholz outlined in an article in *The Spectator* in 1936 – in the early years hid the actual numbers under training:

> *But the actual strength today is far greater, consisting as it does of 530,000 army, 30,000 armed police, 40,000 artillery, 200,000 labour corps. This total of 800,000 men is equal to 1914 strength.*

Prophetically, Buchholz continued:

> *Assuming a fitness-standard of approximately 80 percent the classes from 1910 to 1919 will provide 5,000,000 men, whose training will be completed in 1940. This is exactly 7.5 percent of the population, the same proportionate strength as in 1914. If the classes from 1905 to 1909, which will be partly trained in short-term courses, are taken into account, this total may be reached earlier, say in 1939.*

LEFT On 7 May 1936, 22 divisions of the German Army marched into the Rhineland in violation of the treaties of Versailles and Locarno. Three continued over the Rhine to the east bank. Had the French reacted with troops, there's no doubt they would have been able to push the Germans out. Some feel that this may have averted – or at least postponed – Hitler's subsequent actions in Austria and the Sudetenland.

His figures were close to reality: the 31 May 1940 total for the Wehrmacht was at least 6.6 million.

The size of the population was also increased by acquisition of territory. In 1935, after the 15-year occupation of the Saar by

BELOW The break-up of the Austro-Hungarian Empire after the First World War had left Austria with a sizeable proportion of the population wanting union with Germany. That came in 1938 when the German Army walked in, unopposed. The Anschluß expanded the Reich's manpower, army and industrial base – particularly its ability to produce steel. *(WikiCommons)*

ABOVE AND LEFT The dismemberment of Czechoslovakia between October 1938 and March 1939 by Germany, Poland and Hungary was the result of the Munich Agreement. Far from bringing 'Peace in our time' as British Prime Minister Neville Chamberlain had hoped, on 15 March 1939 Hitler annexed Bohemia and Moravia. *(WikiCommons; Ingsoc/WikiCommons (CC BY-SA 3.0))*

France, nearly 91% of the population voted in a plebiscite to return to German rule. In 1936 the German Army strode into the Rhineland and remilitarised Germany's industrial power base. And then in 1938 Austria and the Sudetenland were subsumed within the Reich. The population of Germany in 1938 was 68 million; with the additional territories this rose to 78 million – Austria, for example, providing immediately five incomplete divisions (two infantry, two mountain and one armoured).

The German Army at the start of full mobilisation in 1939 comprised 51 divisions and two brigades:

- Infantry divisions: 35 – numbers 1, 3–12, 14–19, 21–28, 30–36, 44–46
- Infantry divisions (mot): 4 – numbers 2, 13, 20 and 29
- Mountain divisions: 3 – numbers 1–3
- Light divisions: 4 – numbers 1–4 (became Panzer Divisions 6–9 in winter 1939/40)
- Panzer divisions: 5 – numbers 1–5
- Panzer brigade: 1 – became 10 Panzer Division before outbreak of war
- Kavallerie brigade: 1 partly mechanised.

LEFT From the start of the Spanish Civil War in July 1936 Hitler supported Franco's Nationalists with money, air transport and the Condor Legion – a small but potent fighting force. In all around 16,000 Germans fought in Spain and on 14 April 1939 the Spanish Cross was instituted. Worn below the right breast pocket flap, it had a number of orders. This – the Spanish Cross in Bronze with Swords – was given to the 8,462 Germans who saw frontline combat during the war. *(Gaspar8/WikiCommons (CC BY-SA 3.0))*

LEFT The Free City of Danzig was created by the Treaty of Versailles. Although under the aegis of the League of Nations, the Nazis took over the government in 1935. As part of the invasion of Poland, the League of Nations' High Commissioner was expelled and the city was taken into the Reich. The only real resistance was from the Polish Post Office, whose employees held out for 15 hours. They and most of the city's 4,500 Polish population would be executed.

As well as territorial acquisition, from 1936 to 1939 the Germans provided extensive combat experience for a significant number of men by rotating the personnel it sent with the Condor Legion to Spain, although the legion's total strength never exceeded 20,000 men.

After the practice came the practical, and on 1 September 1939 the German Army attacked Poland. Two army groups (North and South) involved 60 divisions and a number of smaller units. The German losses – some 44,000 casualties including just over 16,000 dead – did not materially affect manpower for the forthcoming attacks.

The Denmark and Norway adventure started on 9 April 1940 and saw nine divisions in action and some 8,000 Wehrmacht casualties including nearly 5,000 dead (1,300 on land). Fighting continued until 10 June, a month after the assault on the West – which saw over 100 divisions, including 97 infantry, attack France through the Low Countries. Casualties were higher than in the other campaigns, with over 150,000, including at least 27,000 dead – although substantially fewer than Hitler's expected million.

The German Army continued to grow as the fighting continued without pause: in the Balkans – after Italy's attack of 28 October 1940 was held, Hitler was forced to help his Fascist partner, sending 337,000 men to invade Yugoslavia on 6 April 1941 – and then after the British and Allied forces evacuated to Crete, the Germans invaded the island on 20 May 1941.

Rommel had already been dispatched to North Africa in February 1941 to bail out the defeated Italians, albeit with only a couple

ABOVE LEFT Germany invaded Poland on 1 September 1939. The German infantry performed competently in its first major conflict, linking well with the Panzers and Luftwaffe in what was a precursor to the Blitzkrieg campaign on the West in 1940. Benefiting from superiority in number of troops, surprise (only half of the Polish armed forces were mobilised) and airpower, the Poles could only withstand the Nazis for five weeks.

ABOVE On 9 April 1940, a month before the invasion of France, German forces attacked Denmark and Norway. The former fell in six hours; the latter put up more of a fight, supported by British forces, before capitulation in early June.

BELOW Few expected the mighty French Army to collapse in the face of the German offensive in 1940. Even with some 80 years of hindsight it is still shocking. The Nazi attack bypassed the defences of the Maginot Line, and six weeks later was master of Western Europe from the Arctic Circle to the border with Spain.

ABOVE **Soldiers at the Parthenon after the successful conclusion of Unternehmen Marita – the German invasion of Greece in April 1941 following the unsuccessful attempt by the Italians in October 1940. While it didn't cause significant disruption to Hitler's planned invasion of Russia, it can't have helped.** *(via RCT)*

of divisions. The battles in the desert would escalate, but the bulk of the Axis forces were Italian. Nevertheless, by the time the Axis forces surrendered in May 1943 the Germans had lost over 12,000 dead and over 100,000 taken POW.

Up until mid-1941 the German Army had sustained casualties, but these had not seriously impacted its effectiveness. Hitler invaded Russia on 22 June 1941 with 153 divisions – 104 infantry, 19 Panzer and 15 motorised infantry divisions in three army groups. Additionally, there were nine security divisions to operate in conquered territories, four divisions in Finland and two divisions as reserve under the direct control of OKH. Finland put up 14 divisions for the invasion, and Romania offered 13 divisions and eight brigades over the course of Barbarossa. All told 3.8 million men – and 625,000–700,000 horses – were controlled by OKH and organised into Army Norway, Army Group North, Army Group Centre and Army Group South.

Initial successes led to the gates of Moscow: on 2 December elements of 259th Infantry Division were within 15 miles of the Soviet capital. It was the high-water mark of the German advance. Unprepared for a sustained campaign in a Russian winter, the German advance was halted and pushed back. German losses and POWs numbered in the millions and of those who disappeared into the depths of Russia – about 3 million – most were released by 1950 although a number didn't return home until the mid-1950s. The Soviets record 380,000 as having died in captivity; Rüdiger Overmans suggests that figure could be nearer a million.

From the close of 1941, apart from a few local successes, the tide had turned and the German Army would reap the whirlwind as it was attacked on four fronts: by the Red Army in the east, and the Western Allies in the Mediterranean, from the air and, in 1944, in France.

The organisation of the army

The German Army was organised in two parts: the Field Army (*Feldheer*) and, from 1938, the Replacement Training Army (*Ersatzheer*). The former – the fighting element – was controlled by OKH, the commander-in-chief and his staff at headquarters in the field. From December 1941 OKH came under Hitler's personal control and by 1942 almost exclusively looked east from his Wolfsschanze HQ near Rastenburg in Poland, with OBW – *Oberbefehlshaber West* – reporting to him through the OKW, *Oberkommando der Wehrmacht*.

OKH	From	To
Generaloberst Werner von Fritsch	February 1934	4 February 1938
GFM Walther von Brauchitsch	4 February 1938	19 December 1941
Adolf Hitler	19 December 1941	30 April 1945
GFM Ferdinand Schörner	30 April 1945	8 May 1945
OBW		
GFM Gerd von Rundstedt	10 October 1940	1 April 1941
GFM Erwin von Witzleben	1 May 1941	15 March 1942
GFM Gerd von Rundstedt	15 March 1942	2 July 1944
GFM Günther von Kluge	2 July 1944	16 August 1944
GFM Walter Model	16 August 1944	3 September 1944
GFM Gerd von Rundstedt	3 September 1944	11 March 1945
GFM Albert Kesselring	11 March 1945	22 April 1945

All other army administration – drafting personnel, training replacements, procuring equipment, permanent military structures, and so on – came under the Home Command in Berlin, part of the Replacement Training Army.

Das Ersatzheer – the Replacement Training Army

The position of *Chef Heeresrüstung und Befehlshaber der Ersatzheer* (Chief of Army Equipment and Commander of the Replacement Army) was held by Generaloberst Fritz Fromm from the beginning of the war until 20 July 1944 when he was executed for his part in the plot to kill Hitler. His position was taken by Reichsführer-SS Heinrich Himmler.

The military districts in Germany numbered seven after Versailles for the seven divisions Germany was allowed to raise. In 1935, after Hitler's repudiation of the treaty, the country was divided into 13 (I to XIII) military districts (*Wehrkreise*) each of whose numbers corresponded to an army corps. The Wehrkreise were responsible for:

> *conscription, training and replacement of personnel including control of mobilization policies and the actual call-up and induction of men; all types of military training, including the selection and schooling of officers and non-commissioned officers; the dispatch of personnel replacements to field units in response to their requisitions; and the organization of new units.*
>
> (From TM-E-3D-451 Handbook on German Military Forces.)

Further Wehrkreise were added after the Anschluß of Austria (XVII and XVIII); another (Wehrkreis Böhmen-Mähren) after the Sudetenland and Czechoslovakia were taken; and three from annexed Polish territory – XX, XXI and the General-Gouvernement.

There were also four independent corps – XIV, XV, XVI and XIX – staffs to control the organisation and training of Panzer and motorised units. These had no corresponding military districts, but were served, as regards personnel and supplies, by the district in which corps headquarters or subordinate units had their peace stations. These ceased to exist as Wehrkreise in 1939 and became:

- XIV – HQ, XIV Panzerkorps
- XV – HQ, Third Panzerarmee
- XVI – HQ, Fourth Panzerarmee
- XIX – unassigned.

Each Wehrkreis was subdivided into two or three *Wehrersatzbezirke* (recruiting areas) and various *Wehrbezirke* (recruiting sub-areas) – but

LEFT **The military districts of Greater Germany following incorporation of Austria, parts of Czechoslovakia and Poland:**
I – Königsberg
II – Stettin
III – Berlin
IV – Dresden
V – Stuttgart
VI – Münster
VII – München
VIII – Breslau
IX – Kassel
X – Hamburg
XI – Hannover
XII – Wiesbaden
XIII – Nürnberg
XVII – Wien
XVIII – Salzburg
XX – Danzig
XXI – Posen, Böhmen und Mähren – Prague, Generalgouvernement – Krakow.

they varied: Wehrkreis VI, the populous Ruhr and Rhineland region, had four.

In peacetime each Wehrkreis held the HQ and administrative components of an active infantry corps (for example II Infantry Corps had its peacetime headquarters at Stettin in Wehrkreis II), and the original divisions and other units were linked to this Wehrkreis and normally received replacements from it. In wartime the Wehrkreis also handled administrative details for the appropriate units of the field army.

In peacetime, the commander of the infantry corps was also commander of the military district. He led his corps into the field, after having developed and maintained the fighting efficiency of the troops under his command. The administration was the responsibility of his Wehrkreis second in command – normally a general officer whose health or age kept him from active service.

On mobilisation, the commander of the infantry corps left for the field army, and the second in command then assumed direct command of the military district with a staff of reserve officers. The field army units included the active units of the peacetime army, which moved out with the active infantry corps and all the units formed after the initial mobilisation in the district.

The replacement training system

The *Chef des Ausbildungswesens im Ersatzheer* (Chief of Training in the Replacement Training Army) was General der Pioniere Walter Kuntze. Organised regionally by military districts, trained replacements were supplied to field units from the Wehrkreis in which the units originated, ensuring a permanent affiliation between each field unit and its home station. To begin with, in general, each replacement training unit carried the same number as the field army unit to which it supplied personnel and was one degree smaller than that unit. For the regular standing army (active divisions in the series 1 to 50) each regiment had two replacement training battalions and each non-regimental battalion had one replacement training battalion. For newly organised divisions of the Feldheer, on the other hand, each regiment had only one replacement training battalion and each non-regimental battalion had a replacement training company. All replacement training units serving the infantry regiments of a division were controlled by an infantry replacement training regiment which carried the same number as the division. Thus the 22nd Inf Replacement Training Regt at Oldenburg controlled all infantry replacement training units of the 22nd Inf Div.

The exigencies of war saw changes from autumn 1942.

a) A number of field replacement units were moved closer to their intended theatre of war.
b) The 33 training divisions became 18 defensive divisions – *Reservedivisionen* – to control training, and 17 administrative divisional staffs to control the flow of replacements from the Wehrkreis. The latter were still designated DivNr, Replacement and Training Divisions, but are probably better-termed mobilisation divisions.
c) The Reservedivisionen were moved into occupied territory, where they came under the control of new HQs and combined the training of recruits with assisting in maintaining internal security. For example, after the French campaign, the replacement training units from Wehrkreis I (East Prussia) moved into Poland. About the same time, many of the replacement training units from Wehrkreis X were transferred to Denmark, where Div Nr 160 (one of the two training divisions of Wehrkreis X) replaced a division of the field army.

From 1942 the process of supplying replacements to the field forces went like this:

a) A new recruit was placed temporarily in an *Ersatzeinheit* (reserve unit) or *Stammeinheit* (cadre unit) in his own Wehrkreis, where he received his papers, personal equipment and very basic training.
b) Next he went to an *Ausbildungseinheit*, a training unit in occupied territory. This transfer was conducted by a *Marschbataillon*, provided by the Wehrkreis.
c) After a period of training the recruit was transferred to a regular *Feldeinheit*. In Russia, many of these carried out anti-partisan duties.

Schattendivisionen – Shadow divisions

When it became apparent that attrition would see divisions reduced to such an extent that they were no longer workable, the Replacement Army set up a system to reconstitute them. Reduced-size shadow divisions were formed with a small divisional staff, and reduced-strength units. When a division was irreparably damaged, a shadow division would take its place.

Das Feldheer – the Field Army

The Field Army was divided into *Heeresgruppen* (army groups) nominally of at least two or three *Armeen* (armies). During the war there were over 30 different units that were given the title Armee, including six Panzer armies, Panzerarmee Afrika (later redesignated Deutsch-Italienische Panzerarmee), a Fallschirmjäger army, two *Gebirgs* (mountain) armies and the Armies of *Norwegen* (Norway), *Lappland* (Lapland), *Ligurien* (Liguria) and *Ostpreußen* (East Prussia). The latter is a good example of a late-war army, created on 7 April 1945, by the redesignation of Second Army (2.Armee), it also included elements of Fourth Army. It was in existence for less than a month.

The constituent elements of armies differed during the war but were, in the main, composed of an HQ, army troops and a number of corps,

ABOVE The German troops in North Africa swelled from two divisions to an army group. Although the term Deutsches Afrika Korps is used to refer to these forces, it's actually only correct for the February–August 1941 period. The infantry component included the Ramcke Parachute Brigade. Over 100,000 experienced German soldiers entered captivity after the Allied success.

RIGHT The adaptability of the German infantryman was shown off to good effect around Arnhem during Operation Market Garden. The British Paras dropped too far from the bridge they were to take and hold, allowing ad hoc blocking forces to slow their advance and wipe them out.

RIGHT An MG42 in action in Normandy in 1944. The German infantry kept the Allies penned into their bridgehead for two months before attrition and poor leadership – much of it from the very top – saw the German defence finally succumb. Note the grenades in support and the natural camouflage on the gunner's helmet compared with some of the canvas helmet covers. *(Battlefield Historian)*

whose elements were dictated by the type – Panzer, infantry, mountain, airborne, corps command (HQ and organic troops – field post offices, police, engineers) and reserve.

As in all armies, the higher formations (army and corps) had a number of specialist units, which they then portioned out as the situation warranted. These units included Flak units, MG companies, heavy artillery, heavy tank units (such as the Tiger units), heavy anti-tank guns, assault gun batteries and flamethrowing tanks.

The building blocks of all of these corps were – as with the Allied armies – the divisions, although the German Army also frequently used *Kampfgruppen* (battle groups), often ad hoc, throwing together units that were available. The closest Allied equivalent unit to the Kampfgruppe was the US Task Force, usually around an Abteilung in size with component units either to suit the mission or – more frequently – what was to hand.

The divisions

There were many different forms of division, such as: *Panzer* (armoured), *Panzergrenadier* (armoured infantry), *Leichte* (light), *Infanterie* (infantry), *Gebirgs* (mountain), *Ski*, *Kavallerie* (cavalry), *Landwehr*, *Artillerie* (artillery), *Festung* (fortress), naval infantry, *Fallschirmjäger* (airborne), Anti-aircraft, Waffen-SS and various

UNIT NOMENCLATURE

The division (Ger: *Division*, pl: *Divisionen*) was divided into one to four regiments (Ger: *Regiment*, pl: *Regimenten*), the size of a British brigade. These were subdivided into *Abteilungen* (sing: *Abteilung*), which were around the same size as the British battalion or tank regiment. The next level was the company (*Kompanie*, pl: *Kompanien*) or battery (*Batterie*, pl: *Batterien*) – the latter used mainly for artillery and equating to a British troop. The company had a number of platoons (*Zug*, pl: *Züge*). The German term *Brigade* equated to two or more *Regimenten*. Below the Zug were the *Gruppe* (group, pl: *Gruppen*), the *Halb-Zug* (half platoon), and *Trupp* (troop, pl: *Truppen*) The *Bataillon* (note spelling, pl: *Bataillone*) was composed of battalion-sized engineer and recce units.

Another important unit to mention is the column (*Kolonne*, pl: *Kolonnen*), a transportation unit often associated with bridging.

It is important to remember that the German infantry division included over 5,000 horses as well as around 1,000 vehicles.

named divisions (such as the Hermann Göring Division). There were also a number of training and replacement divisions given a variety of different titles: *Feldausbildungdivisionen* (Field Replacement Divisions) were part of the Feldheer on the Eastern Front and provided extra training for troops fighting in Russia; the Ersatzheer provided replacement divisions (*Ersatzdivisionen*) handling the training of recruits; advanced training took place in the Ausbildung elements of these divisions which – later in the war – were redesignated Reservedivisionen. And as the war progressed, other types of division were constituted – such as *Sicherheits* (security) divisions used to administer captured territory and static (*Bodenständige*) divisions used for coastal defence. The first of these were 15 under-strength (they had only six infantry battalions) divisions of the 15th wave numbered in the 700s raised during summer 1941 and destined for France, Belgium, Holland, Norway, Greece and Yugoslavia. Others were formed for OBW von Rundstedt in the 18th to 20th waves of 1942. Initially, they had three regiments and nine rifle battalions, but no recce battalion and only three battalions of artillery. Towards the end of 1943, the demands of war saw many lose their third regiments. A number were enhanced by the influx of Ost battalions in late 1943/early 1944, but it's difficult to compare them because their personnel numbers varied depending on location. As with other German units, the supply trains were manned by Hiwis – *Hilfswillige* – mainly Russian volunteers. The number of static divisions was increased in early 1944 when training divisions were upgraded to replace infantry divisions.

Later still, as manpower issues became a problem, the Volksgrenadier divisions came into existence as will be discussed on page 38.

There's no doubt that the most feared German infantry units in 1944 were the so-called *Fallschirmjäger* (paratroop) divisions, although few of the men would ever jump in combat after the invasion of Crete. These divisions fell under the Luftwaffe administratively but were always under Army command in the field.

Infantry divisions

It's important to remember that few things in any wartime army are as identified in official organisation tables. This is particularly true in armies that are sustaining heavy casualties and unable to replace them or those in retreat and losing, as happened to the German Army in 1944–45. Replacement of men and armaments is anything but instantaneous and few wartime divisions are up to strength once they enter the combat zone.

The German divisions were formed in waves (see Chapter 3) and the equipment and organisation of the divisions in each wave was along the same lines; however, as the war progressed, few of the German divisions had exactly the same organisation or equipment.

In general terms, the 1939 Infantry Division was very similar in organisation to that of 1918, and remained very much the same until October 1943 – with three regiments providing nine rifle battalions. A regiment's three battalions provided 12 companies – 9 rifle and 3 heavy weapons – to which were added an artillery and an anti-tank company, making 14 companies in all. On top of this, divisions had one anti-tank and one reconnaissance battalion and a regiment with one medium (15cm howitzer) and three light (10.5cm howitzer or gun) battalions. Between 1939 and 1943 that meant just over 17,700 men, over 3,000 horses and around 1,000 motor vehicles.

After nearly four years of war, the organisation of the standard infantry division underwent a major change in 1943: the creation of the Neues Art or Type 44 Division. The Type 44 saw the reduction of the number of infantry battalions necessitated by the losses in Russia. The personnel numbers were reduced from some 17,000 to around 13,500 by cutting the battalions to three regiments of two. This wasn't new. In spring 1941, the Germans created a number of two-regiment, six-battalion infantry divisions with reduced strength and firepower. However, the new Type 44 Division – at least notionally – saw its firepower increased by supplying more automatic weapons.

The new division's rifle companies were cut to 140 enlisted men and two officers. The number of squads per rifle platoon was reduced from four to three, but firepower was helped by having heavier mortars and anti-tank guns in spite of the reduction in LMG numbers in the rifle companies. The squad personnel was reduced from ten to nine, and the strength of the supply trains on all levels was also reduced. The Type 44 also saw the replacement of the Recce battalion with a Fusilier battalion.

The other major change to infantry division organisation was the creation of the Volksgrenadier (VG) division in late 1944. When Heinrich Himmler — the Chief of the SS and Minister of the Interior — became the Chief of Army Equipment and Commander of the Replacement Training Army, he introduced the reorganised division under the Volksgrenadier name to stress the patriotism of those chosen to defend the Fatherland – and, it was hoped, to increase the number of men joining up. Necessitated by the manpower losses, the name change (not to be confused with the later Volkssturm militia) was supposed to build morale, appealing to nationalism (the people, *Volk*). These divisions had three infantry regiments, each of two battalions and a reduced complement of 10,000 men. A Fusilier company also replaced the Recce Bn. With beefed-up artillery, and the adoption of automatic weapons, *Panzerfaust* and *Panzerschreck*, the divisions created were potent in spite of reduced numbers.

The VG divisions were not, as some sources would have you believe, made up of poor troops and were certainly not incompetent. They were not up to Waffen-SS Panzergrenadier standard, but many fought well: for example, in the Ardennes the 18th Volksgrenadier Division inflicted a heavy defeat on US forces when the 105th Infantry Division was enveloped on the Schnee Eifel.

However, by 1944 many of the divisions were not up to strength: as the year went on losses on every front meant that divisions were both short of manpower and weapons. They were also short of vehicles: many of the divisions were lucky if they had troops equipped with motorcycles – indeed several were dependent on the horse. Problems with equipment losses meant that obsolete and *Beute* (booty) equipment was extensively employed.

Panzergrenadier divisions

Originally known as *Schützen* regiments, Germany's motorised infantry were highly trained and well equipped, noted for their speed, mobility and firepower.

The Spanish Civil War showed that trucks couldn't do the job in many circumstances, particularly off road, and their passengers were vulnerable to enemy fire. The solution was the SdKfz halftrack, the best-known being the 'Hanomag' SdKfz 251; 15,000 Hanomags were built during the war (along with over 6,500 of the smaller SdKfz 250s) and they carried assault troops into battle. They could carry ten men (a squad after the 1943 reorganisation) and were used alongside trucks in Panzer divisions.

In 1939, for the attack on Poland, the motorised infantry division of 16,445 men was formed of an *Aufklärungs Abteilung* (Recce Bn) – armoured cars and motorcycles; 3 × Infantry Regiments each of 3 × Inf Bns, 1 × Panzerjäger Coy and 1 × Inf Gun Coy; 1 × Panzerjäger Bn of 1 × Heavy MG Coy (equipped with Flak 30s) and 3 × Panzerjäger Coys; 1 × Pionier Bn; 1 × Artillery Regiment (mot) of 3 × Light Artillery Bns and 1 × Heavy Artillery Bn and 1 × Observation Bn; 1 × Signal Bn, with transport, admin, supply and medical units.

After Poland, before the attack on the West, the divisions lost an infantry regiment and one of the light artillery battalions.

In 1943 the first Panzergrenadier divisions were formed but steadily their complement of men and armour was eroded. Attrition killed off experienced soldiers, the training times were reduced and fewer vehicles were available for use. As examples of this, the German Army's flagship *Großdeutschland* Division – which had started out as a regiment, became an infantry division in 1942 and then a Panzergrenadier division in 1943 – had only a few SdKfz 251s, and most of its Panzergrenadiers moved by truck. There were over 200 Panzergrenadier battalions in 1943: around 10% used halftracks, the rest used trucks.

There were more halftracks available for the well-equipped Panzer Lehr, 2nd and 21st Panzer divisions, but in February 1944, 17. SS-PzGr Division Götz von Berlichingen had only 245 trucks out of the 1,686 it should have had, and an almost complete absence of prime movers for the artillery!

The divisions were planned to have two motorised infantry regiments of three battalions each, but were otherwise organised similarly

LEFT The Gebirgsjäger proved tough and resilient fighters, although their lack of heavy weapons and dependence on mule transport hindered their usage outside mountain areas.

to the Panzer division except that they had a tank or assault gun battalion instead of a tank regiment. The motorised infantry battalions originally were organised exactly as the normal infantry battalions, but they used trucks as means of transportation. During the year 1944, however, the components of the motorised infantry battalion were reorganised along the lines of the Panzergrenadier battalions in armoured divisions. The two infantry regiments were usually designated *Infanterieregiment (mot)*, but in some divisions they officially adopted the designation of Panzergrenadierregiment.

The 1944 division had an *Aufklärungs Abteilung* (recce bn) – but it was equipped with armoured cars and the motorcycle component was minimal; 3 × infantry regiments (mot) each of 3 × infantry battalions, 1 × heavy gun company and 1 × Pionier company; 1 × Pionier battalion; 1 × Panzerjäger Bn with 2 × Panzerjäger Bn and 1 × heavy Panzerjäger company; 1 × Sturmgeschütz Bn with 3 × Sturmgeschütz batteries; 1 × army Flak battalion; 1 × artillery regiment (mot) of 2 × light and 1 × heavy artillery battalions; 1 × Signal Bn. This set-up included (on paper at least) 42 Sturmgeschütze, 322 Kettenkräder and significant numbers of AA guns.

Gebirgsjäger

The Germans and Austrians had built a tradition of bold mountain infantry during the First World War and this continued under the Nazis. The Anschluß incorporated the Austrian units into the German Army: three divisions were ready at the start of the war and a fourth in 1940. All told, ten Wehrmacht and six Waffen-SS mountain divisions were formed during the war. They took part in a number of significant operations including the invasions of Poland, France, Denmark, Norway and Russia – during the latter they raised a flag on Mount Elbrus, the highest mountain in Russia. They were also associated with a number of war crimes against civilians.

Throughout the war each division had two mountain infantry regiments of three battalions each but the additional units changed. The regiments included a heavy company with 2 × 7.5cm leIG and 6 × 8cm mortars and an HQ company that included a Panzerabwehr company with 12 × 3.7cm Pak 36s. Additionally, in 1939 there was an artillery regiment with two light battalions of 4 × 7.5cm mountain guns or 10.5cm mountain howitzers and a heavy battalion with two batteries each of 4 × 15cm howitzers; a horse-mounted recce battalion, and Panzerjäger, Mountain Pionier, Signals and Ersatz battalions.

The 1944 organisation saw a beefed-up division with significant heavy weapons: the HQ company included a 120mm mortar company, as did each of the Gebirgsjäger heavy companies in the two regiments, which also included a Panzerjäger company with 3 × 7.5cm Paks and 36 Panzerschrecke. Additionally, there was a recce battalion with a heavy squadron including 6 × 8cm mortars, 3 × 7.5cm Paks and 4 × 7.5cm leIGs; a Panzerjäger battalion with a Flak company (12 × 2cm mountain guns), a Sturmgeschütz battery of 10 or 14 × StuGs and a PzJr company of either 7.5cm Paks (10–14) or 14 × SP 7.5cm (or 7.62cm) Paks; an artillery regiment of four battalions (two equipped with 3 × 7.5cm batteries each of 4 × Geb 36 guns, one with 3 × batteries of 10.5cm howitzers, and one with 3 × 15cm sFH howitzers); a Pionier battalion with three companies each armed with 6 × flamethrowers and 2 × 8cm mortars; a Feldersatz battalion of five companies (armed with 6 × 8cm and 4 × 120mm mortars, a 5cm Pak, a 7.5cm Pak, a 2cm Flak, a 10.5cm leFH 18 and two flamethrowers).

Much of the transport involved horses, mules and pack; there were bicycle troops and latterly a degree of motorisation.

BELOW The Fallschirmjäger proved to be the most effective of all the Wehrmacht's infantry. Rarely inserted by parachute or glider drop after the losses over Crete, their distinctive smock and helmet made them instantly recognisable. They fought alongside army units and were under army control unless they were dropping as paratroops.

Fallschirmjäger

Probably the toughest of all the troops encountered by the Allies in the West, the Fallschirmjäger fought with distinction from Eben Emael in Belgium 1940, in their one and only mass-drop on Crete in 1941, in Russia, in the North African desert with Rommel, in Italy at Monte Cassino and in epic battles with US paratroopers in Normandy. General Ramcke, whose men had fought bravely in North Africa and Italy, finally surrendered as garrison commander of Festung Brest after a tough battle.

The first Fallschirmjäger unit, 7th Fliegerdivision, was raised in 1938 and it was under this name that it launched into the Second World War. Combining the short-lived Army Parachute Battalion with its Luftwaffe counterpart, under the aegis of Generalmajor Kurt Student, it saw action in Poland but not from the air: the Panzer divisions had moved too quickly for that. It was as motorised infantry that 7th Flieger took its first objectives and sustained its first casualties. The initial battle drop by the Fallschirmjäger was in Denmark on 9 April 1940. There were a number of drops into Norway and fierce fighting before they returned to Germany to prepare for the audacious *coup de main* on Eben Emael fortress that successfully captured bridges over the River Maas (Meuse) and Albert Canal. Further operations in Holland were not as successful and casualties were high, but the paratroopers were ready to play a role in Operation Sea Lion (against England) until it was called off.

XI Fliegerkorps was formed in January 1941 as the Fallschirmjäger forces were expanded and they took part in Operation Marita (Greece) and Merkur (Crete), where they helped take the island, albeit at great cost. XI Fliegerkorps lost a staggering 3,352 dead and missing and 3,400 wounded out of a force of 22,000 men. Of the transport aircraft used for the Fallschirmjäger, over half were lost. The losses had an immediate effect: the Germans never again used paratroopers in a set-piece operation. (On the other hand, of course, the Allies took the opposite view and immediately began to build up their airborne forces.) They would drop on Elba and Leros, and play the major role in the successful operation to free Mussolini on the Gran Sasso in September 1943, but for the rest of the war they fought mainly as elite ground troops.

Until autumn 1943 there had been only one Fliegerkorps of two parachute divisions. Each had three rifle regiments of three battalions with additional artillery, MG, Panzerjäger, Pionier and signals units. In late 1943 the 3rd and 4th Divisions were formed (the latter including some Italian Paras). The four were split into two Fliegerkorps, one in Italy (1st and 4th Divisions) and the other in France. By the end of the war there would be 11 Fallschirmjäger divisions, those in France collected with other Luftwaffe units (including the Hermann Göring Fallschirm-Panzerkorps) under the grandly titled First Fallschirmarmee, most of whose units were decimated in the Normandy fighting and in the Falaise Pocket. Reconstituted units fought bravely in Holland and the Reichswald, and the Panzerkorps ended the war in Silesia. In 1945, three more divisions were formed, although they had little or no parachute training and were not of the same quality as the earlier units.

Luftwaffefelddivisionen – Air Force field divisions

The Air Force field divisions were formed in the latter part of 1942 from AA personnel, air signal troops, ground and administrative units. Most served on the Russian front in winter 1942/43 but some saw action in Italy and some in France. In autumn 1943 the Luftwaffefelddivisionen left Luftwaffe control to come under the army. Many of them had suffered heavy losses and were disbanded in 1943 and 1944, a number joining the Fallschirmjäger and the remaining few forming divisions reorganised along the lines of the 1944-type infantry division.

LEFT The Luftwaffe ground divisions were set up in 1942 when infantry manpower began to be an issue. Some 200,000 men were employed – not all of a high standard because they lacked the training of their army counterparts. In 1943 they gave up their Luftwaffe uniforms and became regular army troops. *(PK KBK Lw 4 WikiCommons/ Bundesarchiv, Bild 101I-395-1513-06/ Haustein/CC)*

Kriegsmarine land units

As with the Luftwaffe, a number of Kriegsmarine troops fought as infantry during the war. There was some land fighting: the *Marinestoßtruppkompanie* took part in one of the first battles of the war on 1 September at Westerplatte in Poland and other actions by Marines – for example in Norway in 1940. Kriegsmarine units were involved in the occupation of the Channel Islands. Subsequently, as the Atlantic Wall was built, naval coastal batteries, Flak and radar units were staffed by Kriegsmarine personnel but it was in 1944–45 that the main infantry units were formed, some 40 regiments and, latterly in 1945, six divisions (1st, 2nd, 3rd, 11th, 16th and Gotenhafen). None reached full strength. At the end of the war Großadmiral Karl Dönitz (commander-in-chief of the Kriegsmarine) sent a couple of companies to Berlin on Hitler's orders.

THE HITLER OATH

Ich schwöre bei Gott diesen heiligen Eid, daß ich dem Führer des Deutschen Reiches und Volkes, Adolf Hitler, dem Oberbefehlshaber der Wehrmacht, unbedingten Gehorsam leisten und als tapferer Soldat bereit sein will, jederzeit für diesen Eid mein Leben einzusetzen.

I swear by God this holy oath, that I shall render unconditional obedience to the Führer of the German Reich and people, Adolf Hitler, the commander-in-chief of the Wehrmacht, and be prepared as a brave soldier to risk my life at any time for this oath.

Chapter Three

The soldier

The Hitlerjugend and RAD did their job well. When young men were called up they had the equivalent of basic military training, were physically robust and well indoctrinated. This meant that their army training could concentrate on developing their tactical and battlefield acumen. After August 1934 – when Hitler declared himself Führer and Reichskanzler – each one of them had to swear the *Führereid*, the Hitler oath.

OPPOSITE A training march just before the start of the war. The uniforms of the soldiers lack badges and medals. Less than two years later, some of these men will walk most of the way to Moscow. *(Tanis)*

ABOVE The Sturmabteilung was an excellent recruiting ground for young soldiers. Here we see a photograph of a special *Fahnenweihe* flag consecration ceremony, where SA flags were 'sanctified' by coming into contact with the original bloodstained flag carried during the Beer Hall Putsch. *(Bundesarchiv, B 145 Bild-P049613/Weinrother, Carl/CC-BY-SA 3.0)*

Chapter 1 outlined the work of the Hitlerjugend and RAD in preparing young men for army duty. One other organisation also needs to be mentioned: the Brownshirts or *Sturmabteilung* (SA).

Today remembered for its paramilitary actions – particularly those against the Jews such as Kristallnacht in 1938 – the SA had grown in strength in the 1920s until in 1933 it had more than 3 million men – far more than the Reichswehr. But its leader, Ernst Röhm, had put many noses out of joint, not only those of senior Nazi leaders but also of the army establishment.

Röhm and other leaders were murdered in the 1934 Night of the Long Knives and Viktor Lutze took over. The SA was reduced in size and essentially became a training organisation. In January 1939 Hitler ordered that the SA should provide training for men aged between 18 and 65 outside military service. The SA Military Training Defence Group – *SA Wehrmannschaften* – was set up to do this. Initially this training consisted of military exercises over a period of up to three weeks. After this, members were expected to serve for two evenings a week and six hours on Sunday. It was estimated that 13,400 Reserve officers and 30,000 Reserve NCOs were among its members.

BELOW The medical examination at the Musterung. Standards were lowered during the war. From 1943 the categories were: *Kriegsverwendungsfähig* (fit for regular service), *bedingt kriegsverwendungsfähig* (fit for limited service), *arbeitsverwendungsfähig* (fit for labour service), *wehruntauglich* (totally unfit), *zeitlich untauglich* (temporarily unfit).

Conscription

Germany had been used to universal conscription for many years, so it was no major issue when Hitler reintroduced it in 1935 when the period of active service was fixed at one year. This was extended to two years in August 1936 for all men aged 18–45.

In peacetime the registration (*Musterung*) – at age 18 – included a medical examination as well as a provisional assignment to a branch of service. The actual drafting (*Aushebung*) involved a second physical examination, a definite assignment to an arm of the service and a decision regarding any request for deferment. If found fit (*tauglich*), they were then called to the colours (*Einberufung*) and inducted (*Einstellung*) into the military. Between their first registration and induction, the men usually performed their required period of labour service (*Arbeitsdienst*), entering military service at age 20. During the war, however, everything was speeded up: the age limits were varied, the length of service extended and women were conscripted as well as men. The Musterung and Aushebung happened at the same time with induction taking place at 18 initially – and then 17 or younger. Occupational and other deferments, fairly widespread in the early war years, were strictly limited later. Steadily, older and older men were also called up until Ersatzreserve II and Landwehr II were subject to call; the Landsturm, too, would finally serve in the extreme conditions of 1945, as did youngsters from the Hitlerjugend.

The flexibility of the Replacement Training Army meant that the call to arms came in *Wellen* – waves. John Mulholland quotes Dr Leo Niehorster's description of this system:

> *Welle was the German designation for groups of infantry divisions raised at approximately the same time, with approximately the same type of organization and equipment, and that shared a similar type of personnel and level of training.*

In 1939, in the lead-up to war, there were five waves adding strength to the existing army. Note, at this stage the Panzer divisions were doubled in number as the Leichte Divisionen were given tanks. The wave system continued throughout the war, but numbers, organisation and equipment varied depending on availability. The 35 first-wave infantry divisions each had a strength of 17,700 men, whereas the second wave had 2,460 fewer. This reduction in fighting strength continued through the war, during which at least 294 infantry divisions were created in 35 waves.

As the war progressed and more and more waves were called up, divisions that had sustained serious numbers of casualties – and there were many – needed to be remanned and rearmed. To simplify this, shadow divisions were created, with reduced staff and personnel elements, often formed from reserve divisions, who only took a unit designation when they were used to reinstate a front-line division.

German men over 18 and fit for service were placed into the following categories:

Aktiv dienende – on active service.
Reserve I – fully trained, under 35 years of age.
Reserve II – partly trained, under 35.
Ersatzreserve I – untrained, not yet called up, under 35.
Ersatzreserve II – untrained, physically unfit, under 35.
Landwehr I – trained, between 35 and 45.
Landwehr II – untrained, between 35 and 45.
Landsturm I – trained, over 45.
Landsturm II – untrained, over 45.

GERMAN MOBILISATION WAVES FOR INFANTRY DIVISIONS, 1934–44

Wave No	Formed	Number of divs[2]	Divisions[3]	Comments
1	1934–38	38	1–46	Peacetime army units; also 50, 60 and 72 retroactively
2	Aug 1939	16	52–79, 86, 87	From fully trained reservists
3	Aug/Sept 1939	21	205–246	Landwehr (older personnel)
4	Aug/Sept 1939	14	251–269	From reserve units
5	Sept 1939	11	93–98	Reservists
6	Nov 1939	4	81–88	Reservists, all disbanded 1940
Various divisions were formed outside the *Welle* system in the period 1935–39: 9 Panzer, 4 Infantry (mot), 1 Kavallerie, 4 Leichte, 3 Gebirgs, 21 DivNr,[4] 2 named, 35 Div Stab zbV.[5]				
7	Jan 1940	14	161–199	From reserve units
8	Feb 1940	10	290–299	Mostly 1940 draft class
9	March 1940	10+	351–399	Mostly older personnel for static duties. Largely disbanded 1940
			500 series	Disbanded 1940
10	June 1940	9	270–280	Static units, disbanded, 1940

Wave No	Formed	Number of divs[2]	Divisions[3]	Comments
11	Oct 1940	10	121–137	Veterans for Russian Campaign
12	Dec 1940	6	102–113	Veterans for Russian Campaign
13	Oct 1940	9	302–327	For use in occupied Western Europe
14	Nov/Dec 1940	8	332–342	For use in occupied Western Europe
Various divisions were formed outside the Welle system in 1940: 11 Panzer, 9 Infantry (mot), 6 SS, 4 Leichte, 3 Gebirgs, 1 Inf, 10 DivNr, 2 Div Stab zbV.				
15	April/May 1941	15	702–719	Static; for West and Balkans
16	Mar/June 1941	11	201–454	Security Divisions
17	Dec 1941	4	328–331	For use in Russia
Various divisions were formed outside the Welle system in 1941: 4 Panzer, 1 SS, 5 Leichte, 1 Gebirgs, 2 Inf, 3 named, 1 Div Stab zbV.				
18	Jan/Feb 1942	5	383–389	Static; for use in West; later sent East; 385 disbanded and incorporated with 387
19	Feb/March 1942	4	370–377	For use in West; later sent East
20	July 1942	3	38–65	Static; for use in West
Various divisions were formed outside the Welle system in 1942: 3 Panzer, 2 Infantry (mot), 8 SS, 2 Leichte, 13 Inf, 6 named, 6 Jäger, 1 Festung, 1 Sicherungs, 18 Reserve, 6 Field Training, 22 DivNr, 1 Luftlande, Göring LW, 21 Luft Feld.				
	Spring 1943	14	(44–389)	Bore numbers of divisions destroyed in Stalingrad
21	Nov/Dec 1943	10	349–367	Employment varied
22	Dec 1943	6	271–278	From remnants of disbanded units; used in West
Various divisions were formed outside the Welle system in 1943: 2 Panzer, 14 PzGr, 1 Leichte, 16 Inf, 3 named, 5 lettered (A–E), 1 Div Stab zbV, 5 Jäger, 1 Festung, 8 Reserve, 9 DivNr, 26 Div Group, Korps-Abt A–E, 2 Sturm, 4 Artillerie, 3 FJR, 19 Luft Feld.				
23	Jan 1944	3	52, 390-394	Sicherungs divisions
24	April 1944	5		Shadow divisions used to rebuild infantry divisions
25	Feb 1944	6	77–92	For use in West
26	March 1944	4		Shadow divisions used to rebuild infantry divisions
	May 1944	3	50, 73, 98	Replacing divisions lost at Sevastopol
27	July 1944	5	59–237	Formed from reserve divisions
28	July 1944	6		Shadow divisions used to rebuild infantry divisions
	July 1944	10+	500 series	Grenadier brigades
29	July 1944	17	541–562	Grenadier (later Volksgrenadier)
30	August 1944	6	12–36 VG	Formed from cadres and July 1944 grenadier brigades
31	August 1944	5		Shadow divisions used to rebuild infantry divisions
32	Aug–Sept 1944	12	564–588	Divisions of any previous wave reformed as Volksgrenadier units
Various divisions were formed outside the Welle system in 1944: 6 named Panzer, 2 named PzGr, 20 SS, 16 Inf, 9 named, 5 named Inf, 9 Grenadier, 47 VG, 2 Gebirgs, 1 Festung, 2 Reserve, 2 Field Training, 5 DivNr, 12 Div Stab zbV, 12 Div Groups, 3 Korps Abt, 1 Artillerie, 1 Luftlande, 1 Skijäger, 1 Marine, 6 FJR, 2 Sturm.				
33–35	1945			Many divisions to be formed in March.

Source: There is little agreement in the published and online sources as to the divisions created in the various Wellen. Information in this table is primarily from Mitcham, *Hitler's Legions*, and Mulholland (www.axishistory.com).

Notes:

[1] See http://www.axishistory.com/axis-nations/145-germany-heer/heer-unsorted/3419-the-german-mobilization-and-welle-wave-system-1939-1945 for detailed listing.
[2] Not all divisions were raised under the wave system.
[3] Number sequences not complete: see website above for more complete detail.
[4] DivNr – Replacement and Training Divisions.
[5] Div-Stab zbV (*zur besonderen Verwendung*) – Special Administrative Division Staff.

Training

Since 1945, it has been the norm to extol the training of the ordinary soldiers and NCOs of the German Army. Their steadfast defence in the face of huge odds, their flexibility, tactical acumen and bravery has been promoted so much that it has passed into fact: the Germans were good soldiers who only lost because of the numbers of the opposition and the depth of the pockets and industrial power base of the United States. They were far better than the Americans, British and Soviets who overwhelmed them; the Germans had better equipment, better officers and were better trained.

While there is no doubt that there are elements of truth in this view – some of the Allies' forces weren't up to scratch; some of their tactical doctrine wasn't suitable; some of their weapons were poor – there are also strong elements of propaganda, just as post-war HIAG (*Hilfsgemeinschaft auf Gegenseitigkeit der Angehörigen der ehemaligen Waffen-SS*) tried to argue that the Waffen-SS was just a regular armed force, the fourth arm of the Wehrmacht. In reality, the German infantryman came in many different guises: some were well-trained Fallschirmjäger, others rather less capable and placed in static divisions.

The training of the German infantryman was, indeed, comprehensive, particularly so in the 1930s. It was certainly brutal. Injuries were frequent and discipline was harsh and, not infrequently, enforced by capital punishment. The training took place in the Replacement Army before recruits moved on to the Field Army. From the moment they had to pack up and send their civilian clothes home, the emphasis was on physical fitness. Next came drill and weapons training with rifle training – marksmanship, stripping, cleaning and loading – an important component. As rifle skills improved, so the machine gun was introduced. In the early years, training started on older equipment – First World War weapons and helmets – but soon the MG15s were replaced by MG34s and K98ks replaced the longer G98s.

The 16 weeks of training included fire and movement, command, ballistics, heavy weapons, tactical field training – map reading, fieldcraft, camouflage – but physical fitness training was never far away with route marches carrying full pack and weapons.

However, later in the war most of the niceties of training were in the past: much of the physical training was handled by the RAD and the new recruits went straight to weapons training. Erwin Grubba was born in Marienberg in East Prussia in 1925. He was 17 in 1942, was called up and spent a few months in Poland in an RAD labour battalion where he dug anti-tank ditches, underwent paramilitary training, did guard duty and had regular visits from Waffen-SS recruiters. After his RAD stint

ABOVE Drill is always a significant part of any military training and the German Army had its fair share. For ceremonial duties they also used what the English-speaking world calls the goosestep.

BELOW Getting ready for roll-call (*Appell*). The German marching boots (*Marschstiefel*) were termed jackboots in the English-speaking world. The soldiers nicknamed them *Knobelbecher* (dice shakers).

RIGHT ***Grundstellung*** **(order arms) – butt on the ground by right foot, trigger guard forward. Grasp rifle in right hand near upper barrel band.** ***Das Gewehr ... Über!*** **(shoulder arms) – in five counts. Only the hands and arms move; the body must stay absolutely rigid** ***Gewehr ... ab!*** **(order arms) – in four counts, and again, the body must stay absolutely rigid, returning to** ***Grundstellung*****.**

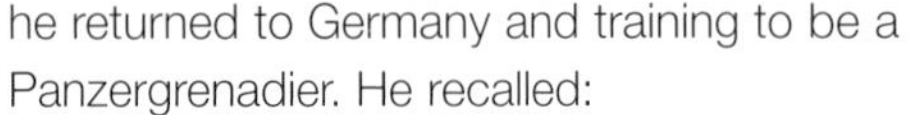

he returned to Germany and training to be a Panzergrenadier. He recalled:

> *But looking back, I can see how skimpy it was. We really didn't have much time. We were hardly through the basics when we were called onto the square again and an officer addressed us: 'Look lads,' he said, 'You're off on a train tomorrow going to the Eastern Front.' … I still think we were raw greenhorns ... but at least we could handle our guns. And we knew what to do and how to react to certain commands … all they really wanted you to do was to fire your rifle and throw hand grenades – that was all you had to do! … I was a civilian in uniform I suppose.*

NCO training

NCOs are the backbone of every army, and the German Army was no exception. During the early years after the Treaty of Versailles, when the army had been restricted in size, the High Command had ensured that the force wasn't top-heavy with officers. Each of the 100,000 was trained to provide a cadre that could itself quickly train conscripts in time of war.

There were two types of NCO: career soldiers who had signed on for 4½ or 12 years – some of whom had applied for NCO training at 16 and joined the army at 17 – and active soldiers who had either applied or had been chosen from the ranks. At first, the latter had to have served a year from conscription. Later, the training period for NCOs was curtailed and much of the instruction instead took place at their unit.

Having applied, the candidates who were in the Replacement Army went to NCO school. Training lasted four months and then there was six months' advanced training for their arm of service: infantry, artillery, armour, mountain troops, etc. By late 1944 there were 22 infantry schools and 13 for other arms, including one Gebirgsjäger and seven Panzer (the latter included Panzergrenadier training).

Officer training

All Wehrmacht officer candidates passed through one of the five *Kriegsschulen* (Potsdam, Dresden, München, Hannover and Wiener-Neustadt). Before 1940, training for officer candidates who had passed the *Abitur* exam and a military test started with *Grund-und Vollausbildung* – basic and advanced military training – that took place over 12–16 weeks in a regular unit.

Next came a Kriegsschule for 8 weeks before the officer candidate moved on to a *Truppenschule* for 16 weeks. This was a branch military school, such as the *Panzertruppenschulen* at Münster (I) or Wünsdorf (II) for tankers or the Infanterietruppenschule at Wien (Vienna). At this stage the candidate had reached the rank of *Fähnrich* (the equivalent of an Unterfeldwebel). His final tour of duty as an Unteroffizier was eight weeks' *Felderprobung* (field probation) as an

Oberfähnrich (Oberfeldwebel equivalent) before he would be commissioned as Leutnant.

After 1940 this training was altered to favour actively serving men and NCOs becoming officers. The training time was shortened and for those active servicemen under 25 included four to six months' weapons training, three to four months' *Offizieranwärterlehrgang* (cadet training course) and 15 months as a *Fahnenjunker-Feldwebel* before promotion to officer level. Those between 25 and 30 became *Kriegsoffiziere* and went straight to *Offizieranwärterlehrgang* (officer candidates' course). Those experienced NCOs over 30 and with 12 months' service in a unit could be promoted to Fahnenjunker-Feldwebel by their CO.

In 1940, US observers estimated that schools were turning out about 6,500 officers every four months, and that 30,000 new officers entered the army between September 1939 and December 1940.

The high standards set by the training schools ensured that candidates had considerable background training, but expanding the German Army for war led to problems. To iron these out, great attention was paid to 'continuation' training of officers, particularly company officers, in the field. This continuation training involved reference to the *Truppenführung* (Manual of Troop Leadership), the field manual published in two parts (in 1933 and 1934) and sometimes named the most influential military doctrinal manual ever written.

It stressed the need for versatility; that the infantry officer must familiarise himself with the capabilities of other arms than his own – a combined-arms view of fighting that certainly assisted the formation of Kampfgruppen. It also stressed that officers must prepare themselves for service in the next higher grade and that it was the responsibility of senior officers to help their juniors in training for advancement, an ideal summed up by one officer: 'We apply simple methods to our leadership. You will find that our lower units are so trained that many in them beside the leader are capable of taking command.'

LEFT AND BELOW As in all armies, grooming was important in the Wehrmacht and facial hair was against regulations other than a small, neatly trimmed moustache and beards in the U-boat service. As the war went on, these restrictions weren't followed strictly. *(both via RCT)*

RIGHT Weapons cleaning – in this case a Maschinengewehr 08. A First World War weapon, it saw continued use in Second World War infantry divisions as there were insufficient MG34s. *(via RCT)*

Personal documentation

Wehrpaß

The basic personal record of the members of all the Armed Forces was the Wehrpaß or service record book. Passport-sized, it was issued to every conscript at the time of his first physical examination for military service, and stamped with their branch of service: Heer, Kriegsmarine, Luftwaffe or Waffen-SS.

It was issued by his *Wehrbezirkskommando* (recruiting sub-area headquarters), where a number of records were opened: the *Wehrstammbuch* (basic military record book – an open envelope with his registration record and containing a *Polizeibericht* (police report) on his conduct prior to registration) into which is pasted his *Wehrstammkarte* (military registration card); the *Gesundheitsbuch* (health record book); and *Verwendungskarte* (classification card). Before 1944, the Verwendungskarte held the soldier's training record, but from autumn 1944, a detailed training record sheet (*Ausbildungsnachweis*) was inserted in the *Soldbuch* (paybook).

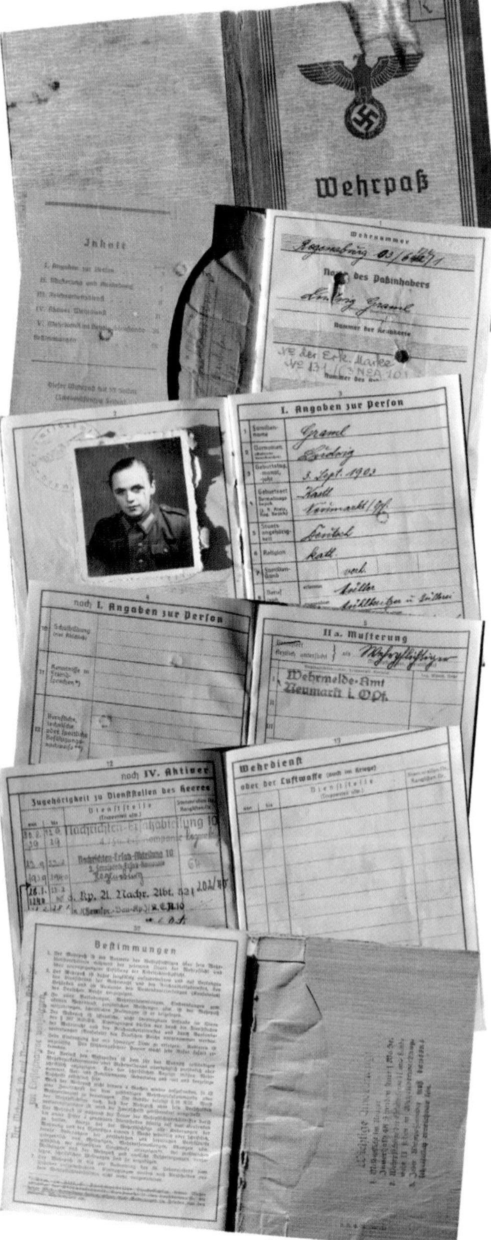

RIGHT The Wehrpaß was the official record for all men who were eligible to serve in the Wehrmacht. It stayed with the unit and was only returned if he left service or was killed. The first two points on the inside back cover emphasise this:

1. The Wehrpaß is the conscript's identity card for the whole of his compulsory military service and on the previous fulfilment of his compulsory labour service obligation.

2. The Wehrpaß must, therefore, be kept carefully and presented on demand to departments of the Wehrmacht and the Reichsarbeitsdienst, the authorities and abroad to the diplomatic missions (consulates) of the German Reich. *(Ken Adams collection)*

Physically, there were a number of variations to the form the Wehrpaß took during the war. The early-war versions have a Wehrmacht-style eagle with downward-facing wings; later in the war the open-winged eagle was used. There were colour variations, too, from grey to black to bluey-grey.

The Wehrpaß opens with the person's Wehrnummer (service number), name, book number and issuing details. The Wehrnummer is an important, permanent, identification feature that was retained whether he is in active service or not. It consisted of five elements:

1. The name of the Wehrbezirkskommando.
2. The last two digits of the year of the soldier's birth.
3. The number of the military registration police precinct (in certain larger cities, number corresponding to first letter of family name).
4. The serial number of the conscription (or volunteer) roster sheet (*Wehrstammrollenblatt*).
5. A number indicating registrant's place on that sheet (from 1 to 10).

Next there's a personal photograph and *Angaben zur Person*, information about the person – name, date of birth, birth place, nationality, religion, family details – including details of foreign languages known and other technical or sporting abilities that could be useful: driving, riding, sailing, flying, swimming, etc.

The second section covers the registration; the third Reichsarbeitsdienst service; and the fourth active military service.

The Wehrpaß was handed over when the person became a soldier. In return he received a Soldbuch. The Wehrpaß was returned to him when he was discharged from the military.

ABOVE The Soldbuch served as the soldier's personal ID and had to be carried at all times. The Spieß would ensure it was kept up to date with promotions noted, any awards listed, etc.

THE FIVE RULES OF THE SOLDBUCH

Read through carefully!

1. The Soldbuch serves the soldier as personal identification in wartime and gives him the authority to receive pay from his own or other duty stations. It may also be used as identification for purposes of travelling on trains, detached service, leave and for receiving mail.
2. The Soldbuch must always be carried by the soldier in the tunic pocket. Leaving the Soldbuch in baggage, in quarters, etc., is not allowed. Taking good care of the Soldbuch is in the best interest of the owner.
3. The Soldbuch must be kept in an orderly manner. The owner himself is required to make certain that changes in pay rate due to transfer or promotion are promptly entered by the responsible duty station.
4. The Soldbuch is an official document. Entries in it are only to be made by a Wehrmacht duty station. Unauthorized changes to the Soldbuch are punishable as falsification of official documents.
5. The loss of the Soldbuch must be reported at once by the owner to his unit or duty station, where a request to issue a new Soldbuch will be made.

Soldbuch

When the soldier entered service he handed in his Wehrpaß and received his Soldbuch – paybook – which was his official means of identification, and acted as an identity card to the police. It carried his Wehrnummer and the number and inscription on his *Erkennungsmarke* (identity disc).

Like the Wehrpaß it contained his personal data and a record of the units in which he served. At 24 pages long, it included his current and past units; his clothing and equipment record; details of his inoculations and hospitalisation; promotions, pay rate group and payments received from units other than his own – the Soldbuch didn't record the payments made from his regular unit but gave him the authority to receive them. In it were also recorded his decorations, periods of leave and other data relating to his active service.

Erkennungsmarke

The oval identity disc – the equivalent of the dog tag – was worn by every member of the Wehrmacht. It was made of aluminium until 1941 when zinc began to be used. Steel came in towards the end of the war. It was divided in half, each half identical and bearing a number and inscription (*Beschriftung und Nummer der Erkennungsmarke*). The disc was issued by the soldier's first unit, normally at company level, and the inscription included the name of this unit, his serial number and (after 1941) his blood type. Should he lose the original, his unit may supply a new disc, in which case it would be issued with that unit's own name and a new serial number.

If the soldier was injured or killed in action,

LEFT This replica dog-tag (Erkennungsmarke) shows that the bearer (number 1066, blood group A) was first enrolled with the 2nd Company of Panzergrenadier-Ersatz-Bataillon 2, before being sent on to his unit. The half attached to a body was left there; the lower half was collected. *(Ken Adams collection)*

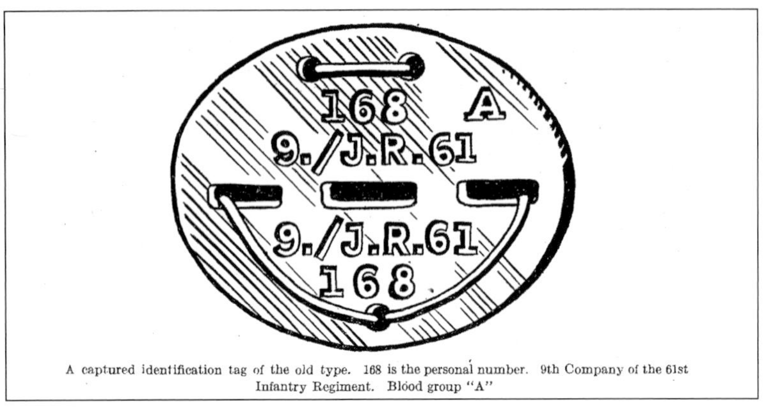

A captured identification tag of the old type. 168 is the personal number. 9th Company of the 61st Infantry Regiment. Blood group "A"

ABOVE The German dog-tag identification system wasn't particularly successful. Bodies discovered in the last 20 years have shown that many soldiers didn't wear them; that they were often exchanged in error; that the aluminium and zinc composition does not stand up to fire (and also corrodes); and that if a single piece of unit information is lost – either on the dog-tag or the record book – they are rendered useless. This diagram shows a soldier who was the 168th to be enrolled with the 9th Company of Jäger-Regiment 61. *(From Handbook of German Army Identification)*

RIGHT AND BELOW Infantry and Panzergrenadier divisions had commissary support in the form of bakery, butchery and commissary companies. Hypothetically a division needed over 10,000 loaves on a typical day. *(both via Tanis)*

the part with the cord/chain was left with the body, while the bottom half was broken off and returned to the unit for processing.

When discharged from active service, the soldier gave up his Soldbuch. It would remain on file at his home recruiting station until such time as he returned to service. He received in return his Wehrpaß. Discharged soldiers were also given a discharge certificate (*Entlaßungsschein*). If the soldier were killed in action, his military records were filed by his home recruiting station but the Wehrpaß was given to the next of kin. A report on his death and burial, together with the lower half of his Erkennungsmarke and a description of the grave, was sent to the Armed Forces Information Bureau for War Casualties and Prisoners of War.

Life in the field

Food and rations

We all know that an army marches on its stomach and feeding the Heer was just as important as ensuring it had enough ammunition. However, as with so many things in the Heer, the rations and the delivery system were a mixture of the excellent and the awful.

First, it's worth remembering that men with guns can always get shelter and food in populated areas simply by billeting themselves – or turfing out – the locals, the likelihood of this happening dependent on the weather, the morale of the troops and the strength of the officers. But when there are no suitable buildings, when the local populace is starving or when the war is mobile, the soldier must depend on the system and in the Heer, it creaked.

Soldiers in the field were supposed to get two hot meals a day – lunch being the most important – from the field kitchens staffed by the *Feldkochunteroffizier* and the *Küchenbullen* (his assistants). Lunch amounted to half of the *Portionsatz* – daily ration quantity – the evening meal to a third and the next morning's breakfast to one-sixth.

The hot food usually came from a horse-drawn rolling field kitchen, although motorised units sometimes had a vehicle. The large rolling field kitchen served 125–225 men; the small rolling field kitchen, 50–125.

FAR LEFT Another photograph taken during training in Germany when supplies were plentiful. *(via Tanis)*

LEFT A commissary unit in a rifle company would have had a *Goulaschkanone* – field kitchen – two cooks and various assistants who were known as *Küchenbullen*. *(via Tanis)*

Food was taken to the frontline soldiers who couldn't mess at the kitchen in hot food carriers – but depending on the distance from the kitchen and the danger of the route could – and often did – arrive cold. There were, of course, other options, as one of James Lucas's contributors remembers (in *War on the Eastern Front*): 'Some of us tied tins of food around the [vehicle] exhausts. It was quick, but if they were left in position too long the tins would nearly explode when they were opened, pouring scalding liquid over hands that were freezing.'

As well as the hot food, soldiers received a daily bread ration with cheese, ham and jam for breakfast and iron or half-iron rations (*eiserne Portionen* or *halb-eiserne Portionen*) as necessary:

- March rations (*Marschverpflegung*) – total weight about 1kg (2.2lb) split into 700g of bread, 200g of cold meat or cheese, 60g spreads, 9g of coffee (or 4g of tea), 10g of sugar and six cigarettes.
- Iron rations (*eiserne Portionen*) – around 650g of food: 250–300g biscuits (Zwieback, Hartkeks or Knäckebrot), 200g cold meat (*Fleischkonserve*), 150g preserved vegetables (*Gemüse*), 25g coffee (*Kaffe-Ersatz*) and 25g salt (*Salz*). Iron and iron half-rations could only be eaten with the express permission of the unit CO.
- Iron half-rations (*halb-eiserne Portionen*) – about 0.5kg (1lb) of biscuits (250g) and a tin of preserved meat (200g).
- Towards the end of the war the Germans tried to emulate the US K rations by producing the *Großkampfpäcken* (combat package) and *Nahkampfpäcken* (close combat package) for troops in combat. Contents varied but included chocolate bars, fruit bars, sweets, cigarettes and possibly biscuits.

As well as 'liberating' food from the local population and living off the land, captured rations were in demand – particularly from the Americans, the quality of whose food amazed the Germans. Jeff Johannes quotes Hebert

ABOVE AND BELOW The Goulaschkanone might look antiquated, horse-drawn and wood-burning, but it did the job. They came in different sizes and, once cooked, the food had to be taken up to the troops, either in individual mess tins or in an *Essenträger*.

RIGHT The Kochgeschirr 31 cooking pot/mess kit, whose body had a capacity of 1.71 litres and the lid 0.54 litres. A full mess kit lid held roughly 500g of rice and 425g of sugar. *(Ken Adams collection)*

Brach, of the 6/ II.GR 916 during the Battle of the Bulge who arrived at Bettendorf and

> *appropriated an American food and clothing storehouse. ... Everybody feasted on the tasty U.S. field rations, and nobody asked where our field kitchen was ... the field kitchen finally came to Diekirch to supply us with hot food, but nobody was hungry. ... The supply chief himself came on the scene and was annoyed to have to take the watery stew away again.*

RIGHT, FAR RIGHT AND BELOW The Essenträger was a large double-skinned aluminium flask that helped keep food warm between leaving the field kitchen and reaching the troops. It wasn't a vacuum flask: there was hot water between the skins. Carrying it forward could be a dangerous occupation if there were snipers about.

Bodily functions

'Life was basic,' said one soldier on the Eastern Front, 'Eat the food, evacuate the food, sleep, guard and fight.' What few mention is how debilitating even the most mundane of tasks became in a Russian winter where 'ears must not come in contact with the metal of the helmet' or skin will freeze to metal and 'Special protective measures for the genitals should be taken if the weather is very cold or the wind very strong.'

Defecation was a tiresome procedure in Russia:

> *... many were glad that they were constipated even though this brought headaches and stomach cramps. An unpeeling of layers of clothing, a few agonising minutes and then, once again, the putting back of layers. Those with dysentery suffered more than most ... the first traces of blood were often a sentence of death. A ravine, a dip or even a low snow wall would protect against the wind. ... We had many cases of cystitis, unable to urinate quickly and an intense burning sensation made this simple procedure a long and painful business. Out of fear of frostbite most of us wrapped that part of our body in a thick cloth. ... Together with all the odours from unwashed bodies, feet and clothing you can imagine we didn't smell very sweet.*

In Africa, the problems were of a different nature:

> *excrement and refuse are the breeding places of flies, and these carry to foodstuffs or direct to people the germs of dangerous illnesses (especially dysentery) ... the virus of many different kinds of diseases can come from the water of this country. Therefore, never drink unboiled water, also do not rinse out your mouth with it, as long as your superior officers do not designate the water pure! ... Do not eat raw meat. Never drink unboiled milk, especially not goat milk!*

Feldpost

Post is immensely important for troop morale and the German Feldpost system worked hard

LEFT Newspapers were important propaganda tools – particularly when the news at the front wasn't good. They were regularly sent from home to remind the troops of what they were missing. *(via RCT)*

to ensure that letters and packets reached the appropriate units. Each division had a field post office and each unit had a randomly assigned field post number (*Feldpost-Nummer*/FPN). Of five digits initially, in late 1939 a prefix L or M was added to indicate Luftwaffe and Marine. Heer FPNs gained a suffix letter A–E that indicated company. Military post was free within Germany until war broke out; after that packages up to a kilo attracted a 20-pfennig fee.

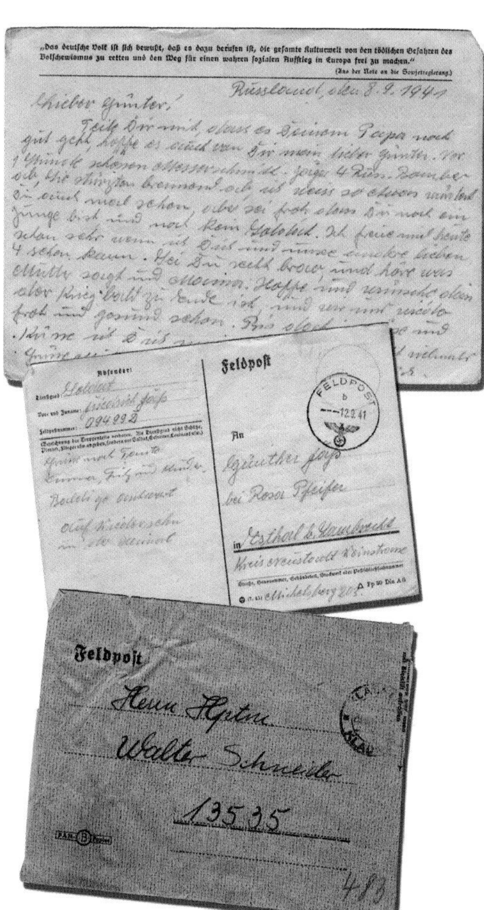

„Das deutsche Volk ist sich bewußt, daß es dazu berufen ist, die gesamte Kulturwelt von den tödlichen Gefahren des Bolschewismus zu retten und den Weg für einen wahren sozialen Aufstieg in Europa frei zu machen."
(Aus der Note an die Sowjetregierung.)

Russland, den 8.9.1941

Lieber Günter,

Feldpost

Feldpost

Herrn Hptm.
Walter Schneider
13535

LEFT Soldiers crave information from their friends, family and loved ones – and vice versa. The German Feldpost system had to cope with the immense – and speedy – expansion to its services required as outposts were spread from Norway to the south of France; from the Channel almost to Moscow. *(via RCT)*

Chapter Four

Uniform and equipment

German Second World War uniforms and equipment mixed of old and new. Much, from Stahlhelm to Iron Cross, was derived from earlier versions of comparable equipment. The German infantryman of 1939 was equipped very similarly to his First World War counterpart. However, there was also much that was new: new insignia and new decorations (with the swastika to the forefront), new ammo pouches for new weapons, cold weather gear for the Eastern Front, and new equipment for the new arms such as the Fallschirmjäger and Panzerjäger.

OPPOSITE A group of captured Panzergrenadiers from 15 Panzer Division in the North African desert in 1943. The unit was destroyed in Tunisia in spring of that year. They are wearing tropical cotton twill M40 five-button tunics and peaked caps.

Introduction

In the run-up to the outbreak of war, the uniforms worn by German Army troops were typical of most modern peacetime armies – that is, they were worn to regulation standards, with the slightest infraction being harshly punished. The basic designs used had been directly inherited from the Reichsheer of the Weimar Republic (1921–35), and as the army grew massively following Hitler's militarisation of the country, little changed. The standard Heer uniform at that time was the grey-green M36 (Model 1936 – here and elsewhere uniform patterns are abbreviated to M for model and the last two digits of the year) pattern. Among other features it had a dark-green collar and *Waffenfarbe* (corps colours) on the shoulders.

After hostilities broke out, however, the practicalities of the battlefield took over, and dress codes were significantly relaxed. This was exacerbated by stores' shortages and the widespread use of captured enemy equipment. Sometimes, however, the regulations were deliberately flouted, especially among the officers, who were meant to wear the same uniform as the other ranks. On paper this was to make them less conspicuous, but many ignored the rules and continued wearing the *Dienstrock* (officer's tunic) as they felt that it helped boost morale among the men. As time went on, many official changes were also seen, often as the result of attempts to reduce costs and/or production time.

The M36 pattern uniform (*Felduniform*) went through various small changes over the next few years, but was extensively revised in 1943 with the introduction of the M43 version, which consisted of a tunic, trousers and shirt. This was influenced by two major factors: the first being practical improvements; the second being the requirement to make economies wherever possible, both in materials and in production time. The tunic was shorter, had six buttons (in place of five), and no longer had the pocket pleats or the dark green facings. The liners were also made of inferior materials such as synthetic silk or viscose.

A final version of the battledress uniform was the M44. Although this was meant to be manufactured to a certain specification, the reality was that it was produced with whatever materials were available. The amount of cloth required to make it was reduced further still by shortening the length of the tunic, and as dyes were in particularly short supply, the colours were extremely variable. The trousers no longer required braces (although they could still be attached) as they were self-supporting, the pockets had flaps and the legs were designed to be used with ankle boots and gaiters.

Alongside the standard clothing, a summer uniform was produced in 1942. This was composed of a *Drillichbluse* (tunic) and matching *Drillichhosen* (trousers). Two versions were produced during the war: the first was dark green and made of linen, but as material shortages got worse, they were increasingly manufactured from synthetic substitutes which were greyer in colour.

One point to remember is that a key element throughout the war was the German – and to a lesser extent the Allies' – mix-and-match approach to keeping everything functional and working. This nightmare for collectors means that cannibalisation was the order of the day. Often what soldiers wore depended on the climate and conditions, summer and winter. A lot of cold weather kit was made locally and each soldier modified his kit to suit the situation and his personal preference. For example, not everyone likes kit banging around their hips.

Rank and insignia

From 1 May 1934, Germany's National Emblem (*Hoheitsabzeichen*) – the Nazi Party eagle-and-swastika – was worn in the army format as part of the uniform on both tunic and headgear. It featured a stylised silver eagle with outstretched wings clutching a wreathed *Hakenkreuz* (swastika).

The breast patch, which was worn on the right side above the pocket, was made of cloth and measured 3.54in (90mm) across. Other ranks initially had theirs constructed from silver-white rayon, while those for officers up to the rank of general were embroidered. This was either done by hand or by machine, using white silk or aluminium thread; generals, being more important, had theirs made in gold. On the outbreak of war, however, it was considered

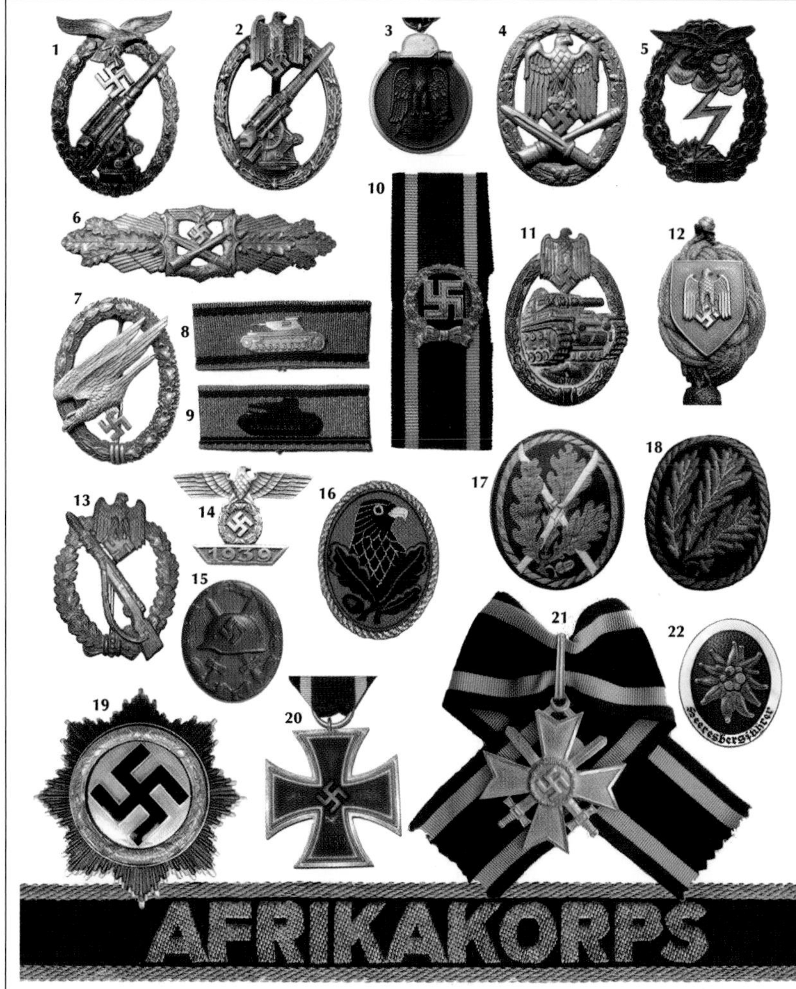

Medals and badges

1 *Flak-Kampfabzeichen der Luftwaffe*
2 *Heeres-Flak Abzeichen*
3 *Medaille, Winterschlacht im Osten 1941/42*
4 *Allgemeines Sturmabzeichen*
5 *Erdkampfabzeichen der Luftwaffe*
6 *Nahkampfspange*
7 *Fallschirmschützenabzeichen*
8/9 *Sonderabzeichen für das Niederkämpfen von Panzerkampfwagen durch Einzelkämpfer (8 in gold, 9 in silver)*
10 *Ehrenblatt des Heeres*
11 *Panzerkampfabzeichen*
12 *Schützen Abzeichen des deutschen Heeres*
13 *Infanterie-Sturmabzeichen*
14 *Spange zum Eisernen Kreuz*
15 *Verwundetenabzeichen*
16 *Scharfschützenabzeichen*
17 *Skijäger* arm badge
18 *Jäger* arm badge
19 *Deutsches Kreuz*
20 *Eisernes Kreuz*
21 *Kriegsverdienstkreuz*
22 *Heeresbergsführer* badge

LEFT *Afrika Korps cuff title*

that the patches on enlisted men were too visible, so more muted versions using matte grey thread were used. As the war progressed, many different variations of the breast eagle were produced, but as none were delisted, they were often seen side by side. By the end of the war resources were so limited that the patches were simply printed on thin cloth.

The National Rosette (*Reichskokarde*), a small circular insignia in black, white and red, was worn on all headgear below the national insignia, except on the steel helmet. It was flanked by oak leaves on all peaked caps except the mountain cap and field cap.

Litzen

The First World War had ensured that most of the gaudy 19th-century uniform displays had been toned down; in particular the amount of braid was reduced. But in spite of this, the German infantryman of the Second World War still enjoyed a range of insignia and symbols of rank and service.

First and foremost were the *Litzen*, the characteristic bars that appeared on the collar patches of German soldiers (other than generals) throughout the Second World War.

By 1938, the collar patch had become a universal design worn by all ranks below officer, with the individual units being identified by the Waffenfarben (see pages 63-64). In peacetime the Waffenfarbe showed through the spaces in the Litzen; in wartime the patches were woven in silver-grey rayon and the Waffenfarbe was relegated to the shoulder boards. Although wartime regulations stated that officers should wear the enlisted field uniform, many added their own green-and-silver collar patches.

All that remained of the braid was the *Tresse* worn by NCOs around the collar – the *Unteroffizierslitze* or *Kragenlitze* – a dull silver braid all around the collar.

Schulterklappen and *Schulterstücke* (shoulder straps)

Schulterklappen and Schulterstücke are essentially the same thing, the former referring to the shoulder straps of enlisted men and the latter to those of officers. To save confusion I have used the English shoulder straps throughout. Shoulder straps were attached to the uniform at the shoulder.

In 1938 the shape of the shoulder straps was changed: until then they had pointed ends; afterwards they had rounded ends, with the pattern then remaining unchanged throughout the war. On three sides the shoulder straps were edged with the relevant Waffenfarben (for the infantryman that would be white) with numbers and letters often identifying units – although the colours and unit designations were phased out as a security measure during wartime.

The different variations of shoulder straps are a minefield of confusion: generals, officers, NCOs and other ranks all have shoulder straps of different materials. A myriad of attached badges, numbers and Gothic script were used to identify units. Each arm of service had a different Waffenfarbe, these increasing in number through the period. There are variations in colour caused by material shortages and wear, and those of the *Wehrmachtbeamte* – civilians serving as army officials – involved different colours.

To add to the confusion, the *Anwärter* – candidates aspiring to be promoted to NCO (*Unteroffizieranwärter*) or officer (*Offizieranwärter*) rank – wore bars of braiding across the shoulder straps.

Finally, introduced in 1939–40 were different rank insignia for use on the denim uniform jacket (*Drillichbluse*) from 1942, and on clothing without shoulder straps (in particular camouflage and winter clothing).

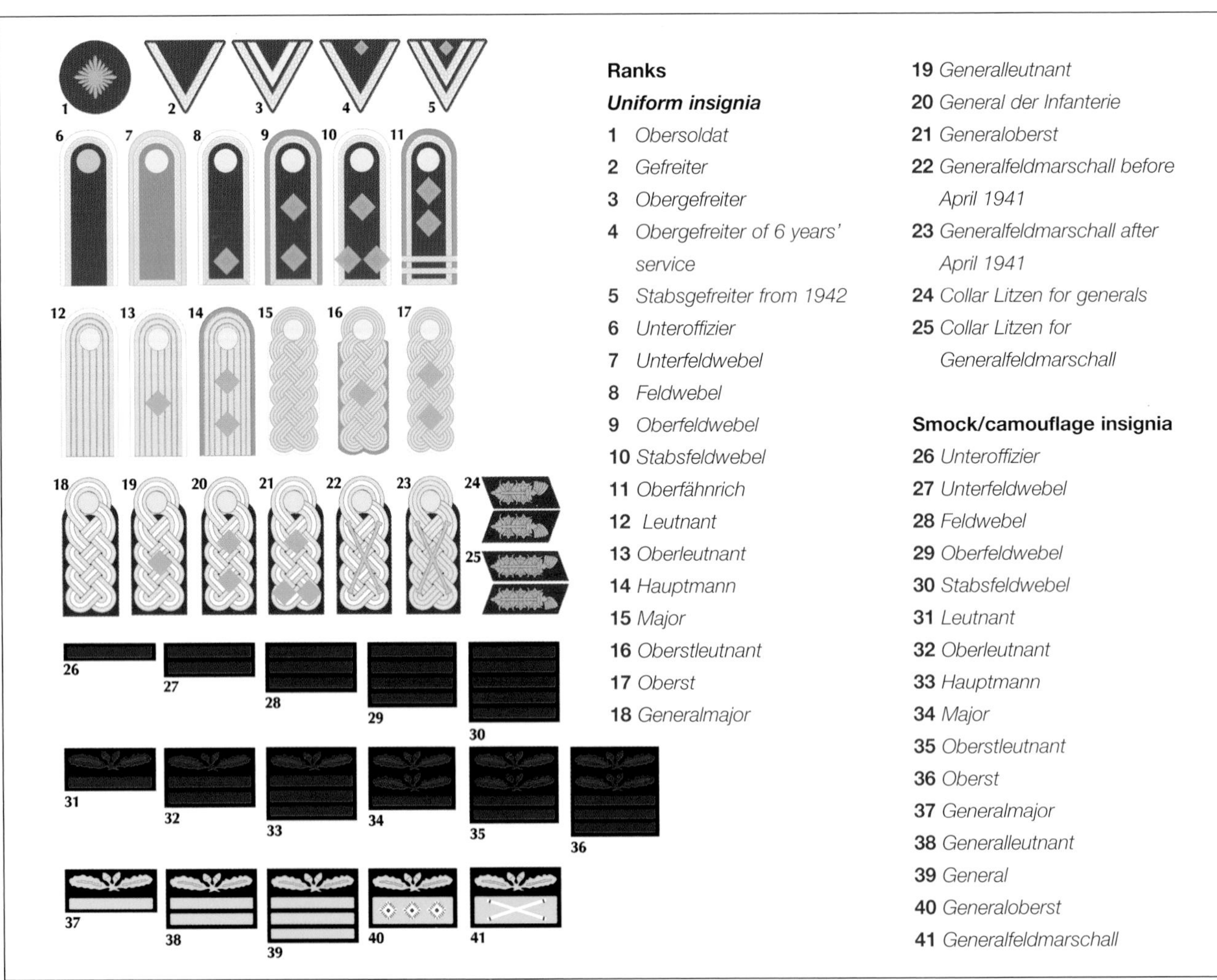

Ranks

Uniform insignia

1 *Obersoldat*
2 *Gefreiter*
3 *Obergefreiter*
4 *Obergefreiter of 6 years' service*
5 *Stabsgefreiter from 1942*
6 *Unteroffizier*
7 *Unterfeldwebel*
8 *Feldwebel*
9 *Oberfeldwebel*
10 *Stabsfeldwebel*
11 *Oberfähnrich*
12 *Leutnant*
13 *Oberleutnant*
14 *Hauptmann*
15 *Major*
16 *Oberstleutnant*
17 *Oberst*
18 *Generalmajor*
19 *Generalleutnant*
20 *General der Infanterie*
21 *Generaloberst*
22 *Generalfeldmarschall before April 1941*
23 *Generalfeldmarschall after April 1941*
24 *Collar Litzen for generals*
25 *Collar Litzen for Generalfeldmarschall*

Smock/camouflage insignia

26 *Unteroffizier*
27 *Unterfeldwebel*
28 *Feldwebel*
29 *Oberfeldwebel*
30 *Stabsfeldwebel*
31 *Leutnant*
32 *Oberleutnant*
33 *Hauptmann*
34 *Major*
35 *Oberstleutnant*
36 *Oberst*
37 *Generalmajor*
38 *Generalleutnant*
39 *General*
40 *Generaloberst*
41 *Generalfeldmarschall*

FAR LEFT This Feldwebel shows off the Tresse on his uniform collar and an early, pointed shoulder board.
(via RCT)

LEFT A pre-war photograph showing an Obergefreiter. Note the dark green collar and pointed shoulder boards.
(via Tanis)

Enlisted soldiers (*Mannschaften*): These wore their rank insignia (if they had any) on their upper left sleeves, whereas NCOs and officers had theirs on the shoulder straps, with those of the latter being either represented as shoulder boards or epaulettes.

NCOs: Non-commissioned officer rank insignia on the shoulder straps consisted of braid and stars. They were also trimmed with *Tresse* – a dull silver lacing all around the collar, and on the shoulder straps of an Unteroffizier on three sides and from Unterfeldwebel to Oberfeldwebel all round.

***Hauptfeldwebel*:** Hauptfeldwebel was the title given to the German equivalent of a company sergeant-major. Usually – but not always – an Oberfeldwebel, he was nicknamed *der Spieß* (the spear) which is altogether too martial an epithet for the administrative centre of the Kompanie. He was responsible for the paperwork – from the updating of a soldier's Soldbuch, to organising inventories and reports. Identifiable by the twin Tresse on the lower arms of his jacket – the *Kolbenringe* (piston rings) – he also kept his papers in a leather pouch (the *Meldetasche*) in his jacket, leaving the second button of the tunic open to accommodate it.

BELOW LEFT Money changes hands between a Gefreiter and a group of NCOs, including the unit's Spieß, a Stabsfeldwebel, who is identified by his double Kolbenringe. Note also his specialist's badge; an anchor and wheel indicated he's a Steuermann – that he is qualified to helm an engineer assault boat.
(via RCT)

LEFT This Spieß is carrying an MP40 and a Stielhandgranate 24. Note also binoculars and torch (on his left hip).

RIGHT Rudolf Witzig commanded the Fallschirmjäger Pionier Platoon at Eben Emael, and was awarded the Knight's Cross. He commanded the 3rd Luftlande-Regiment during the Battle of Crete before seeing action in Tunisia, Russia and in Germany. *(via RCT)*

FAR RIGHT Generalfeldmarschall Erwin Rommel shows off his Pour le Mérite (the 'Blue Max', won during the First World War) and Knight's Cross of the Iron Cross with Oak Leaves, Swords and Diamonds. He was the sixth recipient of this honour, awarded on 11 March 1943 for his actions as commander-in-chief of Army Group Afrika.

Officers: Officers' shoulder straps were made from *soutache*, also known as Russia braid, sewn to a same-size Waffenfarbe underlay until 1938 when they were made wider. For lieutenants and captains the braid was in parallel lengths; for majors and more senior ranks it was in plaits, from Oberst in silver aluminium, above in gold and silver bullion.

Generals: Wehrmacht generals' shoulder straps are shown on page 60.

The collar patch consists of a gold leaf on a red background.

Generals' shoulder straps were similar to officers', with silver Russia braid between two braided cords of gold bullion or later in the war celleon (or cellon – both spellings are seen). This thread was introduced to replace the more expensive metal-based bullion in various insignia. It involved a rayon-type central thread wrapped in a spiral winding of cellophane, giving an almost metallic sheen. There were four plaits rather than the five on the officers' shoulder straps. Note the crossed batons for field marshals. The underlay was scarlet, but from 1944 generals of staff corps used the relevant Waffenfarbe instead.

Generals had neither regimental nor company numbers on their shoulder straps and no piping on their straps. However, they did have red strips down the seams of their trousers.

Waffenfarben (See table opposite.)

These were arm of service colours, seen on the shoulder straps and edges of the shoulder boards and/or as piping around caps, with that of NCOs and officers also denoting rank. (Note the Waffen in Waffenfarbe is short for Waffengattung – arm of service.)

Medical, veterinary and reserve officers

All medical officers additionally carry a caduceus on their shoulder straps, while all veterinary officers carry a winding snake (a caduceus without a stick). Reserve officers have their shoulder straps on a second mouse-grey underlay.

Luftwaffe ground troops

The bluish-green (blue-grey) uniform had shoulder straps of the same shape and with the same insignia as the army rank and grade, but in the colour of the air force uniform. Silver braid (like the army) from Unteroffizier up and silver stars from Feldwebel up. They also had Waffenfarbe piping.

The collar patches differed from the army's in that the background was in the

Waffenfarbe		
Unit	**Waffenfarbe**	**Insignia on shoulder strap**
Army group HQ (*Heeresgruppenkommando*)	White (*weiss*)	G and Arabic number
Army corps HQ (*Generalkommando*)	White (*weiss*)	Roman number of corps
Infantry division HQ (*Infanterie-Divisionsstab*)	White (*weiss*)	D and number of division
Infantry regiments (*Infanterie-Regimenter*)	White (*weiss*)	Number of regiment
Infantry Regiment *Grossdeutschland* (*Infanterieregiment Grossdeutschland*)	White (*weiss*)	GD
Guard Battalion Vienna (*Wachbataillon Wien*)	White (*weiss*)	W
Machine-gun battalions (*Maschinengewehr-Bataillone*)	White (*weiss*)	M and number of battalion
Motorcycle units (*Kradschützen-Bataillone*)	White (*weiss*)	K and number of battalion
Mortar battalions (*Mörser-Bataillone*)	White (*weiss*)	GW
Parachute units, infantry (*Fallschirmjäger-Einheiten*)	White (*weiss*)	FJ
Anti-aircraft battalions (*Flak-Bataillone*)	White (*weiss*)	Gothic Fl
Local defence units (*Landesschützen-Einheiten*)	White (*weiss*)	Latin L plus Arabic number of regiment
Generals (*Generale*)	Bright red (*hochrot*)	No numbers
Artillery regiments (*Artillerie-Regimente*)	Bright red (*hochrot*)	Number of unit
Army Heavy Flak units (*Heeresflakabteilungen*)	Bright red (*hochrot*)	
Assault guns (*Sturmgeschütze*)	Bright red (*hochrot*)	
General HQ of armed forces (*Oberkommando der Wehrmacht*)	Carmine red (*karmesin*)	No numbers
General HQ of army (*Oberkommando des Heeres*)	Carmine red (*karmesin*)	No numbers
War Department and General Staff (*Reichskriegsministerium und Generalstab*)	Carmine red (*karmesin*)	No numbers
Veterinary units (*Vetinär-Abteilungen*)	Carmine red (*karmesin*)	Number of division
Mountain Jäger regiments and Jäger battalions, infantry (*Gebirgsjäger-Regimenter und Jäger-Bataillone*)	Light green (*hell-grün*)	Number of regiment
Panzergrenadier units	Grass green (*wiesengrün*)	Number of unit
Reconnaissance regiments or battalions, infantry (*Aufklärungsregimenter und -abteilungen*)	Copper brown (*kupferbraun*)	A and number of regiment or battalion
Cavalry (*Kavallerie*)	Golden yellow (*goldgelb*)	
Motorcycle units (*Kradschützen-Bataillone*)	Golden yellow (*goldgelb*)	R and number of battalion
Smoke units (*Nebelwerfer*)	Bordeaux red (*Bordorot*)	Number of unit
Engineer battalions (*Pionier-Bataillone*)	Black (*schwarz*)	Number of battalion
Signal battalions (*Nachrichten-Abteilungen*)	Lemon yellow (*zitronengelb*)	Number of battalion
Transport battalions (*Kraftfahr und Fahr-Abteilungen*)	Light blue (*hell-blau*)	Number of battalion
Medical battalions (*Sanitäts-Abteilungen*)	Cornflower (dark) blue (*kornblumen-blau*)	Number of division
Chaplains (*Heeresgeistliche*)	Violet (*violet*)	No shoulder straps
Field signal command (*Feldnachrichtenkommandantur*)	Lemon yellow (*zitronengelb*)	Latin K
Military police (*Feldgendarmerie*)	Orange (*orange*)	No number. Nazi eagle and swastika surrounded by oak wreath on upper left arm; brown band with *Feldgendarmerie* in silver inscribed on lower left arm
Armoured units (*Panzer*)	Pink (*rosa*)	Number of battalion

LUFTWAFFE WAFFENFARBEN

White	*weiß*	Generals and men of the General Göring Regiment
Golden yellow	*goldgelb*	Aviation units (*Fliegerverbände*)
Red	*rot*	Anti-aircraft artillery (*Flakartillerie*)
Carmine	*karmesin*	General Staff officers (*Generalstabsoffiziere*)
Pink	*rosa*	Engineer Corps (*Pioniere*)
Golden brown	*goldbraun*	Air Signal Corps (*Luftnachrichtendienst*)
Light green	*hellgrün*	Air Raid Warning Service (*Luftmeldedienst*)
Black	*schwarz*	Air Ministry (*Reichsluftministerium*)
Dark blue	*dunkelblau*	Medical (*Sanitätsdienst*)
Dark green	*dunkelgrün*	Officials (*Wehrmachtbeamte*)

Additional colours are worn by the following:

Bright red	*hochrot*	NCOs and men of the General Göring Regiment wear this colour as an edging to the collar patches
Yellow	*gelb*	Corps of navigational experts as a second shoulder strap underlay (*Nebenfarbe*)

The ranks of the air force correspond, on the whole, to those of the army with the exception that the lowest grade is known as Flieger, Kanonier or Funker. There is no Oberschütze. The equivalents of General der Infanterie, and so on, are General der Flieger and General der Flakartillerie.

ABOVE This Gefreiter shows off the Luftwaffe rank badges carried on his collar. The Luftwaffe Waffenfarbe was yellow. Until they became army units, Luftwaffe troops kept their own insignia and uniforms. *(via RCT)*

BELOW Oberst Bernhard-Hermann Ramcke (back to camera) decorating some of his men – at left an Oberfeldwebel and in the centre a Feldwebel – after the Battle of Crete. *(Bundesarchiv, Bild 101I-166-0526-30/Weixler, Franz Peter/CC-BY-SA 3.0)*

Waffenfarbe. Wings (a type of rank insignia in silver) were mounted on the collar patch. Silver lace was worn on the lower front edge from Unteroffizier up.

The Luftwaffe steel helmet was the same shape as the army, except that the national insignia used was a flying eagle – as is the national insignia on the right breast of the blouse. Enlisted men and noncommissioned officers wore grey national insignia, while officers' were silver.

The cap insignia consists of the rosette (*Kokarde*), flanked by oak leaves on spread wings.

Fallschirmjäger

The Fallschirmjäger were part of the Luftwaffe and incorporated the Heer's pre-war Fallschirm-

RIGHT **These veterans show off a range of badges. Both are wearing Iron Crosses 1st and 2nd class, a Close Combat Clasp and Infantry Assault Badge. The man at left has two Tank Destruction Badges.** *(via RCT)*

Infanterie-Kompanie/Bataillon at the beginning of 1939 as II./Fallschirmjäger-Regiment 1. This meant their Waffenfarbe was yellow. There were, however, slight variations in rank, although most followed the Luftwaffe. For Fallschirmjäger the other ranks were:

- Unterfeldwebel (sergeant)
- Oberjäger (corporal)
- Hauptgefreiter (most senior lance corporal)
- Obergefreiter (senior lance corporal)
- Gefreiter (lance corporal)
- Jäger (private).

When a recruit had successfully completed his jump training he received the *Fallschirmschützenschein* (parachute rifleman's licence) and the coveted *Fallschirmschützenabzeichen* (parachute rifleman's badge). The Heer unit had used army ranks – Schütze and Oberschütze – but adopted Jäger and Oberjäger. However, specialists retained their designation: so a Funker or Oberfunker serving with a Fallschirmjäger signals platoon remained a Funker, etc.

German naval personnel

Those serving ashore in coastal batteries or as troops in the field (not as landing parties) wore the army field grey. They were distinguished from the army by having gold buttons and insignia.

Medals, badges and cuff titles

Everyone's heard of the Iron Cross, but that certainly wasn't the only medal awarded to infantrymen and Panzergrenadiers by the Third Reich. There were also a number of badges and other insignia worn regularly by all ranks. The main ones are identified in the box overleaf.

BELOW LEFT **This man wears an Imperial German Army (*ie* First World War) Wound Badge as well as a Marksman Lanyard and an Iron Cross.** *(via RCT)*

BELOW RIGHT **This portrait of General der Infanterie Johannes Frießner shows a number of medals: the Iron Cross 2nd Class that he won in 1914 is indicated by the ribbon in the second buttonhole. The Iron Cross 1st Class (won in 1916) is pinned to his pocket. The clasp on the ribbon shows the award of a second Iron Cross 2nd Class (in 1942) and that above the Iron Cross on his breast pocket the award of a second Iron Cross 1st Class (later in 1942). He's also wearing a German Cross in Gold on his right breast pocket (awarded in 1943), at his neck a Knight's Cross awarded in 1943 (he would go on to receive Oak Leaves in 1944). He also has a Wound Badge and (on his left breast pocket) the War Merit Cross with Swords.** *(via RCT)*

DECORATIONS (see page 59)

- Anti-aircraft Flak Battle Badge (*Flak-Kampfabzeichen der Luftwaffe*)
- Army Anti-aircraft Badge or Army Flak Badge (*Heeres-Flak Abzeichen*)
- Close Combat Clasp (*Nahkampfspange*): three grades – Bronze for 15 close combat battles; Silver for 25; and Gold for 50+
- Eastern Front Medal (*Medaille, Winterschlacht im Osten 1941/42*)
- General Assault Badge (*Allgemeines Sturmabzeichen*): one grade; later (1943) adapted by adding a plate identifying 25, 50, 75 or 100 attacks
- German Army Parachutist Badge (*Fallschirmschützen-Abzeichen des Heeres*)
- German Cross (*Deutsches Kreuz*): two grades, gold and silver
- Ground Assault Badge of the Luftwaffe (*Erdkampfabzeichen der Luftwaffe*)
- Honour Roll Clasp of the Army (*Ehrenblatt des Heeres*): four additional grades introduced on 10 November 1944 based on the number of combat operations – 2nd for 25 eligible operations; 3rd for 50; 4th for 75 eligible; 5th for 100
- Infantry Assault Badge (*Infanterie-Sturmabzeichen*): silver footsoldiers; bronze Panzer
- Iron Cross (*Eisernes Kreuz*): three grades – the Iron Cross (two versions), the Knight's Cross (various versions) and the Grand Cross
- Clasp to the Iron Cross (*Spange zum Eisernen Kreuz*)
- Luftwaffe Panzer Badge (*Panzerkampfabzeichen der Luftwaffe*): silver for tank crew, black for Panzergrenadiers and crews of other armoured vehicles
- Panzer Battle Badge (*Panzerkampfabzeichen*): silver for tank crew, bronze (instituted 6 June 1940) for Panzergrenadiers and crews of other armoured vehicles
- Parachute Rifleman's Badge (*Fallschirmschützenabzeichen*)
- Sniper's Badge (*Scharfschützenabzeichen*): Third class (no cord) for 20 witnessed kills, Second class (silver cord) for 40, First class (gold cord) for 60
- Tank Destruction Badge (*Sonderabzeichen für das Niederkämpfen von Panzerkampfwagen durch Einzelkämpfer*): gold for five tanks (replacing four silver badges when the fifth was destroyed)
- War Merit Cross (*Kriegsverdienstkreuz*): four degrees; related civil decoration
- Wound Badge (*Verwundetenabzeichen*): black (3rd class), for those wounded once or twice; silver (2nd class) three or four times; gold (1st class, which could be awarded posthumously) for five or more.

Campaign shields

During the Second World War, Germany awarded campaign shields for particularly hard-fought campaigns. The following five shields were definitely instituted, produced, awarded and worn in recognition of these campaigns – others, such as the Dünkirchenschild, Memelschild and Lorientschild – may have been awarded but not produced before the end of the war.

- *Narvikschild*: The battle of Narvik in the Norway Campaign took place 9 April–8 June 1940; 8,577 were awarded
- *Cholmschild*: Kampfgruppe Scherer held out at Cholm until the siege was lifted on 21 January–5 May 1942; 5,500 were awarded
- *Krimschild*: The Crimean Campaign lasted from 26 September 1941–4 July 1942 until Sevastopol was taken; 100,000 Crimean shields were awarded
- *Demjanskschild*: Over 100,000 men were trapped in the Demyansk pocket 8 February–21 April 1942; 100,000 were awarded
- *Kubanschild*: From February to October 1943 German 17th Army attempted to maintain a bridgehead against Soviet 4th Ukrainian Front. Many awarded.

Trade and specialist badges (*Heeres Laufbahn und Sonderdienststellung Abzeichen*)

Mostly worn by NCOs from Unteroffizier to Feldwebel, these insignia appeared on the right forearm of the tunic with some exceptions (the *Nachrichtenpersonal* and *Steuermann* badges were worn on the upper left sleeve; the gunners' on the lower left). The insignia were usually in yellow on a dark green circular patch, except as identified below. Not covered are the armoured mechanics whose badges were pink *Zahnrad* (cogwheel).

There were insignia for the following:

- Artillery gun layer – *Richtabzeichen für Artillerie* (*Richtkanonier*) on lower left arm
- Clothing stores NCO – *Zeugmeister*
- Gas defence NCO – *Gasschutzunteroffizier*
- Medical personnel – *Sanitätsunterpersonal*
- Motor transport NCO – *Schirrmeister*

- NCO artificer/ordnance technician – *Feuerwerker*
- Ordnance NCO – *Waffenfeldwebel*
- Paymaster trainee – *Zahlmeisteranwärter*
- Pigeon postmaster – *Brieftaubenmeister*
- Qualified assault boat helmsman – *Steuermann* (anchor and steering wheel in silver)
- Signals mechanic – *Nachrichtenmechaniker*
- Signals operator (in a non-signals unit) – *Nachrichtenpersonal* (lightning insignia was in various Waffenfarbe)
- Smoke projector (*Nebelwerfer*) operator – *Richtabzeichen für Nebeltruppen* (mortar projectile in white) on lower left arm
- (Supply) admin NCO – *(Gerät) Verwaltungsunteroffizier*
- (Master) Technical artisan – (*Vor*) *Handwerker*
- Transport (or tank) mechanic 2nd and 1st classes – *Kraftzeug (oder Panzer) Warte II und I.*

Horse-related

- Farrier candidate – *Hufbeschlagmeister (Geprüfte Anwärter)*
- Farrier instructor – *Hufbeschlag Lehrmeister*
- Qualified farrier – *Geprüftes-Hufbeschlagpersonal*
- Regimental NCO saddler – *Regimentsuntersattlermeister*
- Troop NCO saddler – *Truppensattlermeister*
- Veterinary personnel – *Vetinärpersonal.*

Fortifications-related

- Fortifications sergeant-major – *Wallfeldwebel*
- Fortress construction sergeant-major – *Festungsfeldwebel*
- Fortress engineer sergeant-major – *Festungspionierfeldwebel.*

Army proficiency badges (*Heeres Leistungs Abzeichen*)

There were four of these, three worn on the right upper arm and the *Bergführer* (mountain leader) badge on the left breast pocket.

1. Bergführer breast badge – *Heeresbergführer-Abzeichen*

Introduced in 1936 for the Heeres Gebirgsjäger who qualified as mountain guides with a year's active service. Worn on left breast tunic pocket.

LEFT Studio portrait of a Gefreiter wearing a *Tätigkeitsabzeichen für Nachrichten-personal* – a specialist signals badge – above his rank chevron. The badge is worn in the Waffenfarbe of the unit (white for infantry). *(via RCT)*

BELOW This Feldwebel wears a *Schirrmeister* trade badge showing he was a specialist for vehicle equipment (usually motor but could also cover horse-drawn). *(via Tanis)*

RIGHT Der Spieß was the administrative centre of the platoon. Note the double rings on the sleeve, identifying him. Note also the Edelweiß badge of the Gebirgsjäger. *(via RCT)*

FAR RIGHT The marksmanship lanyards – *Schützenschur*, on right shoulder – were instituted for infantrymen on 29 June 1936. Later, in October 1938, a second version was instituted expanding the recipients to tank and artillery soldiers. In all there were 12 grades, 5–8 being silver and 9–12 gold. In each group (plain/silver/gold) the grades were identified by 0/1/2/3 acorns (infantry) or miniature shells. They were lined with silk to protect the uniform.

2. Gebirgsjäger arm badge
Introduced in 1939 for the Heeres Gebirgsjäger, the Edelweiß was worn on right upper arm of tunic and greatcoat.

3. Jäger arm badge
Introduced on 2 October 1942, the oak leaves were worn on the upper right arm of Jäger units.

4. Skijäger arm badge
There is some doubt whether this badge reached the unit: oak leaves and skis, worn on upper right arm.

RIGHT Desert uniform and an Afrika Korps cuff title; note the Iron Cross ribbon on the edge of the left side of the tunic. *(via RCT)*

Army marksmanship lanyards (*Schützen Abzeichen des deutschen Heeres*)

- Introduced by an order of 29 June 1936, the award of these lanyards was intended to improve the accuracy of soldiers' shooting. They attached near the button of the shoulder board with the other end on the second button of the jacket. Every time the award was earned an acorn was added. Over 400,000 marksmanship lanyards were issued during the war.

Other badges

- There were many others – from the gorgets (*Ringkragen*) and arm badge of the Feldgendarmerie to the standard bearer's arm shield and *Schwalbennester* (swallows' nests). There were some cap emblems – the chaplains' Gothic Cross (*Gotisches Kreuz*) and the Edelweiß of the Gebirgsjäger.

Cuff titles

These were produced for three different groups: battle honours, elite units and special formations. Examples are:

- Battle honours – 1936 *Spanien* (Spain) 1939, *Kreta* (Crete), Metz 1944

LEFT Clothing and equipment

1 Later war green shirt, two-ringed socks (covering sizes 5–7).

2/3 *Rundbundhosen* trousers with braces (*Hosenträger*), tie cord at ankle (necessary if worn with ankle boots) and khaki cloth belt. Note the fob pocket to his front right.

4 On goes the tunic. Note the aluminium hook to support the belt.

- Elite units – Großdeutschland, Brandenburg and Feldherrnhalle (various Waffen-SS units – Leibstandarte, Das Reich, Hohenstaufen, etc. – also wore cuff titles)
- Special formations – Feldpost, Führerhauptquartier and Stabshelferin des Heeres.

Uniform and equipment

This section examines the standard uniforms, headgear, webbing, footwear and kit used by German infantrymen. Today, there are so many replicas and fakes on the market that it's sometimes difficult to tell whether kit is from the period or not. Added to this, towards the end of the war quality, markings and manufacturers altered depending on availability and locality; and many armies post-war made use of German-pattern equipment.

The standard combat uniform

Unterkleidung: There were essentially two kinds of lower underwear issued – shorts and long johns. The latter came in various forms, including thick ones for use in winter as well as lighter versions for the summer, all usually having a three-button fly. Both lengths were typically manufactured from white, green or field grey cotton. Once the troops reached the battlefield, however, stark practicality took over and any items that were too dirty or damaged beyond use were simply replaced with whatever could be found, be that military or civilian. Undershirts were produced in many thicknesses and forms, including those made from wool, cotton, rayon and Aertex. Colours ranged from white to grey, field grey and several shades of green.

Hemden: Shirts were longer than usual and worn under the tunic, and from 1933 to 1940 were white and collarless. This format proved to be totally impractical on the battlefield, however, and they were superseded by new ones that were typically pale grey and made of either cotton or wool. In 1941, the colour was changed again to field grey, although some shirts were also made in various shades of green. Early in the war most shirts were made without pockets, but later on two were often added. If the temperature was high enough, the shirt was sometimes worn without the tunic or replaced by the *Drillichanzug* (working uniform).

Socken: Socks are a vital part of any soldier's kit – if they are allowed to get wet and/or dirty for any length of time, foot disease is sure to follow, which, when advanced, renders that person

in the M36 version, but this was changed to field grey to match the rest of the uniform in 1940. They were manufactured from the same material, and featured straight legs (*Langhosen*) with a high waist, small side pockets, and a buttoned fly. There was also a dedicated watch pocket and a strap on the back of the waist to allow for girth adjustment. They were designed to be held up with braces and the legs tucked straight into jackboots.

A new version was released in 1943, designated M43. These had narrower ends to the legs to allow them to fit under gaiters and into ankle boots, and the waist featured belt loops to avoid the necessity for braces. The seat was also reinforced, making them a much more robust article of clothing. This was a good design that was popular with the troops and as a result it was produced unchanged until the war ended. Some officers still chose to wear breeches with high boots, though, while generals and general staff officers wore trousers with wide red stripes down the sides.

ABOVE A group of junior soldiers on the ranges to practise shooting (complete with comedy moustaches). They are wearing M36 service tunics and most are wearing Marschstiefel boots. *(via Tanis)*

unfit to fight. Consequently, most armies have very strict regulations concerning foot hygiene, and the German Heer was no exception. Those items issued to the troops – originally labelled 'stockings' – were typically of grey wool and reached up to the mid-calf. They were supplied by many companies and came in four different sizes, these being typically denoted by one to four coloured rings. As an example, two rings covered sizes 5 to 7, and three rings denoted sizes 8 to 9. The markers were usually about 3mm wide and coloured white, although others were produced in red, green, yellow and blue. A permitted alternative was for there to be one to four stitches of white thread near the top of the sock.

As was typical of all German supplies, the quality fell dramatically during the war. This was particularly so with the advent of synthetic rayon (reconstituted cellulose fibre) and Perlon (a commercial name for nylon) yarns that replaced the original wool. A much-simplified version came into service in June 1944 – these knitted tubes with no heel came in one size and were referred to as 'Finn socks'.

Feldhosen: The trousers that accompanied the Feldbluse were of a slate grey (*steingrau*) colour

Gürteln: Belts were made of leather that was black on the outside and tan on the inside. There were many different buckles used to hold them together; however, most had a depiction of the *Heeresadler* (Army eagle) together with the inscription *Gott mit uns* (God with us). The ones used by enlisted men were box-shaped and either made from aluminium or pressed steel. In the field these were painted a drab colour to reduce their visibility, but for dress occasions they were usually silvered. Likewise, officers used both field and dress versions that were constructed using a two-pronged frame. Dress buckles were in the shape of an oak leaf around a Heeresadler. They were made of silvered aluminium and worn with a belt of silver braid, except for generals who replaced the silver with gold.

Feldbluse: The M36 version of the field tunic issued to the other ranks, formally known as the *Heeres Dienstanzug Modell* 1936, kept the traditional *feldgrau* (field grey) colour of the Imperial and Reichswehr uniforms. The exception to this was where the collar and shoulder straps were concerned – these were dark bottle green. It also featured a variety of small changes, including to the format of the pockets (*Aufgesetztetaschen*) and the number of buttons (five). The national emblem (*Hoheitsabzeichen*) was also positioned over the right breast pocket. The overall length of the Feldbluse was reduced to make it more suitable for use in mechanised transport, and it featured an internal webbing system so that equipment could be suspended on the outside without requiring an extra harness.

The next version was referred to as the M40 Tunic – this was the same as the earlier model except that the previously green collar and shoulder straps were now field grey. The M41 came soon after – this featured six buttons (instead of five), but was made from inferior synthetic and/or recycled materials. When the M42 appeared, it was more or less the same, but with all the pleats removed to save materials and costs. Likewise, the M43 was cheapened yet further by having simpler pockets and simplified or no internal webbing. The last version of the Feldbluse was the 1944 model – the M44. This was drastically shortened to reduce production costs once again, and instead of field grey, came in a drab greenish-brown referred to as Feldgrau 44. Since it was produced late on in the war, it was mostly used by the badly trained replacement troops of the Flakhelfer, Hitlerjugend and Volkssturm militia.

The tunic used by officers did not undergo the same cost reduction exercises as those for

LEFT This Panzergrenadier is wearing the M43 Feldbluse and carrying his K98k. On his head is an M43 *Einheitsfeldmütze*. He's wearing *Gamaschen* (gaiters) and short boots (*Schnürschuhe*). Note, also, the enlisted man's belt buckle.

BELOW LEFT AND BELOW A classic *Signal* propaganda magazine photograph. Festooned with their kit, led by a decorated NCO, these soldiers look very different to the ragtag collection of POWs whose uniforms show what much of the German Army looked like after weeks of war and few opportunities to pick up replacements or supplies: torn and dirty with broken shoelaces (below). *(via RCT)*

RIGHT Still wearing his M36 tunic and old-style field service cap (*Feldmütze*), officers' breeches and riding boots, but beltless, this officer was photographed by his captors in Normandy, 1944. *(Battlefield Historian)*

BELOW Obviously a hot day for cobbling! This photograph shows off the toe and heel plates and 40+ hobnails. *(via RCT)*

the other ranks because they had to buy their own uniforms, and usually had them tailor-made from higher quality materials.

Marschstiefel: The German boot – known the world over as the jackboot – was made to a high standard from brown cowhide blackened with polish. Those produced early in the war were very long, measuring between 35 and 41cm (13.8–16.1in), and were fitted with an iron plate over the heel, as well as doubled leather soles that had between 35 and 45 hobnails in them. Referred to by the troops as *Knobelbecher* (dice shakers), the design of the boot had changed little since the First World War. Those worn by officers were very similar, but tended to be tailor-made items, usually designed to be worn with breeches (in spite of orders to the contrary). As the economic situation got worse, the boots were first reduced in height to between 29 and 35cm (11.4 and 13.8in), and then later still were restricted to combat soldiers. These included the infantry, artillery, cyclists and motorcyclists as well as specialist troops like the Pioniers. By the end of 1943, production ceased completely, although any remaining stocks were still issued.

Schnürschuhe: The M37 lace-up ankle boot was designed to be worn with gaiters, and was usually only used for light duties such as basic training and fatigue work. From 1941 onwards, however, they became more common on the battlefield due to the jackboot being in short supply. The M44 version became the standard footwear issued with that year's uniform.

Drillichanzug: The working uniform was what the troops wore while working or on campaign. It was unlined and featured no insignia, originally made in a pale grey colour, although after February 1940 it was produced in a dark olive or reed-green denim. Drillich is recognisable by the herringbone pattern – much the same as the herringbone twill or HBT well known to US Army soldiers. In German HBT is *Leinen-*

LEFT These soldiers wear the Drillichanzug in grey or off-white; later versions would be in green. *(via RCT)*

Drillich. In 1942 the reed-green Drillich M40 Feldbluse was produced as summer uniform (*Sommerfeldanzug*); there was a later version without front-pocket pleats and pocket-flap scallops similar to the M43.

Mantel: The double-breasted M36 greatcoat as issued to the troops in the Second World War owed its ancestry to the previous century; however, even though it did not suit the odern mechanised battlefield it remained in use until the end of the war. Constructed from a thick woollen material, it reached down to the knee and provided a significant degree of protection

ABOVE LEFT In the summer soldiers began to wear their Drillich as hot-weather clothing and soon reed-green (*Schilfgrün*) herringbone denim versions were made for soldiers and officers alike.

ABOVE The standard army greatcoat – double-breasted with a dark-green collar – was worn by all ranks (other than generals) from before the war started. *(via Tanis)*

BELOW LEFT Generalmajor Robert Sattler, commander of Cherbourg Arsenal, surrenders on 27 June 1944. He's wearing the standard greatcoat for generals and above, whose lapel facings are bright red (the lighter grey in this photo). Note his torch attached to a button and the officer's *Schirmmütze*, which had gold cap cords instead of the usual silver. *(Battlefield Historian)*

LEFT This infantryman wears regulation gloves and scarf with his 1943 greatcoat, which has a larger collar.

ABOVE, RIGHT AND BELOW Blankets, greatcoats and Zeltbahn sections were often rolled and attached to the Tornister. First, the arms were pulled inside out; next the greatcoat was squared off ... then rolled tightly; finally, it was attached to the Tornister with straps.

against the cold. It featured a turn-down collar and had shoulder straps that were faced with dark green as well as turn-back cuffs and a half-belt at the rear. In spite of all the development work put into it, the greatcoat became very heavy if it got wet, and when temperatures were low enough it froze solid. Under these conditions it made movement incredibly difficult. Attempts were made to improve it as the war progressed – these included the addition of two side pockets, a longer collar and a hood, and some versions also had extra linings. The lack of fabric availability meant that much of the material used was recycled and the quality got worse.

Headgear

Stahlhelm: The distinctive shape of the M35 pattern helmet was derived directly from the M18 version by Eisenhüttonwerke of Thule. It came into service in June 1935, and was worn by all members of the Wehrmacht, SS, police, fire brigades and Party organisations. Although it was shorter and lighter than its predecessor, it was nevertheless difficult to manufacture, and supplies were still limited after the war began. In

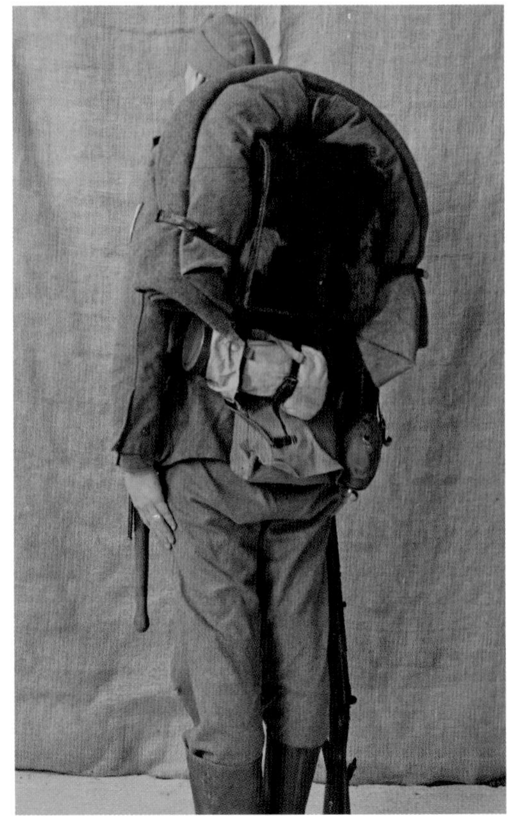

FAR LEFT AND LEFT **Luftwaffe helmet decals were placed on the sides of the Stahlhelm, the Wehrmacht on the left and the national colours on the right. The Luftwaffe used their eagle and the Kriegsmarine version was gold instead of silver. Note the Luftwaffe M35 version of the helmet. The M42, later, version can be identified on page 41.** *(Gerald Zehetner/ WikiCommons (CC BY-SA 4.0))*

order to reduce production time, a new model was developed which first saw service in March 1940. This relied more heavily on stamped components that were faster to manufacture. Overall, however, it still looked very similar to the earlier pattern, and although it is sometimes called the M40, this was never an official designation.

The M42 helmet replaced the M35 pattern in August 1942, with cost cutting being the principal driver. The main difference was that the rolled edges were removed, reducing the amount of material and time it took to make the finished item. It also had a cheaper paint finish and a poorer quality lining. Heer units typically had them issued in a grey-green colour (although they were originally green), but most soldiers then added their own camouflage to suit their surroundings. From 1942, elite units were issued with camouflage helmet covers, but these were unavailable to most soldiers. Instead they made their own, by using chicken wire or some kind of netting to hold local foliage, whereas others added splinter-pattern poncho fabric or painted their helmets to better match the surroundings.

As was mentioned earlier, decals were affixed to both sides of the M35 pattern helmets up until 1940, when the one on the right was deleted. This single decal was later removed in 1943 by order of the Supreme Commander of the Wehrmacht, in order to lower costs, speed up manufacture and reduce visibility on the battlefield. The insignia used on the left denoted which branch of the forces the wearer belonged to; Heer units used a silver-coloured Heeresadler on a black shield. The decal on the right (when it was used) bore the German national colours of black, white and red in diagonal stripes within a shield.

Schirmmütze: The peaked cap came into use in 1934, and was issued for dress, service and walking-out. Often referred to as the crusher cap, NCOs were allowed to wear it whenever the field cap was specified in orders, and officers wore their own version. Those used by enlisted men had a crown that was made from field grey wool over a wire frame with a dark green velvet band. In front of this was a stiff visor that could be made from a variety of different materials, including various synthetic fibres, plastic and leather. Officers' caps were of a higher quality, lacked the wire frame and had a soft visor.

Insignia on the front came in the form of

LEFT **The interior of the Stahlhelm showing leather liner, which was tightened to the head size. The Stahlhelm came in different sizes to fit different-sized heads.**

LEFT **Camouflage helmet cover.**

RIGHT A replica officer's Schirmmütze with Waffenfarbe of grass green showing the owner was a Panzergrenadier.

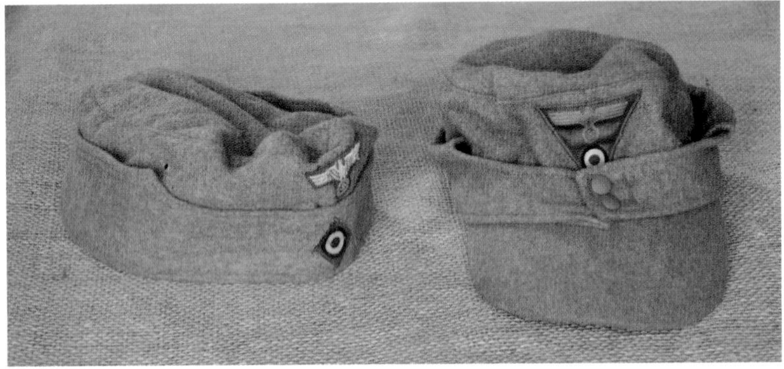

ABOVE Re-enactors' copies of the Feldmütze (left, in this case without the inverted soutache chevron) and the Einheitsfeldmütze (right). By undoing the clip buttons on the front of the latter, ear flaps could be lowered.

a red, white and black cockade that was surrounded by an oak leaf wreath. Above this was the *Wehrmachtsadler* (national emblem), which was usually made of stamped aluminium for the enlisted men, while those used by officers were typically embroidered in silver (or gold for generals). The edges of the cap were piped in Waffenfarbe, and while the enlisted men had black leather chinstraps, officers – who usually bought their own caps – often had cords made from silver or aluminium. Again, generals had theirs in gold. The 1934 pattern officer cap, which came to be known as the *Knautschmütze*, was officially replaced by the *Schiffchen* (little ship) M38; however, the old-style cap was more popular and continued to be used until the end of the war.

Feldmütze: The Feldmütze or forage cap, sometimes called the field or side cap, was a popular piece of soft headwear that was first introduced to the Heer in 1934. It was given the nickname Schiffchen and was usually made of field grey wool, although variants were also produced in cotton in both black and olive green. It carried insignia in the form of an embroidered *Wehrmachtsadler*, together with a red, white and black cockade, and early in the war there was also an inverted chevron made of soutache in the relevant Waffenfarbe. The field caps worn by officers had silver or aluminium piping, unless they were of general rank, in which case it was gold. The M43 Dienstanzug field cap came into service in 1943 – this was again made in field grey (except for Panzer units, for whom it was black), but differed in that it had a built-in visor.

Einheitsfeldmütze: The M43 forage cap as issued to men of the Heer owed its origins to pre-First World War mountain troops who wore a visored ski cap called a *Gebirgsmütze*.

RIGHT Officer's M38 Feldmütze, here worn by Major Wilhelm Bach, an Afrika Korps Ritterkreuzträger who was captured after defending the Halfaya Pass, Egypt, in January 1942. Note inverted chevron.

FAR RIGHT Portrait of a soldier wearing an M43 Feldbluse and an Einheitsfeldmütze. *(via RCT)*

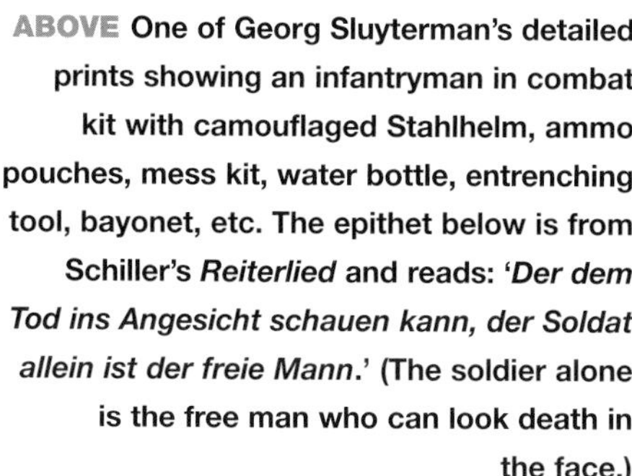

ABOVE One of Georg Sluyterman's detailed prints showing an infantryman in combat kit with camouflaged Stahlhelm, ammo pouches, mess kit, water bottle, entrenching tool, bayonet, etc. The epithet below is from Schiller's *Reiterlied* and reads: '*Der dem Tod ins Angesicht schauen kann, der Soldat allein ist der freie Mann*.' (The soldier alone is the free man who can look death in the face.)

ABOVE LEFT Rear view of a Panzergrenadier re-enactor showing off his equipment attached to assault pack webbing: entrenching tool and bayonet; gas mask holder and gas cape; mess tin, Zeltbahn section; Stielgranate 24; small additional equipment bag; Brotbeutel; water bottle; and K98k rifle. This equipment didn't change much throughout the war. He's also wearing M43 tunic and trousers, gaiters and ankle boots.

ABOVE RIGHT This soldier has a different rig to the last with his mess tin attached to the Brotbeutel and a Tornister (pack – see detail overleaf) attached to his webbing.

Modelled on the same lines, it was made from a field grey material with ear flaps that folded across the front and secured in place by two buttons when not in use. It featured similar insignia to the side cap, and was very popular with the men who used it widely on the battlefield. Officers often had stiffening boards added to the peak to make the cap look more official.

Equipment

Feldausrüstung: The field equipment issued to the German infantryman consisted of a variety of items. Starting with those hanging from his webbing, they included:

- ammunition pouches (*Patronentaschen*)
- bayonet (*Seitengewehr*) in a leather frog
- entrenching tool (*Schanzzeug*)
- bread bag (*Brotbeutel*)
- water bottle (*Feldflasche*)
- gas mask container (*Blechbüchse für Gasmaske*)

Troops were also issued with delousing powder and small sewing kits, and were ordered to shave every day when possible. Likewise, clothing was washed whenever the opportunity arose, typically in lakes, streams and rivers. Although the German High Command put a great emphasis on hygiene, the reality was that in the battlefield the Heer did not adhere to the rules as strictly as the Allies did. This was especially so in places like the desert, where the loss of men to sickness caused by poor hygiene was much higher. A good example was where lice were concerned – one of the consequences of an infestation is that typhus

RIGHT AND FAR RIGHT Exterior and interior of a Tornister, showing the approved position for boots, mess tin, etc. The metal container is a rifle cleaning kit. There were fewer cowhide exteriors, with their distinctive coarse hair and different colours, as the war went on.

RIGHT Equipment in the field. This Gefreiter is wrapped in his Zeltbahn section and is wearing a Feldmütze. To his right one can see the handle of his entrenching tool; to his left his helmet (behind him), Brotbeutel, mess tin, gasmask container and gas cape, Kar98k and the top of his water bottle.

will occur, usually sooner rather than later. Since this has a mortality rate of 10–60%, great efforts were made to avoid it breaking out. A standing order was issued that anyone who discovered they had lice had to report it immediately.

Tornister: Although various other versions had been used since the mid-19th century, the M34 *Tornister* (knapsack) was brought into service in November 1934. It was basically a soft pack with an internal pocket designed to hold the mess kit. Predominantly made of olive drab-coloured water-resistant canvas with a calf leather flap, it had riveted leather straps to hold the flaps down as well as long carrying straps. A slightly improved model known as the M39, which looked more or less identical, was released in 1939. This had added short

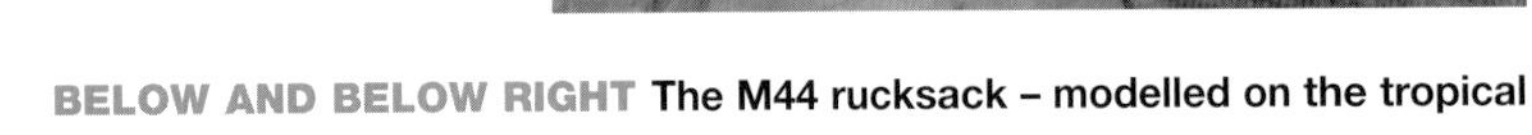

BELOW AND BELOW RIGHT The M44 rucksack – modelled on the tropical rucksack used in the desert (see page 88) – became more used during the war.

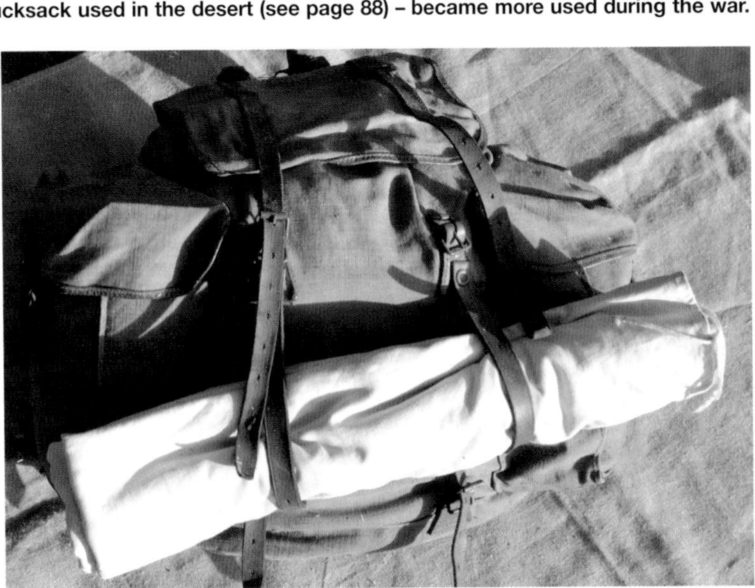

straps to make it possible to attach the pack to the Y-strap combat webbing, but no internal pocket. Although the leather components on early production items were left in their natural brown state, when the war started new ones were painted black. Over the course of hostilities, quality fell as a consequence of the economic situation and recycled materials were often used, although different suppliers used different methods to finish their products.

Brotbeutel: The bread bag was a small cloth haversack used to carry rations and personal items. Made in a wide variety of colours – mostly shades of green or grey – it was introduced in 1931 and used in various forms until the end of the war. Early versions had aluminium buckles and studs, but as rationing bit ever harder, these were replaced by more readily available materials like steel and zinc. Likewise, the leather reinforcements seen on early examples were also deleted. Produced from water-resistant canvas, the bags had a leather or webbing carrying strap as well as small loops and D-rings to allow alternative methods of attachment. Inside, there were two compartments separated by a cloth divider.

Feldflasche: The water bottle issued to the Heer was a derivative of those used in the First World War. Brought into service in 1931, it held 0.8 litres (1.4 pints) of water, and was made of aluminium with an olive drab or brown cover made of wool. It had a carrying strap made of canvas webbing or leather and a cap that doubled up as a drinking cup (*Trinkbecher*). This could be made of steel, aluminium or Bakelite. If the woollen cover were wetted down with water on a hot day, evaporation would help lower the temperature of the contents. In 1940, this cover was replaced with a type of plastic to improve durability. The design remained more or less unchanged until the end of the war.

Kleines Schanzzeug: The entrenching tool was a short shovel that formed a standard part of the soldier's kit. More or less unchanged since its introduction in the 1880s, it was about 55cm (1ft 9.5in) long and had a blade that measured around 14.5cm (5.5in) wide by 18.5cm (7in) in height. This was made of two pieces that were

LEFT The Brotbeutel came in various colours from green to grey, the latter often being Luftwaffe equipment. Typical contents include wallets, personal grooming gear, a toque (neck warmer), and two Bakelite circular containers – these in black and orange – to contain butter or fat.

LEFT There were various versions of the water bottle – nicknamed the coconut for obvious reasons. All of them had a cover (which if dampened kept the contents cool), a large drinking container that could also be used for food (usually aluminium but occasionally Bakelite), and an aluminium 'bottle' although there were examples in the desert and elsewhere made from phenolic resin. The volume was generally 0.75 litres, but there were medical and Gebirgsjäger versions which had a capacity of 1 litre.

LEFT A range of different entrenching tools: the *Schanzzeug* one-piece tool and the *Klappspaten* foldable spade. The latter came in around 1938 and was later copied by the US forces.

RIGHT ***Scherenfernrohr*** **– periscope-extended binoculars – were usually used from a tripod for artillery spotting. The most common version was the SF 14Z.**

spot-welded together and then attached to the handle by means of rivets. It was stowed in a belt-carrier that was initially made of leather, but later constructed from a pressed cardboard that was called *Press-stoff* or *Ersatz Leder* (replacement leather). This had a leather retaining strap to secure the shovel in place. While the standard entrenching tool had a fixed handle, there was also a folding variant.

RIGHT AND BELOW The German infantryman used ***Dienstglas*** **(service binoculars) which were 6× 30s (6× magnification; 30° field of view) but also a range of different** ***Ferngläser*** **(binoculars), many captured or self-provided. The official cases were usually leather or Bakelite (right).** *(via RCT)*

Doppelfernrohr: Binoculars were issued to certain personnel, but were often 'acquired' by others who either wanted them as status symbols or felt they needed them to do their jobs. Although there were many kinds around, the two most common types could be roughly divided into long-range and general observation categories. The former tended to be around 10 × 50 – in other words, they had ten times magnification with 50mm objective lenses. These were good for studying things in detail at reasonable distances and were good in low light, but were both large and heavy. Consequently, they were cumbersome to carry around, and thus best suited for use by people like infantry commanders and artillery observers. More suited to general-purpose use were those rated at 6 × 30 (six times magnification with 30mm objective lenses) – these were far easier to carry, being much lighter and smaller. They also had a wider field of view, but didn't perform as well in low light or have as much magnification. German optics were among the best in the world at the time, with manufacturers like Zeiss being the main suppliers.

Meldekartentasche: The map case was only issued to certain personnel, such as unit commanders, messengers and observers. Directly derived from the First World War era, the design of the M35 version received various small modifications during the war, mostly to the front flap as well as the addition of a small front pocket. They came with various specialist tools, such as reading instruments, and the maps they contained were usually only issued when required, being both named and numbered for security reasons.

Patronentaschen: The type of ammunition pouch issued depended on the type of weapon being carried. The standard service rifle, however, was

RIGHT AND FAR RIGHT **A Panzergrenadier Leutnant armed with an MP40 (note the dedicated ammunition pouches). He's also carrying an M35 map case, some typical contents shown at far right. These include a mechanical map measurer, compass, kilometre gauges and paper pads, as well as a *Deckungswinkelmesser* (indirect fire calculator) which helped to calculate distances and height differences in terrain.**

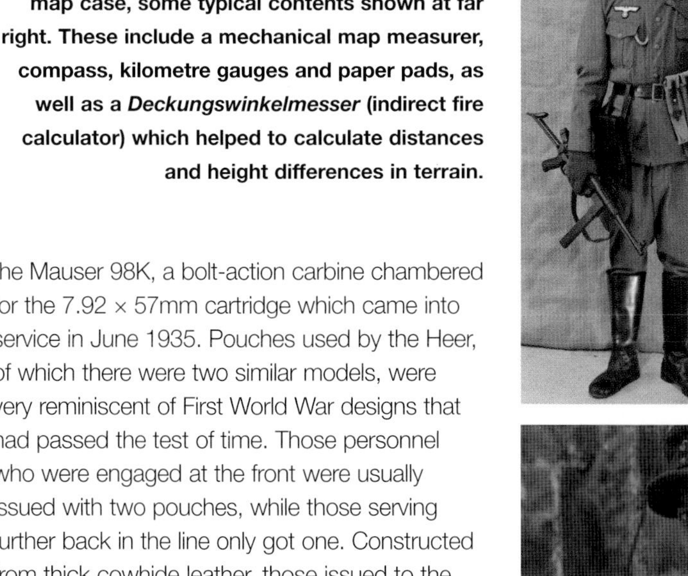

the Mauser 98K, a bolt-action carbine chambered for the 7.92 × 57mm cartridge which came into service in June 1935. Pouches used by the Heer, of which there were two similar models, were very reminiscent of First World War designs that had passed the test of time. Those personnel who were engaged at the front were usually issued with two pouches, while those serving further back in the line only got one. Constructed from thick cowhide leather, those issued to the Heer were usually black with a rough pebbled texture and were held together by heavy cotton threads and steel or aluminium rivets. There were compartments inside with catgut bands to keep the ammunition clips apart.

LEFT **The real thing: this man carries his map case and also his belt – with equipment attached – over his shoulder ready to surrender it to his captors, US 26th Infantry Division at Bütgenbach during the Ardennes Offensive. He's wearing a reversible parka (*Wendbarer Winteranzug*).** *(Battlefield Historian)*

BELOW AND BELOW RIGHT **The ammunition pouches for MP38 and MP40 (below) came in pairs as did those for the K98k (below right). The former carried six magazines with a total of 180 rounds; the latter had two clips of five in each pouch: 60 rounds in total.**

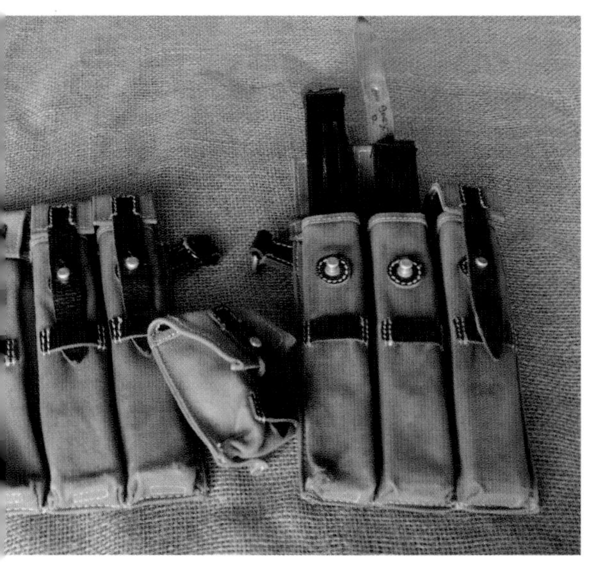

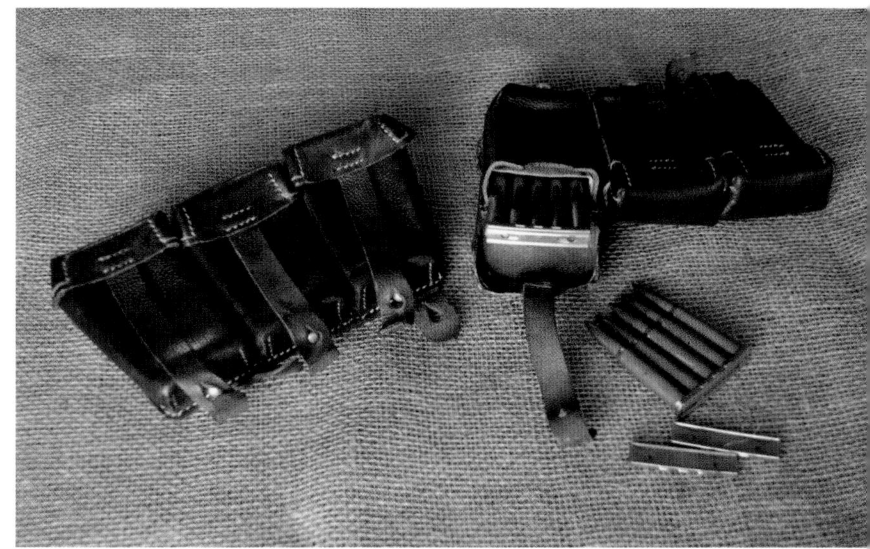

ABOVE Luckily they were never needed: almost every photograph of a Second World War German infantryman shows a gas mask holder. They were carried throughout the war.

BELOW Gas mask drill, including walking for miles wearing it. *(via Tanis)*

Blechbüchse für Gasmaske: There is much debate about why Germany did not use chemical weapons on the battlefield in the Second World War. Legend has it that Hitler experienced the horrors of gas himself during the First World War, and that he realised they were just as much of a threat to the troops using them as to the enemy, and thus forbade their use. Despite this, the troops still had to be able to protect themselves against chemical attack by the enemy, and so were issued with gas masks and sturdy waterproof canisters (*Blechbüchse für Gasmaske*) to contain them. These were made from stamped steel and came in various lengths depending on the model. They were fitted with straps that allowed them to be carried in the small of the back. The lid of the canister folded back and had a spring clip on the inside that held the anti-fog lenses in place. The mask was meant to fit below this, but many troops simply dispensed with them and used the canisters to carry personal effects, ammunition, or extra food instead.

Other items

It is impossible to identify or illustrate all the items of German infantry equipment and uniform here. Six years of war saw not only many official variations but also a myriad unofficial ones: the subject is enormous. Varying quality and material changes forced by wartime exigencies; the extensive use of captured equipment and industrial facilities; improvements following testing in the field and in combat; changes of command and control;

LEFT This 1944 photograph shows items found in German soldiers' pockets when they were taken prisoner – some unusual items include ladies' suspender attachments.

inventions and technological improvements – all these things play a part in creating a huge official inventory swelled by in-the-field usage of civilian or locally made uniforms or equipment. Above all, the Nazi propensity for duplication – caused by the empire building of the big hitters and inter-faction and inter-service bickering – means that there is less homogeneity than, for example, the US inventory. Added to this, the post-war faking of German equipment and genuine reproductions propelled by a lucrative collecting market and re-enactors means it can be difficult to know what is real.

Camouflage

During the First World War the Germans had been the first to use printed camouflage on aircraft and then introduced disruptive camouflage for tanks and steel helmets. In the interwar period (1930) they brought in *Splittertarnmuster* 31, which was used on *Zeltbahn* (tent) sections; in turn these were often used as camouflage ponchos by the troops. When war started, the use of disruptive-patterned camouflage accelerated. In 1941 Fallschirmjäger received camouflaged smocks before *Unternehmen Merkur* (Operation Mercury – the invasion of Crete). In 1943 *Sumpftarnmuster* (swamp pattern) was introduced in two forms: M43 and M44.

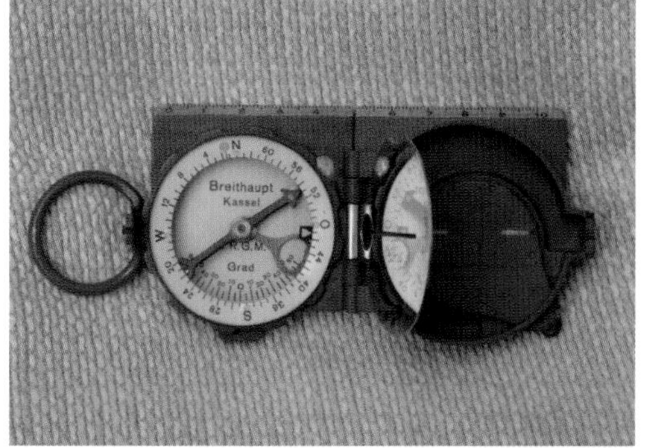

LEFT Another example of a German wartime compass.

LEFT Mosquitoes and flies in the Pripet Marshes: 'The stink is indescribable. The flies and mosquitoes are a plague and I wonder what these blood-sucking pests lived on before we came along. We wear nets but . . .' *(via RCT)*

RIGHT This soldier wears a pair of MP40 ammunition pouches and a lightweight camouflage smock, with tan and water (*Sumpftarnmuster*) pattern outside and white inside (the edges can just be seen on the tips of the chest 'pockets' – openings to allow the wearer access to his tunic jacket's breast pockets).

CENTRE The Fallschirmjäger smock (in *Luftwaffesplittermuster* – Luftwaffe splinter pattern also called Splinter Pattern 41 – camouflage) first used during the Battle of Crete proved too expensive to mass-produce and so the Luftwaffefelddivisionen used a simpler three-quarter length over-jacket using Sumpftarnmuster camouflage.

The Waffen-SS had patterns designed by Johan Georg Otto Schick that were used from 1935.

- *Platanenmuster* – plane tree pattern (1937–42)
- *Rauchtarnmuster* – smoke pattern (1939–44)
- *Palmenmuster* – palm tree pattern (from 1941)
- *Eichenlaubmuster* – oak leaf pattern (A and B versions 1942–45)
- *Erbsenmuster* – pea dot pattern (1944–45)
- *Leibermuster* – body pattern (1945).

Quite often these were reversible with camouflage for two seasons – summer and autumn, or summer and winter (snow).

Winter clothing

The only significant item of cold weather clothing issued to the Heer at the beginning of the war was a heavy woollen greatcoat. After experiencing the horrors of the Russian winter for the first time – soldiers had to stuff newspapers under their shirts to survive – a thorough review was conducted that resulted in a full set of winter equipment being made. This included hooded waterproof parkas and heavy water-resistant trousers, tunic and gloves. All these were white on one side with conventional colours, either green camouflage or field grey, on the other. There was also thick underwear in white and field grey as well as thick woollen scarves. These were machine knitted with a mix of mottled grey wool and rayon, and featured a black stripe at either end. Although all this was a massive improvement, the boots used by the Russians were still considered superior and whenever possible the German soldiers did their best to obtain some. Those who had to use the standard items often filled them with straw in an attempt to keep out the cold, and many also relied on other captured Red Army equipment to get through the harsh eastern winters.

LEFT The Zeltbahn came in sections, with each man carrying one section along with poles and tentpegs. Another important use of Zeltbahn sections was as camouflage smocks – as shown by our two re-enactors.

ABOVE An evocative photograph of a group of winter warriors carrying K98ks and map cases. They are wearing reversible snowsuits, as exemplified by our re-enactor. These suits stained easily, but the Sumpftarnmuster camouflage was very effective. Note the mitts worn by the man at left (photo above left) attached by a drawstring. *(via RCT)*

The Winter Relief Organisation – *Winterhilfwerk* – collected public donations of furs and suitable warm clothing, including underwear, socks and gloves, to supplement equipment issued, and therefore non-standard items were sent to the front.

Straw boots were issued, based on Russian versions. Cumbersome – they fitted over a standard marching boot – they were effective in keeping feet warm while on static duty (sentries for example) but they weren't robust in wet conditions. As a consequence, pressed felt overboots were produced, also based on a Russian design. These proved to be useless in wet or slushy conditions, so an improved version was provided.

These latest overboots had a wooden sole, calf-length 1cm compressed felt, and leather front, toe, heel and lower side. They were front-opening and secured by two leather straps with metal claw buckles. They could be worn over footwear or stockinged feet and were robust enough for most conditions other than constant immersion. The weakest point was the felt/leather stitching. Many manufacturers produced these, including Paul Otto Hartha.

Skijäger

Ski-mounted troops were issued with a complete set of equipment that differed from that given to conventional infantry because their

BELOW The variety of winter coats – many made in situ – used in Russia served two purposes. First, and most obviously, they were necessary to keep the wearer warm. Many were, therefore, made from skins. The other prime reason for white coats was camouflage: because of this many were smocks or even, on occasion, looted white sheets. *(via Tanis)*

RIGHT German war artists were important proponents of propaganda. Published in 1944, Kurt Kranz's *Winteralltag im Urwald Lapplands* (Winter Life in the Lapland Forest) provided nearly 40 wonderful sketches of the snowy war fought in Lapland – the northernmost region of Finland. This image shows ski troops armed with an MP40 and K98k carbines and single-piece snowsuits. *(via RCT)*

role was to operate in very cold environments. Since a lot of heat is lost from the head, they were given an insulated skullcap manufactured from an off-white heavy cotton; this was secured with two green celluloid buttons. Below this there was a green or grey cylindrically knitted woollen neck warmer that could be worn either as a scarf or as a tube over the head. To keep the chest area warm, a long sheepskin parka was provided. This had lots of buttons in the relevant places, such as at the cuffs and collar to keep the wind out, as well as ventilation slots under the armpits and on the chest to minimise overheating. Under the parka a woollen shirt was worn that could vary in colour from green to grey.

Since the ability to use small arms was paramount for a soldier, keeping his hands warm was critical and to this end canvas mittens with a thick woollen lining were provided that had a special compartment for the trigger finger to slide into.

Alpine trousers made of grey wool were worn on the lower half and were partially lined with an off-white linen to provide extra insulation. As with so much military kit, exact designs varied depending on the year and the supplier, but typically the trousers had four pockets, each with its own flap, including one dedicated to holding a watch. The legs also had tie-down straps to secure them while the footwear was being pulled on: this comprised of long leather boots worn over woollen socks. They were substantially constructed with leather laces that went through steel eyelets. The soles were also made of leather and then reinforced with steel plates, five at the toe and one at the heel. There was also a special groove for the ski bindings to clip into.

The Skijäger used to carry his kit and belongings in an extra large backpack, including one of his most important pieces of equipment – the ski furs. These were designed to go over the skis to allow the user to walk up hills without sliding back down again. Made of seal fur, the orientation of the hairs was such that the ski would slide forwards but not backwards.

Desert clothing

The desert clothing used by the German infantry was typified by that worn by the Afrika Korps. This centred on the M40 tropical tunic, which was issued to all officers and men and made of a medium-weight olive drab material. It was cut in more or less the same style as the standard item, but with an open collar and lapels. Although intended for use in Africa, it was later also approved for the hotter areas of southern Europe. A matching shirt was used, and occasionally a similarly coloured neck tie. Insignia were embroidered in grey on a tan background. Officers also had privately

FAR LEFT AND LEFT **The troops in the North African desert will always be remembered as Rommel's Afrika Korps, although many of them were Italian and Rommel wasn't there for the whole period. One of the iconic images of the desert is the M40 peaked cap with its bright red cotton interior. The sketch by Wilhelm Wessel shows Obergefreiter Hartnagel wearing his peaked cap. It's dated 18 April 1942. Wessel is perhaps best-known for his book *Mit Rommel in der Wüste*.** *(Ken Adams collection; via RCT)*

purchased M35 cotton tunics, which could be khaki, olive or mustard-yellow in colour.

Early in the war, M40 tropical breeches were issued to be worn above boots, but the heat made them very unpopular and most were cut down to make shorts. By 1941, new lightweight cotton trousers and shorts in olive cotton replaced most of the despised breeches. Since the desert can be extremely cold at night, a long overcoat was issued as well – this was the same as the European version, except that it came in a brown colour.

The head was meant to be protected from the sun by a pith helmet; however, this did not suit frontline combat, and so was mostly used further back in the line. Instead, the conventional steel helmet, painted in one of several shades of a sandy colour, was issued.

LEFT **Early days: many of the German troops reached North Africa by transport aircraft from Italy. The troops boarding the 'Tante-Ju' Junkers Ju52m are wearing the German *Tropische Kopfbedeckung* – the British called them solar topis – made of pith covered in fabric.**

RIGHT Heavily burdened troops march with all their gear: bed rolls, rucksacks, even a solar topi. It looks heavy going in the sand.

When not in contact with the enemy, the soft M40 peaked cap was generally used. The feet received ankle boots with puttees or lace-up canvas knee-boots. Once again, the heat made the use of puttees and long boots impractical, so the former were rarely seen and the latter were usually cut down to ankle length.

Scharfschützen

Snipers had their own specialist kit too, with the smock being the most noticeable item. This was either of splinter or tan and water camouflage pattern, both being derived from First World War designs. The former first

LEFT AND BELOW This group shows off the tropical uniform, including shirt and tie, in light green. The uniforms soon bleached in the desert sun. The only thing missing in this photograph is the high lace-up boots shown well in the neighbouring image. Sometimes long gaiters were worn over them. *(both via RCT)*

LEFT These Fallschirmjäger POWs are from 2nd FJR Division who surrendered with Ramcke after the fall of Brest in September 1944. The three nearest the camera are wearing the *Knockensack* (bonesack) jump smocks and Luftwaffe officers' sidecaps. Note the long leather jump gloves worn by the man in the front row.

saw service in 1931, with the latter being introduced in 1934 – a final version was released in 1944. The M42 sniper's smock was hoodless and based on the Waffen-SS version. A subsequent model designated the M43 was introduced a year later; this had an integral hood that was big enough to go over a steel helmet, along with a built-in camouflage face veil. It was made from a light cotton fabric that had the camouflage design printed directly on to it, and had drawstrings both at the waist and at the collar.

Fallschirmjäger as infantry

Although the Fallschirmjäger were supposedly Luftwaffe paratroopers, they were often used as ground troops too, either in support of airfields or as battlefield infantry. They proved tenacious fighters on every front.

They had a range of specialist clothing and equipment although some of the clothing was impractical to use and expensive to issue. The jump smock – at first in grey or grey-green – was a good example: worn over their equipment and clothing, at the start of the war it involved step-in legs, which were at best impractical and at worst dangerous. These were changed and press-studs were fitted in time for the attack on Crete. Most of the smocks were in splinter camouflage, although some were in olive green. They were expensive to manufacture in the quantities required and were later replaced with a camouflaged over-jacket. This came as standard with the Luftwaffe eagle and swastika emblem printed on it. Epaulettes were added after issue to denote the wearer's rank. The combat trousers were gathered at the ankle and had slits on the outer seam to knee level to allow the removal of kneepads. There were special jump boots, but these were usually replaced by short boots when their infantry role took over. The special rimless Fallschirmjäger helmet had an extensive harness, more interior padding and often a cover. It is this helmet and the smock that provide the lasting image of the Fallschirmjäger.

Another important item of equipment was the Fallschirmjäger's K98k bandolier. This was made of cloth and hung around the neck, with loops to attach to the belt. It had six compartments on each side, each holding ten rounds. There was a similar bandolier carrying eight 20-round magazines of the FG42. There was also a grenade bag.

Gebirgsjäger

The true mountain troops of the Third Reich, the early war divisions were well-trained specialists with equipment that had been specially produced for mountain warfare. Later in the war

LEFT AND ABOVE The Gebirgsjäger in their element: heading to the hills, their rucksacks bulging and their heavy weapons carried by horses and mules. In particular the 7.5cm Gebirgsgeschütz 36, 8cm and 12cm mortars and 7.5cm Paks broke down for transport by pack animal. *(via RCT)*

BELOW A group of Gebirgsjäger show off their ***Bergmütze*** caps, the cleats on the sides of their hobnailed mountain boots and puttees or long socks. There are some Edelweiß badges visible on right arms implying that a number are fully fledged Gebirgsjäger; the rest are probably recruits. *(via RCT)*

this wasn't always the case – particularly those created within the Waffen-SS. Take the 5th Gebirgsjäger who trained in the Bavarian Alps after being formed from the 100th Mountain Infantry Regiment of the 1st Division and 10th Infantry Division. They fought in Greece, Crete, Russia and Italy, finally surrendering to the Americans in Turin.

Gebirgsjäger equipment included a purpose-built ankle-length and heavily studded boots; the sage-green *Windjacke* (windproof jacket); and mountain-climbing equipment – skis, snow goggles, ice axe, rope, ice hammer, crampons, pitons and snowshoes, as well as a special Große Knapsack.

Motorcycle troops

The *Kradfahrer* were used for a variety of purposes, from chauffeuring officers to delivering dispatches or transporting hot food, and as fast scouts for forward patrols. Sometimes, they even acted as mobile anti-tank units, and many had to operate in mud that was so thick that horses sank up to their bellies in it. As a result, the riders had to be able to withstand all weathers, from the heat of the desert to the snows of winter. On the Russian front, temperatures fell to -40°C (-40°F), at which point engine oil freezes solid.

Motorcycle troops needed special equipment in order to operate. The outermost layer was usually a rubberised canvas raincoat called a *Kradmantel*. This was first introduced in 1934 and designed to be big enough to go over the standard field uniform and equipment. It had a large flap across the front and reached down to the calf to give maximum protection. Its style and cut was popular enough for it to be worn by many non-motorcyclists, despite regulations to the contrary. Its colours varied, but the field grey version with zinc buttons was the commonest – this had a bottle-green or black woollen collar and featured shoulder boards for the relevant Waffenfarbe. It was held in place by a black leather belt.

The standard battlefield helmet was usually worn with aviator-style goggles over the top, and heavy gauntlets made of leather and canvas were used on the hands – sometimes supplemented with hand warmers. Long black jackboots were provided for the feet.

ABOVE In among the British POWs on Crete, a Fallschirmjäger motorcycle combination. Note the driver's goggles.

BELOW Wehrmacht motorcyclists wore the Kradmantel rubberised overcoat. Note the buttons low down on the coat. With these the garment could be buttoned around the motorcyclist's legs while he was riding. *(via RCT)*

Chapter Five

Weapons

Germany excelled at the manufacture of weapons. The MP38/40 machine pistol is one of the iconic weapons of the Second World War; the Sturmgewehr 44 was the first assault rifle; the FG42 an outstanding design. The infantry squad was built around the machine gun and the Germans had two beauties – the MG34 and MG42. German anti-tank weapons were also particularly effective: the Panzerfaust and Panzerschreck, the Pak 40 and 43 and the 8.8cm Flak 36, the best anti-tank gun of the war.

OPPOSITE Booty. A haul of German weapons collected by American troops. From front to back: PzB39 mags holding 7.92mm anti-tank rifle rounds in boxes and loose; two Kar98k carbines resting on MG34 drum magazines; MG34, ammo boxes and belts and, at back left behind the ammo boxes, two spare-barrel containers.

Introduction

The cutting edge of any infantry unit is its weaponry and in 1939 the German infantry division boasted around 17,000 men, most armed with the K98k rifle, Luger or Walther pistols, hand grenades, bayonets and other personal weaponry. The heavy weapons amounted to:

- 643 × MGs – usually MG34s used as LMGs (527) on bipods and HMGs (116) on tripods
- 90 × anti-tank rifles (PzB 38/39)
- 84 × light (5cm) mortars
- 58 × medium (8cm) mortars
- 20 × 7.5cm leIG
- 4 × 10.5cm sIG
- 75 × anti-tank (3.7cm/5cm later 7.5cm) guns
- 36 × 10.5cm leFH
- 12 × 15cm sFH
- 12 × light (2cm) AA guns.

By 1944, the division had changed composition and weaponry. It had fewer men (around 12,000) and fewer rifles (around 9,000), as there were around 1,500 SMGs (MP38/40s) included on the table of equipment. As far as heavy weapons go, there were:

- 656 × MGs – usually MG42s used as LMGs (566) on bipods and HMGs (90) on tripods.
- 48 × medium (8cm) mortars
- 28 × heavy (120mm) mortars
- 108 × Panzerfausts/schrecks
- 12 × light (2cm) AA guns
- 20 × 7.5cm leIG
- 6 × 10.5cm sIG
- 21 × anti-tank (7.5cm) guns
- 14 × SP anti-tank (7.5cm) guns
- 18 × light (7.5cm) howitzers
- 42 × 10.5cm sIG/howitzers
- 12 × heavy (15cm) field howitzers.

A 1944 Volksgrenadier division had around 10,000 men armed with:

- 423 × MGs – usually MG42s used as LMGs (369) on bipods and HMGs (54) on tripods
- 42 × medium (8cm) mortars
- 24 × heavy (120mm) mortars
- 216 × Panzerfausts/schrecks
- 9 × 3.7cm anti-tank
- 75 × light (7.5cm) infantry guns or howitzers
- 24 × (10.5cm) gun/howitzers
- 12 × heavy (15cm) field howitzers.

A 1943 Panzergrenadier division had around 14,000 men. It was much more heavily armed than an infantry division with armoured cars, SP guns, Sturmgeschütze and mobile Flak:

- 582 × MGs – usually MG42s used as LMGs (534) on bipods and HMGs (48) on tripods
- 24 × medium (8cm) mortars
- 4 × heavy (120mm) mortars
- 33 × 7.5cm Pak 40 (including 3 × SP)
- 42 × 2cm Flak (including 24 × SP)
- 18 × Flammenwerfer
- 42 × Sturmgeschütze assault guns
- 28 × Marder 7.5cm SP guns
- 18 × armoured cars with 2cm guns
- 7 × 7.5cm leIG
- 24 × 10.5cm leFH
- 12 × 15cm sFH
- 2 × 1.5cm sIG
- 8 × 8.8cm Flak.

BELOW The Luger was issued to officers, NCOs and weapon crews. It started with wooden pistol grips but Bakelite came in as the war progressed. The leather holster showed variations of colour throughout the war. It held a spare loaded magazine as well as a roughly cruciform-shaped disassembly tool, which also aided loading. *(Greene Media Ltd)*

Pistols

Pistole Parabellum 1908 (P08)

One of the first semi-automatic pistols, the Luger (nicknamed for its designer) was a well-balanced accurate pistol, with a high muzzle velocity. It fired a 9mm-calibre bullet creating a small clean wound – not a stopping round. This recoil-operated eight-round pistol had a toggle action and was extremely functional but prone to dust and dirt getting into the mechanism. It was difficult to keep clean in desert conditions and worked best if oil was only used sparingly.

Type: Recoil-operated semi-automatic pistol
In service: 1908–45 in various forms
Designed: G.J. Luger
Manufactured: DWM – Deutsche Waffen-und Munitionsfabriken – produced about 38% of all Lugers. Mauser Werke of Oberndorf made about the same percentage. A German Imperial arsenal in Erfurt only made Lugers between 1910 and 1918, but their total was about 21%. The remaining 3% was made by the Swiss factory at Bern, the Vickers factory in England (that's right, England!), Simson & Company and Krieghoff, both of Suhl, Germany .
Number built: About 3 million (give or take a few hundred thousand)
Weight: 0.87kg (1lb 14oz) empty
Length: 22.3cm (8.78in)
Barrel length: 9.8cm (3.86in)
Cartridge: 9 × 19mm Parabellum
Feed: Eight-round detachable box magazine; recoil feed or by pulling back toggle
Rate of fire: 20 rounds/min
Muzzle velocity: 114m/sec (375ft/sec)
Effective range: 20–50m (25–55yd)
Sights: Rear – open v; front – inverted v.

Walther P38

The P38 replaced the Luger because the latter was expensive to manufacture and jammed easily. The P38 became the standard sidearm of the Wehrmacht. It was a dependable, high-quality weapon that was fired without having to cock it first.

Type: Short recoil-operated, semi-automatic and double-action pistol
In service: 1938–45
Designed: Walther
Manufactured: Carl Walther Waffenfabrik, Mauser Werke, Spreewerk; from 1942 to 1945 Neuengamme concentration camp Hamburg using slave labour
Number built: Over 1 million
Weight: 0.907kg (2lb) empty
Length: 21.6cm (8.5in)
Barrel length: 12.5cm (4.75in)
Cartridge: 9 × 19mm Parabellum
Feed/action: Eight-round detachable box magazine-fed, short recoil feed from magazine
Muzzle velocity: 365m/sec (1,200ft/sec)
Effective range: 20–50m (25–55yd)
Sights: Rear – open v; front – blade.

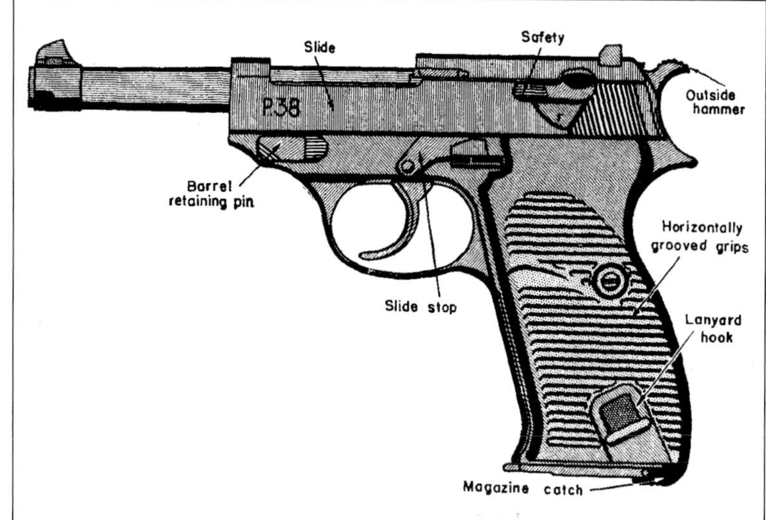

ABOVE The Walther P38 was designed to be mass-produced. Originally it had an enclosed hammer but this was altered at the request of the military, who needed to see the hammer to judge its readiness.

Rifles

Gewehr 98 (G98)

This bolt-action rifle had an internal box magazine holding five clip-fed 7.92mm bullets. Manufactured in 1898, it was the standard German rifle throughout the First World War and continued in service until 1935 when the K98k replaced it. However, many G98s remained in use throughout the war.

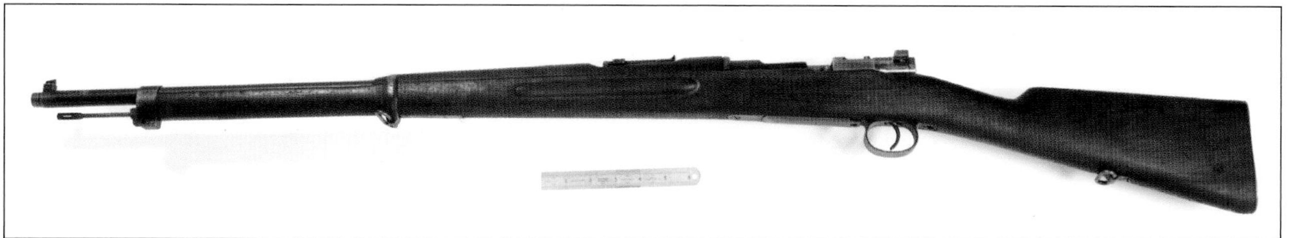

BELOW The G98 was a long rifle with a horizontal bolt. Its variant was the K98b with improved sights and a turned-down bolt handle. The latter was a carbine in name only, to get around the restrictions of the Treaty of Versailles. *(Greene Media Ltd)*

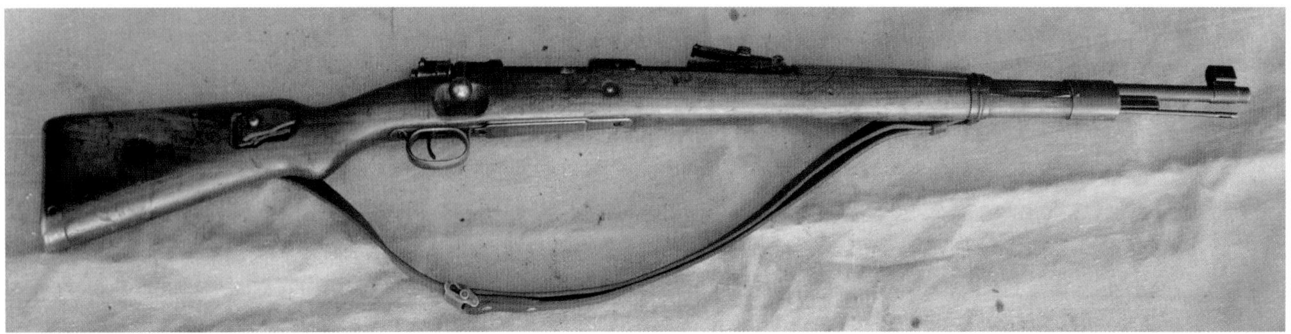

ABOVE Note the differences between the G98 and K98k: the latter is, of course, shorter; it also has an enclosed foresight, the sling is side-mounted and the bolt handle is turned down into the stock.

The rifle stock was oiled walnut wood until shortages towards the end of the First World War necessitated the use of beech, making the rifle heavier. Able to launch grenades from various models of attachable cup, it was adapted to mount a sniperscope. A recess had to be cut into the stock to accommodate a modified bolt because the bolt action would not work if a scope had been mounted. The recess and a higher mounting for the scope solved the problem.

Type: Bolt-action rifle
In service: 1898–35; but seen in use until 1945
Designed: Paul Mauser
Manufactured: Mauser
Number built: Over 9 million
Weight: 4.09kg (9lb) empty
Length: 1.25m (4ft 1.2in)
Barrel length: 74cm (2ft 5.1in)
Cartridge: 7.92 × 57mm spitzer (pointed bullet)
Feed: Bolt – Mauser-designed and still considered one of the finest ever made; five rounds on stripper clip in internal box magazine
Rate of fire: 15 rounds/min by a skilled operator
Muzzle velocity: 878m/sec (864yd/sec)
Effective range: 500m (550yd) using sights; 800m (870yd) with optics. Max range: 3,735m (4,080yd)
Sights: Rear – leaf; front – inverted v; optics: 2.5× and 3×.

BELOW Cross-section of K98k magazine, trigger and bolt mechanism. Note thumb pressure clip feed.

Karabiner 98k (K98k)

This *Karabiner* (carbine) was the shorter (k = *kurz*) version of the First World War G98 and became the standard issue rifle of the German army from 1935 to the end of the war. The change came about when an improved ball cartridge was adopted in 1935. It produced less muzzle flash and greater accuracy than the G98 cartridge. A short, bolt-operated magazine (internal) fed five rounds. The metal parts were blued to guard against rust, but this only provided minimal protection. A more effective system was introduced in 1944.

The hooded front sight post cover was added in 1939 to reduce glare and to protect the post. Laminated stocks were introduced from 1937 after lengthy trials. These were stronger and less likely to warp than the solid wood one-piece stocks. Walnut, beech and elm were used in the process. All stocks had a steel butt plate.

The bolt comes a long way back and this forces the user to drop the rifle from the shoulder to cock and reload it – not the best thing to have to do in a firefight. Ammunition was carried in two sets of three leather ammunition pouches attached to the belt, each of which holds 30 rounds in five-round clips.

How to identify the K98k:

a) Short barrel
b) Upper and lower stock binding bands close together
c) Cleaning rod section fitted into the stock under the muzzle. Three sections (from other weapons) made a full-length cleaning rod

LEFT Firing

1 Firing from a kneeling position.

2 Working the bolt.

3 Firing from a standing position.

d) Open v notch leaf rear sight sliding along a ramp; graduated 100–2,000m

e) Bolt-action with same modifications to bolt as the G98

f) Semi-pistol grip stock

g) Leather sling through butt

h) Metal-lined hole on butt to help with stripping the firing-pin assembly

i) Mod98 stamped on left receiver wall.

Accessories:

- Leather sling
- Muzzle cover
- *Reinigungsgerät* (cleaning kit) 34
  This is contained in an 8.5cm (3.3in) wide × 13.5cm (5.3in) long box with two hinged and clipped lids top and bottom. It holds: an oiler, takedown tool, aluminium linked pull-through chain, a cleaning and oiling brush and short lengths of gauze cleaning patches for the pull-through.
- S84/98 III bayonet
  This differed from its First World War

BELOW Two types of leather bayonet frog. That with a retaining strap was for mounted troops; without for the rest of the military. Interestingly a regulation of 25 January 1939 stated that all frogs were to have the retaining strap, though there is no evidence that this was followed through. For those new to collecting bayonets, in the early days almost all parts were quality stamped, although very close examination is needed sometimes to find the marks. On production both the bayonet and the scabbard would have matching production numbers. This combination is rare now owing to the German system of wasting nothing and reusing parts.

ABOVE Attaching the bayonet

1 Remove from scabbard. **2** Attach bayonet. **3** Complete.

predecessor by having a smaller flash guard and often not having a manufacturer's mark. Unserrated, the bayonet usually had a Bakelite grip (1937–44) although 1935–36 and 1945 models had wooden handles as Bakelite stocks ran out. It was 38.4cm (1ft 3in) in total length, of which 25.1cm (10in) was blade. Millions were made from 1935 to 1945.

- Rifle grenade launcher (*Gewehrsprenggranate*).

The rifle grenade filled the gap between a hand grenade and the small infantry mortar. Developed during the First World War, by the Second World War the Germans had designed a spigot-type launcher and a cup-type launcher.

The cup launcher (*Schießbecher*) holder clamped to the rifle barrel and a rifled cup discharger screwed into it. With experience the sighting attachment was discarded. There were three types of projectile: HE anti-personnel grenade (GSprgr) that could also be thrown

RIGHT Using the K98k to launch rifle grenades

1. Barrel attachment.
2. Attach and lock on.
3. Rifle ready to receive grenade.
4. The rounds available.

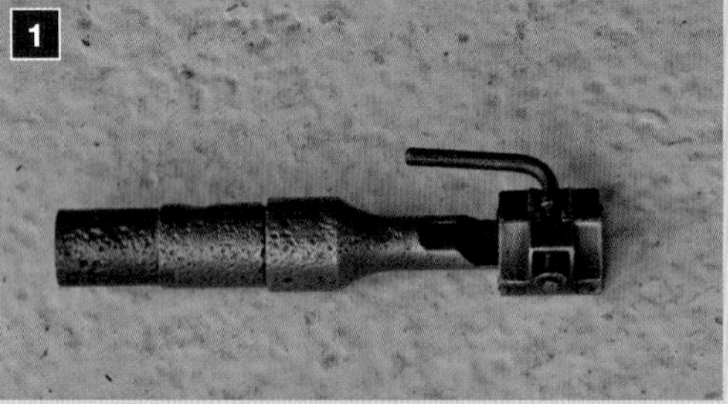

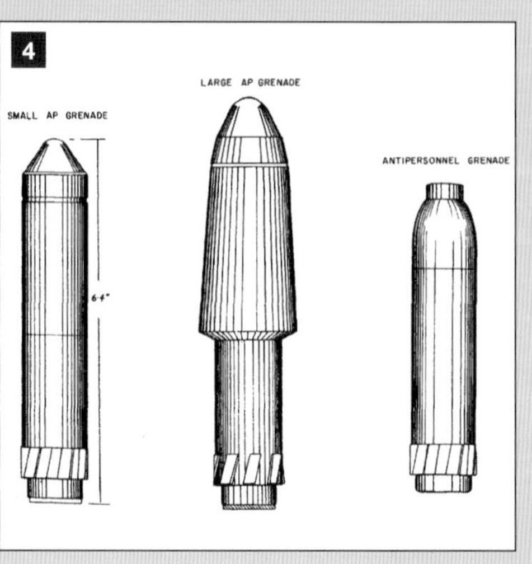

as a hand grenade (range 242m/265yd max); GPzgr – hollow-charge light armour-piercing anti-tank (range 75m/82yd max); gross GPzgr – hollow-charge heavy armour-piercing anti-tank (range 100m/109yd max).

The *Schuß* GG P-40 spigot-type grenade employed a hollow tubular spigot with sight, attached to the K98k the same way as a bayonet. The round had a hollow tubular tail, which fitted over the spigot and was launched by a bulleted blank cartridge, contained within the tubular tail until needed. The hollow-charge head was covered by a convex metal cap. The grenade initiated when it hit or grazed a target. There were HE and anti-tank versions. Its overall length was 23.5cm (9.3in).

One of the rounds was the Panzergranate 61 whose hollow charge could penetrate 89mm of armour.

Type: Bolt-action carbine
In service: 1935 onward
Designed: 1935
Manufactured: Mauser
Number built: 14.6 million
Weight: 3.5–4kg (8–9lb)
Length: 1.1m (3ft 7in)
Barrel length: 59–60cm (1ft 11.4in)
Cartridge: 7.92 × 57mm Mauser spitzer
Feed: Bolt-action; five rounds on stripper clip in internal box magazine
Rate of fire: 15 rounds/min by skilled user
Muzzle velocity: 760m/sec (830yd/sec)
Effective range: 500m (550yd) using sights; 1,000m (1,090yd) with optics; Max range: 2,700m (3,000yd)
Sights: Rear – leaf; front – hooded; optics: Zf41 (1.5×) scope. Over 100,000 made but it had poor eye relief and so German snipers preferred captured Soviet sniper rifles or the G98 with custom-built civilian scopes.

Gewehr 41 (G41) and *Gewehr* 43 (G43)

The German Army needed a semi-automatic rifle to replace the K98k, particularly for use on the Eastern Front. The G41 (41W – Walther or 41M – Mauser) was made by two manufacturers and, therefore, there were slight differences in construction. It was gas-operated. On each shot the propellant gases are forced up (deflected) and push back a long piston rod which in turn forces back the breech to recock the weapon ready for the next shot – a quick system. Mauser's version had – as per the design brief – a bolt-action backup if the semi-auto failed. Unfortunately, Mauser's version was very unreliable and production was halted after only 6,600 were built. Walther's version didn't have the bolt-action backup and was built in larger numbers – up to 100,000. Over-tooled and difficult to strip in field conditions, the Walther version was better than the Mauser but still suffered from gas-fouling problems. It was redesigned in 1943 as the G43 with a detachable box magazine and a piston system copied from the Tokarev SVT40, with gas tapped from the barrel rather than deflected.

Data: G41W [G43]
Type: Semi-automatic
In service: 1941–45 (1943–45)
Designed and manufactured: Walther
Number built: 100,000 (402,713)
Weight: 5.02kg (11lb) (4.2kg/9.3lb)
Length: 1.14m (3ft 9in)
Barrel length: 0.545m (1ft 9.5in)
Cartridge: 7.92 × 57mm Mauser rimless

LEFT The Polish Campaign raised the need for a semi-automatic rifle. The G41W self-loading rifle was the result. However, the ten-round integral magazine was slow to load and the weapon was muzzle-heavy. The G43 – as held by our Panzergrenadier – was an improvement. It had a gas-operated Tokarev system concealed within the stock, and a detachable magazine. The receiver was machined to take the ZF41 telescopic sight. The G43 was much better than the G41 but never overcame its reputation for unreliability.

STRIPPING AND CLEANING

The first step in cleaning a weapon is to ensure it is unloaded; a trained person will do this without thinking. Next, it is important to have a standard operating procedure when breaking down the weapon into its component parts. Each piece will be put down in sequence so that whatever the circumstances it can be reassembled in the dark or by someone else if the circumstances demand.

1 **Remove bolt:** cock the rifle by working the bolt, and set the safety lever halfway between the safe and the locked positions. Pull the bolt back. Then pull out the near end of the bolt stop, which is located on the left side of the receiver near the cut-off. Hold the bolt stop out while you remove the bolt from the receiver.

2 **Disassemble bolt:** press in the bolt-sleeve lock and unscrew the bolt sleeve, firing pin and spring assembly. Now place the tip of the firing pin in the hole in the stock of the rifle. Compress the spring, pushing down on the bolt sleeve until the bolt sleeve clears the headless cocking piece. Turn the cocking piece a quarter turn in either direction and remove it from the firing pin shaft. Ease up on the bolt sleeve so as not to allow the spring to escape suddenly. Remove the bolt sleeve and firing pin spring from the firing pin.

3 **Remove magazine floor plate:** insert the point of a bullet or a pointed tool into the small hole in the magazine floor plate, and exert pressure while at the same time pushing the floor plate toward the trigger guard. This will release the catch, and the magazine floor plate spring and follower can then be removed and broken down into their separate units. Further stripping is not usually necessary.

4 **The cleaning kit:** cleaning brush (*Reinigungsbürste*), oil container (*Öltropfer*), oiling brush (*Ölbürste*), pull through chain (*Reinigungskette*), take down tool (*Hülsenkopfwischer*)

5 **Cleaning the barrel:** Drop the cleaning chain down the barrel ...

6 ... and pull through oiled rag.

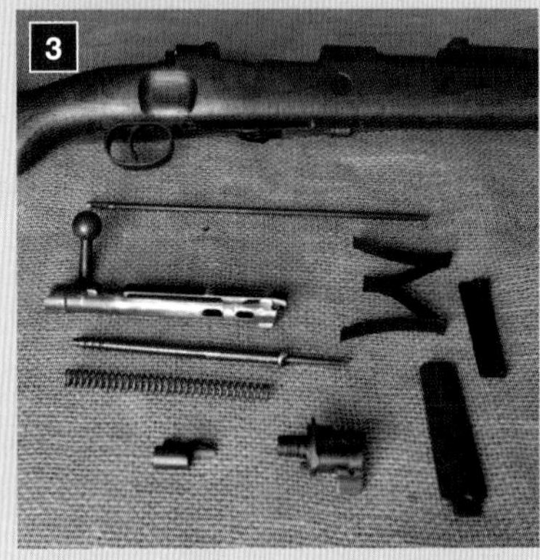

Feed: Gas-operated short piston; ten-round non-removable magazine loaded with 2× five-round stripper clips: a slow loading system
Rate of fire: 20–30 rounds/min (30 rounds/min)
Muzzle velocity: 776m/sec (2,550ft/sec)
Effective range: 1,200m (1,312yd) allegedly! (500m/547yd effective)
Sights: Rear – flip; front – post (also ZF4 telescopic sights).

Fallschirmjägergewehr 42 (FG42)

During the Battle of Crete, Fallschirmjäger were equipped with the standard Heer weapons, but could only carry pistols and hand grenades during jumps; other weapons were delivered by containers. This meant that the German paratroopers were outgunned until they could retrieve their support weapons. To compensate for this – although there were no massed drops by the Fallschirmjäger after Crete – the FG42 was developed.

However, two events altered the FG42 significantly during production. First, supplies of the manganese steel, from which it was initially manufactured, had to be diverted to other needs resulting in a redesign that replaced it with stamped sheet metal. On top of this, user information led to improvements that saw the bipod moved from the front of the hand guard to the muzzle; the grip angle changed; the hand guard size altered; and the stock changed from steel to wood. The spike bayonet under the barrel was shortened from around 250mm to 150mm (from 10in to 6in).

The FG42 proved to be a good weapon but was loud and produced a strong muzzle flash, which when used at night gave away the operator's position.

ABOVE AND LEFT
One of the first service rifles with a straight-line configuration, the FG42 was an outstanding design. It was, however, expensive to make and considered a 'glorious waste of resources'. It had a side-loading box magazine but was difficult to control on fully automatic. It was first used in the rescue of Mussolini from the Gran Sasso (as left). *(Greene Media Ltd)*

Type: Automatic rifle
In service: 1942–45
Designed: Louis Stange
Manufactured: Rheinmetall (limited); Heinrich Krieghoff Waffenfabrik, L.O. Dietrich (limited)
Number built: *c*7,000
Weight: 4.95kg (10.9lb) later model
Length: 97.5cm (3ft 2.4in) later model
Barrel length: 50cm (1ft 7.7in)
Cartridge: 7.92 × 57mm Mauser
Feed: Gas-operated, rotating bolt; 10- or 20-round detachable box magazine
Rate of fire: 750 rounds/min later model
Muzzle velocity: 740m/sec (2,428ft/sec) (SmK bullet)
Effective range: 600m
Sights: Rear – diopter sight; front – flip-up front post; optics: ZFG42 or ZF4 scope.

RIGHT The MP38/40 fired pistol ammunition unlike MGs, which fired rifle ammo. Reinforcing under the barrel allowed it to be fired from within a vehicle with the lug at the end of the barrel preventing it from pulling inwards. The single column-feed magazine (bullet on top of bullet within the mag) was not reliable and prone to stoppages. Our Grenadier fires the weapon from the shoulder, leaning into the weapon when firing. Note the stability provided by the firer's left hand. The MP40 was incorrectly known as the Schmeisser because the original concept was based on a Bergmann-Schmeisser Vollmer design from the First World War.

Sub-machine guns

Maschinenpistole 38 and 40 (MP38/40)

In the form of the German MP38 and 40 the sub-machine gun is, perhaps, the iconic weapon of the Second World War. The Italian Army introduced the first SMG in 1915: the 9mm Glisenti Twin Villar Perosa. The first German weapon was the MP18 (MP = *Maschinenpistole* = sub-machine gun) designed by Hugo Schmeisser of the Theodor Bergmann Abteilung Waffenbau – his name, incorrectly, was used by the Allies to describe all German SMGs thereafter.

The development of the MP38 sprang from the MP18 and its follow-up the MP28, and also through Heinrich Vollmer's EMP and MP36.

The MP38 was the first SMG to have a folding butt; the first to be made solely from metal with no wood; and the first to be designed specifically for a fast-moving army. It could be fired from the confines of a tank or armoured vehicle; from the shoulder or from the hip.

Its drawbacks were an inefficient single-column feed system that caused the magazine to jam, as well as its expense to manufacture because it required high-quality steel and many machining processes. Because of this, a simpler version – the MP40 – which could be mass-produced, succeeded it. The design was

HOW TO OPERATE THE MP40

Safety

The only safety on these guns is the notch marked S (*sicher* = safe) at the butt end of the cut made for the operating handle in the receiver. To make the gun safe, pull the operating handle back as far as it will go and then push it upward into the safety notch. This is not a positive safety, as a jump or a fall may disengage the operating handle from the safety notch and leave the gun ready to fire.

To load and fire

Press the thumb catch above the pistol grip in order to release the skeleton shoulder stock from its folded position. Snap the shoulder stock into extended position and unfold the butt plate. Pull the operating handle back and switch it into the safety notch. Insert a loaded magazine into the feedway on the underside of the receiver until the magazine catch engages. Disengage the operating handle from the safety notch; then aim, and squeeze the trigger. The magazine can serve as a grip while firing.

To unload

Press the magazine catch and remove the magazine. Check the chamber to be sure that it is empty. After pressing the trigger, let the operating handle go forward slowly.

Stripping

Pull out the locking pin located on the bottom front portion of the receiver behind the magazine well, and turn the pin a little to keep it unlocked. Grasp the barrel with the left hand and the pistol grip with the right; press the trigger, and at the same time turn the receiver in a counterclockwise direction, holding the magazine housing in its normal position. It will then be possible to separate the receiver from the barrel and from the magazine housing. Remove the bolt and recoil spring from the receiver by means of the operating handle. The recoil spring may be removed from the telescoping recoil-spring housing.

reworked with spot-welded steel and pressed components. Modifications to the internal components reduced the jamming that often occurred with the MP38 in combat conditions.

The MP40 was one of the standard weapons of the German infantryman, used in particular by squad and platoon leaders.

Type: Automatic SMG
In service: 1938–45
Designed: Heinrich Vollmer
Manufactured: Erfurter Maschinenfabrik among many others
Number built: Over 1 million MP40s
Weight: 4kg (8.8lb) unloaded
Length: 83.2cm (2ft 8.75in) extended stock; 69cm (2ft 0.75in) folded
Barrel length: 24.8cm (9.75in)
Cartridge: 9 × 19mm Parabellum
Feed: Straight blowback, automatic only; 32-round detachable box-magazine
Rate of fire: 500 rounds/min
Muzzle velocity: 381m/sec (1,250ft/sec)
Effective range: 70–80m (up to 90yd); max range: 1,690m (1,850yd)
Sights: Rear – flip up v sighted 100–200m; front – hooded.

Sturmgewehr 44 (StG44)

The StG44 started life as the *Maschinenkarabiner* 1942 (MKb42), which performed well in 1942–43 field trials, but the complex procurement process for new weapons (often curtailed at Hitler's whim) led to its redesignation as the Maschinenpistole 43 (MP43) and, later the 44 (MP44). It was given the name Sturmgewehr in July 1944. Designed to counter the Soviet SMGs, which were very effective in close-quarter battles, it had a shorter range than the K98k with a comparable rate of fire to the Soviet PPS SMG, a greater range and could switch from fully automatic, to single shot, to semi-automatic with good accuracy.

The StG44 was the first true assault rifle. Almost entirely made from pressed steel, it was faster and easier to make than the K98k. It was produced for use on the Eastern Front where close-quarters contact was the norm, especially in built-up areas. It was recognised that close-quarters fighting did not need the power and range of the K98k round, so an intermediate cartridge was developed with less power and shorter range.

Assault detachments (*Stoßtruppen*) of 1st Infantry Division were issued with the StG44 in late 1943 (about a year later than it had been hoped that the weapon would enter service) and, in theory, this allowed the K98k to be retained for sniping and grenade launching, while the StG44 provided added firepower to

LEFT The StG44 in use during the Ardennes Campaign seen FIWA – fighting in a wooded area in today's parlance. The VG divisions made heavy use of automatic and semi-automatic weapons to clear the advance.

BELOW The StG44 assault rifle put production quantities ahead of its finish: note the crude butt and pistol grip. A German report noted: 'Of all infantry weapons the StG44 was the only one which always worked in Russia's dirt, cold and snow, had no misfires and was resistant to stoppages.' *(Greene Media Ltd)*

cover machine guns when loading or moving to another position. When attacking, it was hoped that the K98k grenades would subdue a position with the StG44s suppressing the defenders. However, the Allies were not too impressed with the weapon, considering it poorly made and subject to stress, along with difficulty in maintenance and prone to jamming.

Perhaps its most famous variant was the Krummlauf bent barrel to allow the StG44 to be fired round corners.

Type: Assault rifle
In service: 1943–45
Designed: Hugo Schmeisser
Manufactured: C.G. Haenel Waffenund Fahrradfabrik
Number built: *c*426,000
Weight: 4.6kg (10lb) unloaded; 5.13kg (11.3lb) loaded
Length: 94cm (3ft 1in)
Barrel length: 42cm (1ft 4.5in)
Cartridge: 7.92 × 33m kurz (short)
Feed: Gas-operated full auto (for emergencies only because of wear and tear), semi or single shot; 30-round box magazine (it could actually hold 35–38 but the spring was too weak to take that many)
Rate of fire: 500–600 rounds/min
Muzzle velocity: 685m/sec (2,247ft/sec)
Effective range: 300m (auto); 600m (semi-auto)
Sights: Leaf rear to 800m (876yd); front post with or without cowl
Optics: ZF4 telescopic sight.

RIGHT The MG34 was the first true GPMG (general-purpose machine gun) and used in many roles including anti-aircraft, as here. To prepare the MG34 for this role:

1. Attach the circular front sight.
2. Attach the drum magazine crate to the centre of the tripod as ballast.
3. Attach weapon to tripod.
4. Aim and fire.

Machine guns

Maschinengewehr 34 (MG34)

An impressive and versatile weapon that could meet almost every possible requirement, the MG34 was light enough to be carried by one man, and could be fired from the hip. It could fire up to 800/900 rounds/min, something no other MG could do at that time. Fed by belt or drum, firing singly or on automatic, it had an adjustable-height *Zweibein* 34 (bipod) which folded under the barrel when not in use.

The most advanced MG when produced, it also featured a lightweight *Dreifuß* 34 (tripod) for AA use. When mounted on the MG-Lafette 34 it was considered at that time to be a heavy MG for indirect fire. However, it was a complex weapon that was expensive to make and the manufacturing capability could not meet demand when quantity rather than quality was needed. The MG34 took some 120–50 man-hours to produce and most have as many as six different inspection marks. Under combat conditions it could be difficult to maintain in trying conditions – mud, sand and in extremes of temperatures.

Type: Machine gun
In service: 1936–45
Design: Adapted from the SMM30 by Heinrich Vollmer with Mauser
Manufactured: Gustloff Werke, Steyr-Daimler-Puch, Mauser Werke and others
Number built: Nearly 350,000 (peak production in 1941 81,467)

BELOW The drum magazine carrier could be attached to the AA tripod at various positions to ensure stability. Each drum carried a 50-round belt.

CHANGING BARRELS

The biggest drawback of the MG34 was barrel life (the same was true of the MG42 – see page 107). Each bullet fired increased the barrel temperature to such an extent that firing around 450 rounds left it close to melting. This meant that theoretical rounds/min values were in fact heavily restrained to prevent overheating as well as by ammunition constraints. This overheating meant that MG crews had to carry lots of spare barrels so that they could be replaced after 250–300 rounds in full auto – 400 at the very most and only in an emergency. If used correctly, barrel life was *c*6,000 rounds. It was improved later in the war by chrome-plating.

Procedure:

1. Cock the gun and set the safety lever to the safe position.
2. Push in the receiver catch (located just below the rear sight base on the left side of the barrel jacket) and turn the receiver almost a half turn in a counterclockwise direction.
3. Lower the shoulder stock until the barrel slides out of the barrel jacket.
4. Remove the hot barrel using an asbestos hand pad that is furnished with the spare parts kit.
5. Level the piece and insert a cool barrel into the barrel jacket.
6. Turn the receiver back to the right until the receiver catch again locks together the barrel jacket and the receiver.
7. Set the safety lever to the fire position and commence firing.

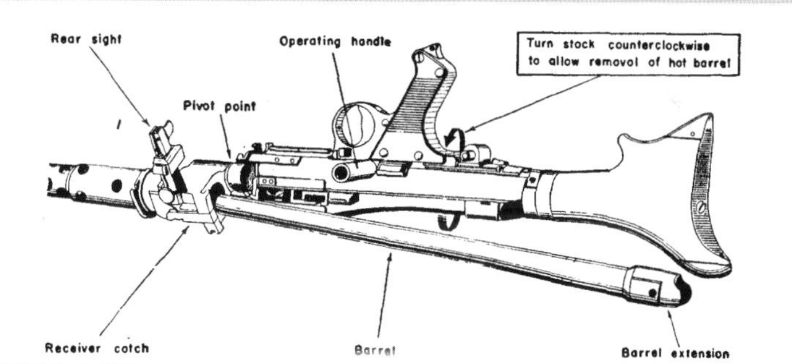

ABOVE AND BELOW Photo and illustration show the spare barrel container and the method of removing and changing the barrel. The MG34 was also the weapon of choice for most armoured vehicles because of the ease of barrel changing. Turn the stock counterclockwise without having to remove the weapon from its mounting/position. It needed to be easy: each squad had to carry six new barrels to replace those that heated up and even bent during sustained firing. *(Greene Media Ltd)*

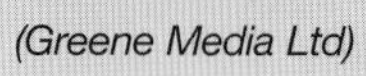

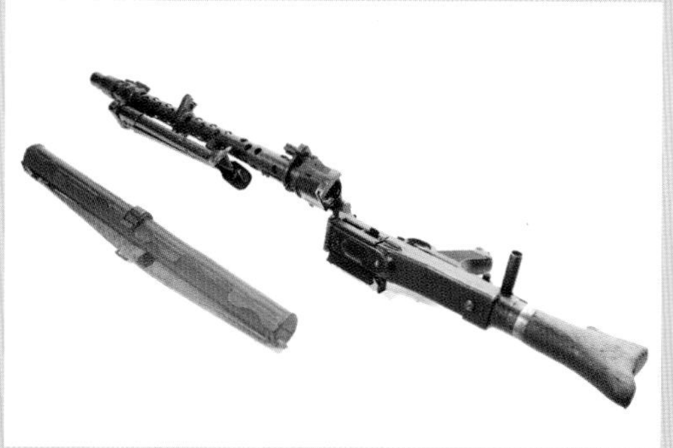

ABOVE Here the MG34 is used in the ground role with AA sight and a spotter. Accuracy was a problem if used in rapid fire, because it climbed during a long burst. Additionally, the operator needed a good position to handle the recoil, but in short bursts it was accurate and in the hands of a skilled operator – and there were a lot of them – it was deadly. Telescopic sights could be fitted. *(via RCT)*

MG34 ACCESSORIES

1. Spare barrels, usually three, in a single- and a double-barrelled holder
2. Tripod for using the weapon as a heavy machine gun (this may have an anti-aircraft mount adapter)
3. Anti-aircraft tripod
4. Belts and belt boxes
5. Belt drums and belt-drum holders
6. Tool kit, containing: 1 spare bolt, 1 ruptured-cartridge extractor, 1 anti-aircraft auxiliary ring sight, 1 open-end wrench, 1 cartridge-extractor tool, 1 oil container, 1 plastic case containing sulphur (used with oil as a lubricant)
7. Canvas or leather breech cover
8. Spare parts (in the belt box marked with a yellow E (*Ersatzstücke* – replacements)
9. 1 brush, 1 screw-top metal container
10. 1 oil container with bristle brush on cap, 1 open-end wrench, 2 complete bolt assemblies, 1 bolt carrier
11. 1 firing pin, 1 firing pin retainer, 1 firing pin lock
12. Asbestos hand pad (for handling hot barrels); package of rubber muzzle caps; 1 belt-feed pawl-slide housing; 1 belt-feed pawl assembly
13. 1 feed-plate lower assembly.

Weight: 12.1kg (26.5lb) with bipod; 19.2kg (43.3lb) with tripod in heavy role
Length: 1.219m (4ft 1in)
Barrel length: 62.7cm (2ft 0.7in)
Cartridge: 7.92 × 57mm rimless GP98 – 1,500 per case (weighing 51.25kg/113lb)
Feed: Open bolt, recoil-operated helped by a recoil booster on the muzzle and a rotating bolt. *Patronengurt* 34 (cartridge belt) non-disintegrating or metallic-link belts holding 50 rounds that could be connected to make longer belts (belt loaded by hand or machine). Alternatively a detachable saddle drum (*Patronentrommel* 34) holding 75 rounds; otherwise, single drums holding a belt of 50 rounds. The belt and drums fed from the left-hand side but could be swapped to the right-hand side by using a special feed arm
Rate of fire: Nominally up to 1,000 rounds/min; in practice 200–500 rounds/min
Muzzle velocity: 765m/sec (2,510ft/sec)
Effective range: As LMG – 200–2,000m (220–2,200yd); as HMG (with telescopic sight) – 3,000m (3,600yd); max – 7,700m (5,100yd)
Sights: Rear – vertical leaf with open v, graduated 200m–2,000m; front – post; AA – peep sight used with AA ring sight; telescopic sights: MGZ40 (same as MG34)
Crew: Nominally 3 – No 1 on gun; Nos 2 and 3 loaders and ammo carriers. However, most members of squad will carry extra ammo as necessary

Maschinengewehr 42 (MG42)

Even as the MG34 was being made, it was realised that it was too complex and expensive to mass-produce. An alternative was needed: one that was capable of mass production, less expensive and keeping the non-disintegrating belt as well as the many accessories – mounts, tripods, etc. The MG42 did exactly that, the wide use of stamping, welding and riveting made it more cost-effective to make. The price difference between the MG34 (327RM) and MG42 (250RM) was substantial. The most obvious visual difference between the two was the MG42's rectangular barrel shroud that vented on the left-hand side, leaving the right-hand side open for barrel changes.

While the gun-making fraternity was appalled

with the lack of tolerance on the working parts, the MG42 proved to be extremely sturdy although crudely made. Among the economies/ simplifications made were:

- the wood of the butt was synthetic injection-moulded
- the bipod was simplified
- straight charging handle was replaced with a toggle grip lever to ease cocking.

A major advantage of the weapon was its high rate of fire, said to be anywhere from 1,200 to 2,000 rounds/min – so fast that the sound of individual rounds being fired couldn't be distinguished, accounting for the Hitler's buzzsaw/chainsaw nicknames. Weather and conditions would have affected rate of fire, the low end would be after, as one commentator put it: 'firing several thousands rounds against attacking hordes of Red Army. Stuffed to gills with carbon residue, grit in rails, feeding from a frozen belt on the bank of the Dnepr during winter 1943/44 when the temperature is -22°C.'

The fast rate of fire meant it consumed huge amounts of ammunition and was difficult to control in the sustained-fire role. Quite often sandbags had to be used to support the tripod legs or they had to be held by the crew. The high rate of fire also led to frequent barrel changes – but to do so was much simpler than with the MG34. A trained gunner could change the barrel in 6 to 7 seconds. The stages were:

- Lock bolt by pulling cocking handle back
- Open hinged barrel release panel
- Remove barrel using asbestos mitt
- Insert new barrel and close panel.

The MG42 was a flexible weapon that could be mounted and fired from bipod, tripod, AA mount and vehicle mounting – in many ways the first GPMG. It could also be fired from the hip, but was not used as a hull-mounted MG in AFVs because of the barrel change method.

As with the MG34, the accessories came in a canvas carry bag containing the tools needed to clean and service the gun in combat: scraper, cleaning rod sections, broken shell case extractor disassembly tools, chamber cleaning tools, flash hider, wrench, bore brush, oiler, solvent and oil cans, asbestos mitt (to grasp hot barrel), pull-through cord. The contents would be subject to gunner and crew as extra pouches would have carried such items as a Bakelite container to hold the recoil and muzzle flash unit overnight in kerosene or in a kerosene/oil solution in extreme cold.

Type: Machine gun
In service: 1942–45
Designed: Werner Gruner who specialised in the technology of mass production; Metall und Lackierwarenfabrik Johannes Großfuß AG
Manufactured: Mauser Werke AG and others
Number built: *c*410,000 (max production 211,806 in 1944)

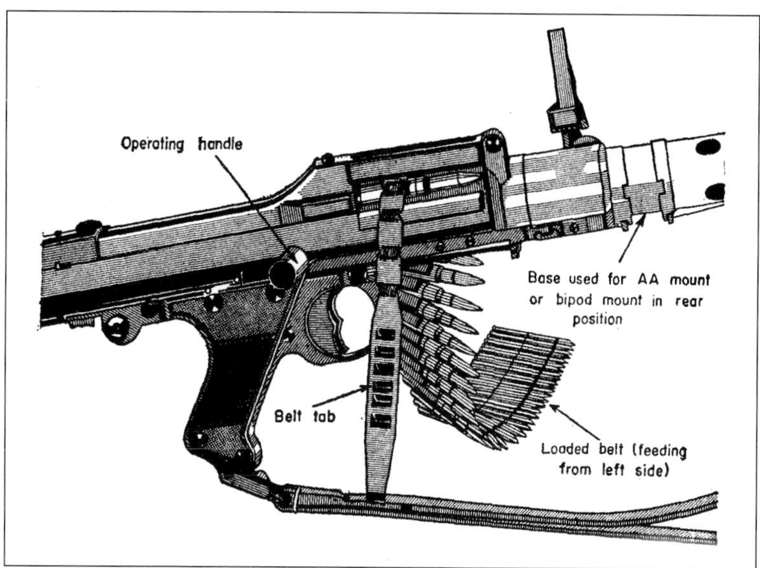

ABOVE AND BELOW
The MG34 and 42 were belt-fed from the left-hand side (as shown in our re-enactor photograph) but an attachment for the MG42 could allow feed from the right. This is rarely seen other than on photographs printed the wrong way round. Both these images show the MG34.

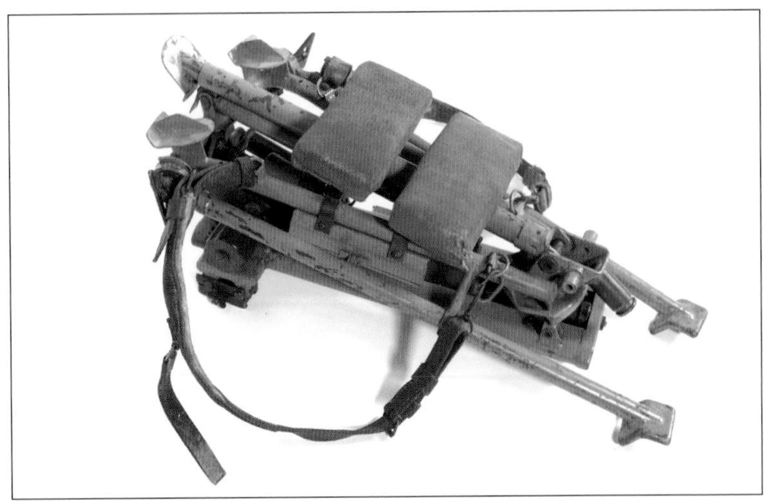

ABOVE **The MG34 and 42 used the Lafette 34 and 42 respectively, a man-portable tripod which folded up and was made with padding to protect the carrier's back. The heavy tripod was in manufacture from 1936 to 1945, changing between the 34 and the 42 around 1942. In 1943 a mountain version with extendable rear legs was also produced.** *(Greene Media Ltd)*

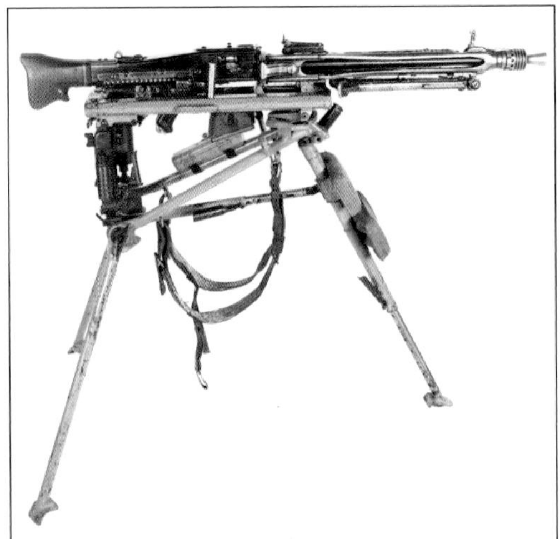

ABOVE RIGHT **The MG42 on its bipod was an LMG but designated HMG when on its tripod. There's no doubt – in spite of the barrel-changing requirement – that it was an effective weapon. Heinrich Severloh and the machine gunners on the bluffs above Omaha Beach showed that on D-Day.** *(Greene Media Ltd)*

RIGHT **Carrying the MG42 was easier with a sling but is often seen over the shoulder. Note the white mitt attached to the gunner's belt pouch (*Werkzeugtasche*) which was used for hot barrel changes. Inside the pouch there was a range of tools, including a ruptured cartridge remover, a wrench, a spare bolt, the AA ring sight, an oil can, muzzle covers, starter tab for the ammunition belt and calibre gauge.**

Weight: 11.5kg (25.8lb) unloaded
Length: 1.22m (4ft)
Barrel length: 53.3cm (1ft 9in)
Cartridge: 7.92 × 57mm Mauser GP98
Feed: Combination of short recoil and blowback. Bolt locked to the barrel by means of two movable locking studs. Easier and smoother than the MG34, it used the same Patronengurt 34 non-disintegrating metal-link belt – the ammo box lid acting as feed system – or drums as per the MG34
Rate of fire: 1,050 to 1,350 rounds/min, cyclic air-cooled automatic (no semi-auto)
Muzzle velocity: 755m/sec (2,480ft/sec)
Effective range: 200–2,000m (219–2,187yd); 3,500m (3,828yd) on tripod using telescopic sights; 4,700m (5,140yd) max
Sights: Rear – open v on slide graded 200–2,000 (219–2,187yd); AA peep sight; front – inverted v (folding post); separate front-mounted AA sight; telescopic sights: MGZ40 (same as MG34)
Crew: Officer commanding; NCO gunner; No 2 loader; support group of three riflemen carrying extra ammunition. As the war progressed manpower shortages reduced the number of crew and support.

Hand grenades

Stielhandgranate 24

With its unique design, the stick grenade, or 'potato masher' as the British slang had it, was the principal German Army hand grenade during both world wars. A friction igniter system was unusual and not used by other nations. It was set off by unscrewing the base cap and pulling down on the porcelain ball attached to a cord in the exposed cavity. The Model 24 was an offensive weapon which generated a blast to stun or incapacitate, unlike the Allied grenade which was primarily a defensive weapon designed to kill by fragmentation.

During the Weimar Republic period, weapons development progressed through clandestine partnerships with industries in sympathetic countries such as Sweden and Switzerland. As the constraints of the Treaty of Versailles eased, the M24 – a new and improved version of the First World War M17 grenade – was introduced with a shorter head and longer wooden handle which was 34.5cm (1ft 2.4in) long and drilled through from top to bottom.

Compared to Allied grenades, it had one main advantage: it could be thrown further. Other benefits were that it wouldn't roll back down a slope; was difficult to catch and throw back; and was safer for the user – there was nothing to snag if not made ready. It could be tucked behind the belt or webbing, in the top of a jackboot, in twin sandbags hung around the neck or in a sleeveless jerkin designed for the grenade with five pockets front and rear.

The disadvantages were that it was less accurate; more difficult to throw into a pillbox slit or any narrow firing point; and slower to arm.

The Model 24 was made from 1933 and used throughout the war. The other main version, the Model 43 (see below), was introduced from 1943. Both would have been painted to suit the area and conditions (so white in snow, ochre in the desert, etc.).

Type: Offensive, concussion grenade
In service: 1924–45
Designed: 1924
Manufactured: Initially Richard Rinker, but many others during the war
Number built: Over 75 million
Weight: 595g (1lb 5oz); 765g (1lb 11oz) with charge
Length: 35.5cm (1ft 1.5in)
Ignition: BZ24 detonator No 8. (White stencilling on head 'Before using insert a detonator'.) Special fuse marked K (*Kalt*) when cold
Delay: 4–5 seconds

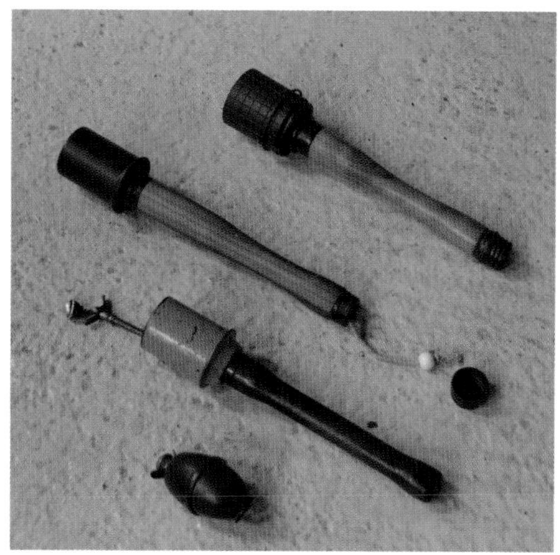

LEFT Replica hand grenades showing from top to bottom:

1. Stielgranate 24 with clip-on fragmentation sleeve.
2. Model 24 showing pull cord with porcelain bead (coral).
3. Model 43 with solid wood handle and friction pull on the head.
4. Eierhandgranate 39. Note the same blue metal igniter cap on both the 39 and 43.

Blast: 12–14yd – because it's a blast grenade, not fragmentation, the thrower doesn't need to take cover – he can continue his advance. The thin iron or steel head casing surrounded a factory-sealed HE

A pressed metal box held 15 grenades with charge screwed or held in a removable clip frame with carrying handle. Fuses were separate in a container that was part of the frame.

Among the variants of this weapon were:

Nebelhandgranate **(smoke grenade)**
Designed to mask operations, activity or signalling, there were two variants: the NbHgr39 and NbHgr39b. They had a ribbed handle for identification at night and a broken white line painted near the base of the head for both models. Smoke-release holes were on the

OPERATING PROCEDURE

- Remove from the carrying case (holds 15 grenades and fuses) Unscrew handle from charge (head) and insert detonator into the open end of the exposed delay fuse
- Screw handle back on, which breaks the protective seal within the charge (head)
- Arm prior to a mission or when told to
- In action, unscrew cap at base of handle
- The coral (the pull-cord has a ceramic grip on it) falls out through gravity
- Grasp coral between fingers
- Pull and throw (4–5 second delay between ignition and blast).

To disarm, unscrew handle from head and remove device, screw back on. Drop coral and cord back into base and screw on cap.

bottom of the head. The delay between ignition and smoke was 7 seconds and the smoke was generated for 1½–2 minutes.

Model 1943 (M43)

As the war progressed, Germany's ability to produce weapons munitions and equipment became increasingly strained and quality suffered. Without compromising safety, weapons had to be easier and more cost effective to produce and be less complex. The M43 was an ersatz version of the M24, with fewer expensive parts and no machine-cut tooled threads on the screw sections (they were machine-pressed instead). The main change was the use of the M39 *Eierhandgranate* self-contained detonator on the top of the grenade head. This meant the coral cord pull ignition system of the M24 was unnecessary and the handle was undrilled.

Special uses of stick grenades

The *Geballte Ladung* was a concentrated charge for anti-tank, anti-pillbox or special demolition work. Six M24 or PH39 heads were wrapped and secured around a seventh (complete) grenade.

Bangalore torpedo

Designed to blow a path through barbed wire or other obstacles avoiding a direct approach and possibly under fire, the German version of the Bangalore torpedo was made by binding a number of heads behind one another on to a board or other suitable object with the nearest grenade complete with handle and detonator. Attached to the draw cord a long wire or cord was used to ignite the weapon.

Anti-personnel stick grenade mine

This was the same as the concentrated grenade with the central throwing handle removed and replaced with a pressure igniter.

Eihandgranate 39 (EihGr39)

Another offensive weapon, the egg grenade was small, grey-green and thin-cased with a distinctive blue knob on top and a central raised rib. The knob had to be unscrewed to prime – the same system that was used on the Model 1943 stick grenade. To use, the soldier simply unscrewed the knob, pulled and threw.

Fuse cap colour codes:
- Grey: booby trap 10-second delay
- Red: 1-second delay
- Blue: 4–5 seconds standard fuse
- Yellow: 7.5 seconds.

In service: 1940–45
Designed: 1939
Manufactured: Many manufacturers during the war
Number built: Over 80 million
Weight: 0.34kg (12oz)
Length: 3in
Ignition: BZE39 (Brennzunder fur Eihandgranate 39)
Delay: 1–10 seconds, depending on colour of cap
Blast: Similar radius to the M24.

Nebelhandgranate 42 (NbEihgr42)

An elongated version of the EihGr39, it had a loop welded to the bottom. It was made from heavy gauge steel with crimped seam, the sections having a one-third/two-third ratio with the larger, lower case containing the smoke compound and the upper the ignition. There were three smoke-escape holes. For identification purposes, the grenade had EihGr39 stencilled on the case, which was green with three broken white bands on the lower section.

Blendkorper 1H and 2H glass smoke grenades

These grenades were glass jars sealed with a plaster of Paris-type material and protected in carriage by a cardboard sleeve/box. Weighing 0.374kg (13.2oz), with a titanium tetrachlorine charge, they were thrown against a hard surface to produce dense smoke with high humidity. The Blendkorper 2H version was boxed in fours, similar to the 1H, but was able to generate smoke in less favourable conditions – desert or cold down to -40°C, having silicon tetrachloride added to lower its freezing point.

Hafthohlladung magnetic anti-tank grenade

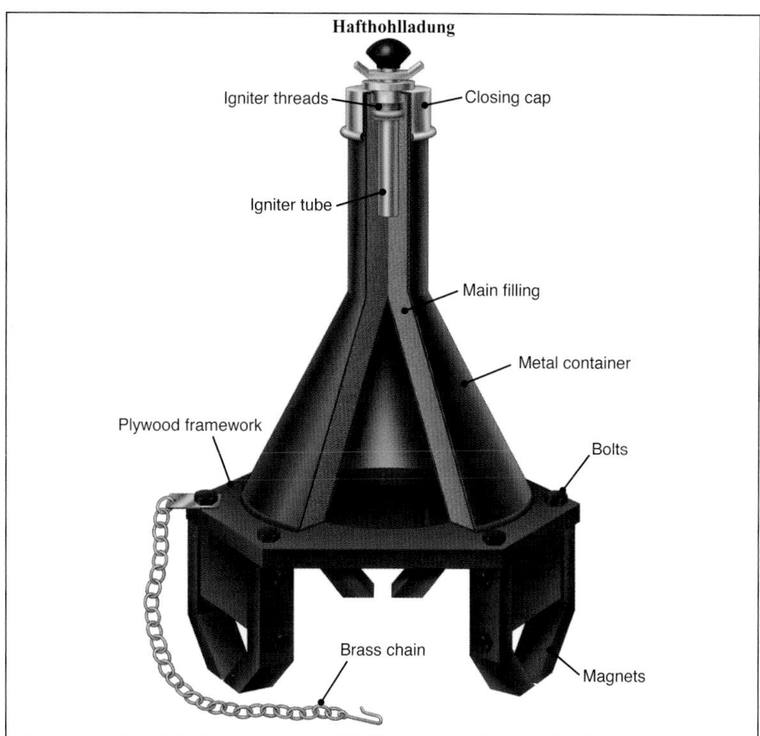

ABOVE LEFT AND ABOVE The Hafthohlladung magnetic grenade/mine was used to fight tanks at close quarters. This was not just a Pionier task but one for the infantry as well. Using a hollow-charge grenade, a young Grenadier in Russia 1944 remembered: 'My T34 was now so close that I was not in any real danger as the crew couldn't see me. The grenade had a safety cap which had to be screwed to reach the rip-cord; my hands were shaking. The tank turned . . .' He was awarded a Tank Destruction Badge **(see pages 59 and 66).**

A conical-shaped pressed metal container with an elongated apex that formed the handgrip and an initiation charge, it was fitted with three horseshoe magnets attached to a plywood frame bolted to the base. This hollow-charge grenade was placed by hand or thrown at its target and could penetrate 110mm (4.25in) of armour. It was 12cm (4.5in) long, weighed 3.63kg (8lb) and had a delay of 4.5–7 seconds. Expecting the Russians to copy this effective design, the Wehrmacht developed the anti-magnetic paste Zimmerit, which produces the corrugated effect visible on German tanks around the middle of the war. In fact the Russians never did copy the magnetic approach and Zimmerit was unnecessary. The Germans stopped applying it in the autumn of 1944 because they thought projectiles could ignite it. They couldn't, and HEAT missiles rendered Zimmerit obsolete.

Mortars

5cm *leichter Granatwerfer* 36 (leGrW36)

Nicknamed *Zigeuner-artillerie* (Gypsy artillery), this was the standard German light mortar of the early war years. It was easy to carry but could be slow to set up. Designed to engage the enemy beyond a grenadier's range with high-angle fire, this close-support weapon was too complex for its intended role, and with too light a round and poor range, it was withdrawn from the front line during 1942 – although it was still in use at the end of the war. A platoon and squad weapon, for short distances it could be carried by one man by use of an integrated handle and the tube fixed to the baseplate. The fuse armed the missile about 55m (60yd) from the tube. With a 'graze' action it could detonate as an airburst in wooded terrain.

Without sights, it was left to the experience of the firer to judge the angle of the barrel when used. In action from the prone position, the layer on the left holds the levelling handles while pressing down on the baseplate. The loader lies to the right and drops the round down the tube. He then squeezes the trigger to fire when ordered to.

ABOVE An abandoned or captured hasty mortar scrape showing two 5cm Model 36 light mortars, two types of mortar bomb and carrying cases, along with K98ks, an entrenching tool and a Stahlhelm.

Type: Muzzle-loaded mortar
In service: 1936–45 though withdrawn from frontline service by 1942
Designed: Rheinmetall-Borsig AG
Manufactured: Rheinmetall-Borsig AG and others
Number built: Many thousands
Weight: 14kg (30lb 9oz)
Barrel length: 490mm (1ft 7in)
Round: 50mm (1.97in) HE, AP and smoke – carried in a transit case of ten rounds each weighing 1kg (2.2lb), maroon-coloured with black stencils

RIGHT The moment of firing a 5cm light mortar by pulling the trigger lever. Note the immediate availability of the next round, and the ammunition carrying case.

Feed: Muzzle-loaded, trigger-fired (as opposed to impact firing pin)
Rate of fire: 40 rounds/min, but firing at that rate would soon burn out the barrel. Realistically, one in 4 seconds
Muzzle velocity: 75m/sec (246ft/sec)
Effective range: 50–92m (94–100yd); max range: 510m (550yd)
Sights: Early models had a telescopic sight. Deemed to be too complex, the later models had a simple white line on the barrel
Crew: 3 with 45 rounds for immediate firing – one man baseplate and traversing and levelling gear; one man tube and elevating pillar; the other ammo.

8cm *schwere Granatwerfer* 34 (sGrW34)

The German Army's medium (originally deemed heavy) mortar was an 81mm (3.2in) variation of the British Stokes model of the First World War. A shorter, lighter tube version, the 8cm Granatwerfer 42, was produced for Fallschirmjäger and Gebirgsjäger.

Smooth-bore (seamless) muzzle-loading with a fixed firing pin, its high trajectory – the angle of firing was 45–90° and the traverse 10–23° varying with elevation – gave it an advantage over light artillery as it could target reverse slope positions. Its main disadvantage – as with all mortars – was its firing position, which had to be near to the forward lines and thus made ammunition resupply dangerous.

It was used in conjunction with aiming stakes. These are only used for indirect fire weapons such as artillery guns, howitzers or mortars. Gun batteries employ an aiming circle or director that relays angles to the guns (or mortars). The gunsights then set that angle and the layer moves the gun left or right until the director is centred in the sight. As long as the director is visible in the centre of the sight, the gun will be pointing towards the desired compass bearing.

The GrW34 had a good reputation for reliability and accuracy and a decent rate of fire: it was considered by troops to be their preferred close-support weapon. Ammunition was carried in a pressed steel container of four rounds and the weapon was man-portable (just about) with each of the three crew carrying the barrel, baseplate and bipod.

It could be packed on one horse or a two-wheeled cart together with 48 rounds in containers – otherwise, all available unit manpower carried ammo.

One unique ammunition innovation was a 'bouncing' bomb. Initially, an airburst to blast shrapnel downwards was trialled but proved to be too problematic. The concept of the bouncing bomb was the same, but with the round hitting the ground and being blasted upward to ignite a short-delay fuse to produce a lethal effect on those underneath. They were effective on hard ground but less so on soft. Proving costly to produce, these rounds were gradually phased out.

Type: Muzzle-loaded, high-trajectory mortar
In service: 1933–45
Designed: Rheinmetall-Borsig AG 1922–33
Manufactured: Rheinmetall and other manufacturers enlisted to keep up with demand as well as producing the projectiles
Number built: Over 50,000
Weight: 62kg (136.6lb)
Barrel length: 1.14m (3ft 9in); GrW42 74.7cm (2ft 5.4in)
Round: HE 3.4kg (7lb 8oz) *Wurfgranate* 38 and 39 were both bouncing bombs to produce airbursts. Smoke and illuminating; also captured rounds that worked
Feed: Muzzle-loading and initiated by impact with firing pin at base of the tube

ABOVE Obviously posed during training, this 8cm GrW34 crew stand by their weapon as an MG team passes them. Note the rectangular baseplate, bipod with cross-levelling wheel between bipod legs and near aiming post stake in front of the mortar. This was used to help align a number of mortars to supply accurate grouped fire. *(via RCT)*

BELOW LEFT As its crew eat in their winter gear, the angle of the tube shows the enemy is close. The tube is pre-set and the cable in the soldier's left hand could be a silent command to fire when pulled by an observer. We will never know!

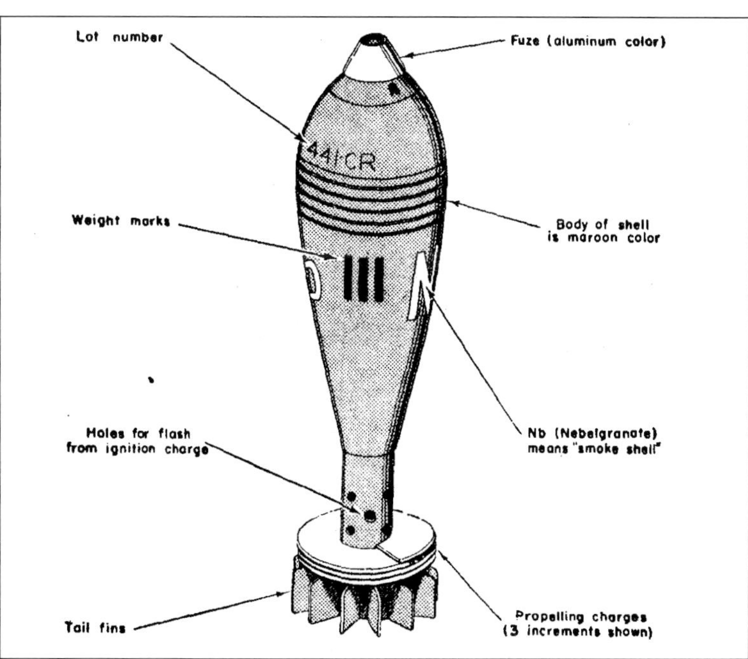

BELOW 8cm mortar shell showing the amount of information on it and the number of propelling charges which are needed for the task.

Rate of fire: Up to 15 rounds/min
Muzzle velocity: 174m/sec (571ft/sec)
Effective range: 549m (591yd) to 2,400m (2,625yd); range was adjusted by alteration of elevation and charges:

Main charge	549m (591yd)
Additional +1	1,000m (1,094yd)
Additional +2	1,460m (1,597yd)
Additional +3	1,900m (2,078yd)
Additional +4	2,400m (2,625yd)

Sights: Integrated optics

Crew: 3 – one to make necessary adjustments for mission; one to manage the ammo; the other to load and stabilise the bipod when firing.

Mines

Schrapnellmine 35 (SMi-35)

This was known as the S-mine or 'Bouncing Betty' (to the Americans). It was activated by pressure or tripwire. A black powder charge sent the mine upwards to about 60cm (2ft) before exploding and blasting 350 steel balls with a radius of about 150m (165yd), although realistically it was lethal within 20m (22yd). The psychological effect with Allied troops was the possibility of emasculation rather than death. Anti-personnel mines were intended to wound rather than kill: that way it took troops off the battlefield as they had to administer and then help their wounded mates away from the fighting. The S-mine was mainly made of metal, so it was easily found by metal detectors if they were available. The SMi-44 was cheaper to produce and had an offset fuse.

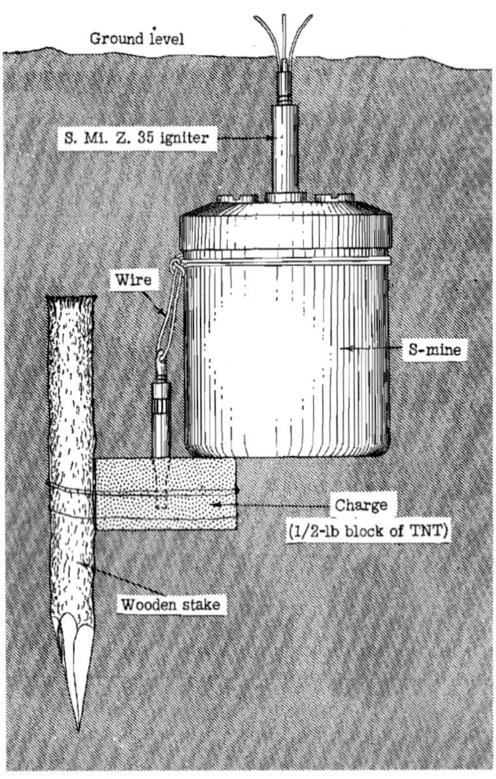

RIGHT The S-mine 35 anti-personnel mine was nicknamed the 'Bouncing Betty' and the 'emasculator'. Troops arriving in Normandy feared the latter sufficiently that occasional mines would spread fear and panic. This illustration shows the mine with an anti-handling device. *(Intelligence Bulletin, Vol. II, No. 11)*

Type: AP mine
In service: 1938–45
Designed: 1930s
Manufactured: from 1935
Number built: Nearly 2 million S-mines (SMi-35 or SMi-44)
Weight: 4kg (8.8lb)
Height: 13cm (5in)
Ignition: Pressure
Delay: 4 seconds
Blast: Lethal within 20m (66ft) but could cause casualties over 100m (330ft away).

RIGHT Component parts of an S-mine. Note the Y adaptor which had two ZZ35 pull ignitors and could be used in place of the Z35 push ignitor. The deadly component was the filling of around 350 steel balls.

Tellermine 35 (TMi-35)

The plate-shaped anti-tank Tellermine (*Teller* = dish) could be used in a wide variety of locations: deserts, forests – even underwater in a special case. The first of the series was the -29, which had 10lb of TNT and was 10in in diameter. The pressure required to set it off meant that only a vehicle or very heavy object would do so. The -35 had more TNT and was 1ft 0.5in in diameter). After the -35 there were two main later versions: the -42 and -43, the latter being a simplified version of the former,

ABOVE American mine clearing and a late war German minefield warning sign. The string/rope in the photograph indicates safe lanes.

saw improved resistance to blast and anti-handling devices.

Data: TMi-35
Type: Anti-tank mine
In service: 1935–45
Number built: More than 3.6 million
Weight: 8.7kg of which explosives were 4.9kg
Height: 7.6cm (3in)
Ignition: Pressure 90kg (200lb) on the edge and 180kg (400lb) on the centre.

Anti-tank guns

Panzerbüchse (PzB) 38 and 39 tank-hunting rifle

The standard German anti-tank weapon at the start of the war, the PzB38 was an expensive and overcomplicated weapon, which jammed easily. A simpler and less expensive replacement, the PzB39 had a falling block action moved by a pistol grip, unlike the recoil action of the PzB38.

ABOVE The retreating Germans were experts at setting booby traps – particularly associated with souvenirs. No one touched a Luger left lying around without very careful checks. *(Battlefield Historian)*

BELOW The Germans had about 40 types of anti-tank mines with the four shown being the most commonly used.

1 Tellermine 35.
2. Tellermine 42.
3 Tellermine 35 (steel) – a heavier version.
4 Tellermine 43 (mushroom).

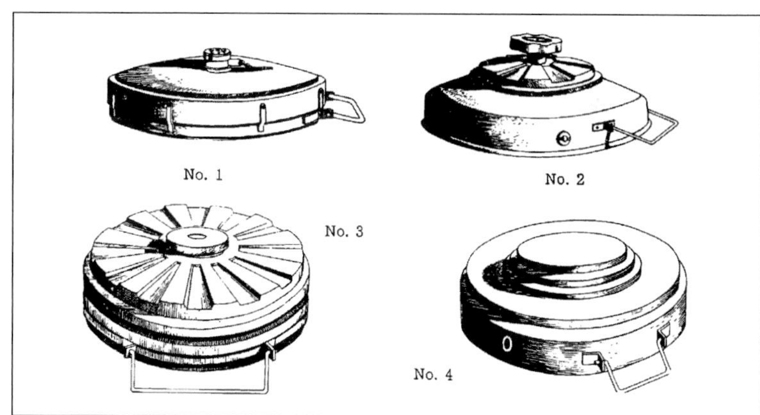

RIGHT The Panzerbüchse 39 AT rifle was an early war weapon that could do little against more modern tanks. With 40,000 produced up to 1941, it was still in use against light vehicles well into the war. *(Bundesarchiv, Bild 101I-213-0254-07A/Gebauer/CC-BY-SA 3.0)*

237mm 8.8cm Pak 43

35mm 3.7cm Flak

8mm 7.92mm K98k

LEFT A graphic indication of the difference between the armour penetration of a rifle bullet and projectiles from a 3.7cm Flak (35mm) and 8.8cm Pak 43 (237mm).

Designed to damage or destroy an enemy tank by killing crew or wrecking optics and weapons, it was very effective against weak spots – giving side and rear spalling. A shortened version was fitted with the K98k firing cup attachment.

Data: PzB39
Type: Lightweight man-portable 7.92mm (.312in) anti-tank rifle
In service: 1940–44 – obsolete by 1941
Designed: B. Brauer
Manufactured: Gustloff Werke, Suhl
Number built: 39,000
Weight: 11.6kg (25.57lb)
Length: 1.62m (5ft 3in)
Cartridge: 7.92mm × 94mm P318 SmKH tungsten carbide core
Feed: Manual; falling-block action and pistol grip
Rate of fire: Single-shot but enhanced by two ten-round point-down bullet containers either side of the stock forearm allowed 10 rounds/min
Muzzle velocity: 1,210m/sec
Effective range: 300m (330yd)

GERMAN ANTI-TANK ARMOUR PENETRATION

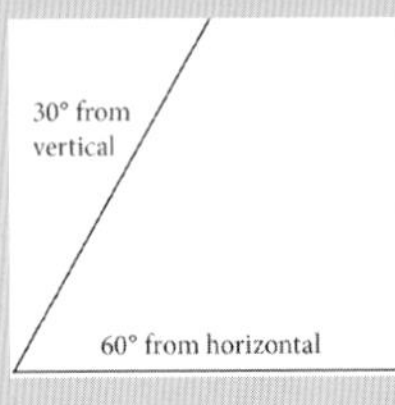

ABOVE Armour penetration is based on impacting a plate sloping at 30° from the vertical.

There's a mass of contradictory information in books and on the internet about this subject, with much analysis of information from various records. In an excellent 1998 introduction to analyses of this sort of information, John D. Salt of Brunel University identified some of the points to keep in mind:

- there are different 'hardnesses' of armour – homogeneous, face-hardened, etc.
- armour penetration is an imprecise science: it may be measured in millimetres but that implies a precision that doesn't exist when firing in combat at a tank and hitting a lifting lug. As one writer states, 'there is a conflict between theory and practice'.
- Penetration is not the only way that anti-tank weapons damage tanks. It takes no account of non-penetrating damage that can destroy running gear or even remove the turret. As he puts it, 'Extremely large calibre rounds can cause catastrophic damage without needing to penetrate the target.'

Weapon	Ammo	Type	Penetration*
Rifles			
7.92mm K98k	SmK	APCR	8mm
7.92mm MG34/MG42	SmKH	APCR	13mm
13mm Mauser T-Gewehr	TuF	AP	21mm
7.92mm Panzerbüchse 38	P318	APCR	34mm
7.92mm Panzerbüchse 39	P318	APCR	34mm
Artillery			
3.7cm Flak 18/36/37/43	Pzgr 18	AP	35mm
2cm Flak 30 and 38	Pzgr 40	APCR	40mm
3.7cm Pak 36	Pzgr	AP-HE	50mm
10.5cm leFH 18 (L/28)	Pzgr	AP-HE	63mm
3.7cm Pak 36	Pzgr 40	APCR	64mm
5cm Pak 38	Pzgr	AP-HE	67mm
5cm Pak 38	Pzgr 39	APC-HE	69mm
7.5cm Pak 97/38 (L/36)	Gr 38/97 HI/A (f)	HEAT	75mm
7.5cm Pak 97/38 (L/36)	Gr 38/97 HI/B (f)	HEAT	75mm
7.5cm Pak 97/38 (L/36)	Gr 15/38 HI/B (f)	HEAT	75mm
7.5cm leIG 18	IGr 38 HL/A	HEAT	75mm
10.5cm leFH 18 (L/28)	Gr 39 HI/A	HEAT	80mm

Sights: Hooded front and v rear notch good to 300m

Crew: 2 – rifleman and No 2 ammunition. Issued one per platoon.

3.7cm *Panzerabwehrkanone* 36 (Pak 36)

The 3.7cm (1.45in) *Panzerabwehrkanone* (anti-tank gun) was developed from the 1928 Pak L/45 and proved successful in the Spanish Civil War. It was the main German early-war weapon, but was quickly seen to lack penetration and was replaced from 1941

LEFT '... We called the 3.7cm anti-tank gun the "doorknocker" because of its inability to destroy Russian tanks at range. We cleaned it and rolled it out to engage the Soviets. As it had no sights we fired it at point-blank range killing two T-34s with four shots ...'.

7.5cm Pak 97/38 (L/36)	Gr 98/97 Hl/C (f)	HEAT	90mm
7.5cm lelG 18	IGr 38 HL/B	HEAT	90mm
8.8cm Flak 36	Gr 39 Hl	HEAT	90mm
10.5cm leFH 18 (L/28)	Gr 39 Hl/B	HEAT	90mm
7.5cm Pak 41	Pzgr 41 (W)	APCNR	97mm
8.8cm Flak 36	Pzgr	APCBC-HE	97mm
7.5cm Pak 39 (L/48)	Gr 38 Hl/C	HEAT	100mm
10.5cm leFH 18 (L/28)	Gr 39 Hl/C	HEAT	100mm
5cm Pak 38	Pzgr 40/1	APCR	116mm
8.8cm Flak 36	Pzgr 39	APCBC-HE	120mm
7.5cm Pak 40 (L/46)	Pzgr 40	APCR	126mm
5cm Pak 38	Pzgr 40	APCR	130mm
15cm sIG 33	Gr 39 Hl/A	HEAT	160mm
15cm sFH 13 (L/17)	Gr 39 Hl/A	HEAT	160mm
15cm sFH 18 (L/29.5)	Gr 39 Hl/A	HEAT	160mm
8.8cm Flak 36	Pzgr 40	APCR	170mm
5cm Pak 38	Stielgranate 42	HEAT	180mm
8.8cm Flak 41	Pzgr 39-1	APCBC-HE	194mm
7.5cm Pak 41	Pzgr 41 (HK)	APCNR	198mm
8.8cm Flak 41	Pzgr 40	ACPR	237mm
8.8cm Pak 43 (L/71)	Pzgr 40/43	APCR	237mm
Mines and grenades			
Geballte Ladung			20mm
Tellermine			20mm
Panzergranate 61 Rifle Grenade		HC	89mm
Hafthohlladung		HC	206mm
Rockets			
Faustpatrone/Panzerfaust 50 Klein		HC	153mm
8.8cm Raketenpanzerwerfer/Panzerschreck		HC	209mm
Panzerfaust 100 Klein		HC	219mm

*at 100m with armour plate at 60° from horizontal (30° from vertical)
Source: Panzerworld (http://www.miniatures.de/anti-tank-weapons-german.html) and (lower set; ranges varied) http://www.miniatures.de/anti-tank-weapons-german.html

by the 5cm Pak 38. Organic equipment of the German infantry regiment, it was usually towed on its own wheels by a prime mover or, occasionally, carried in a truck. Its demise was delayed by ammunition improvements, first the introduction of the tungsten Pzgr 40. This had a mild steel body, an aluminium-alloy ballistic cap and tungsten carbide armour-piercing core. In 1943, the Stielgranate 41 shaped-charge projectile became available. The range wasn't great but they were light and therefore issued to Fallschirmjäger and other light troops. The projectile was attached to a perforated sleeve within which there was a rod that fitted into the muzzle. It proved very effective and extended the life of the weapon – but it took some courage to reload in front of the shield.

Type: 37mm anti-tank gun
In service: 1936–45 – obsolete by 1941
Designed: Rheinmetall
Manufactured: Rheinmetall
Number built: 12,000 (1936–41)
Weight: 327kg (721lb)
Barrel length: 1.66m (5ft 5in)
Feed: Manual
Rate of fire: 13 rounds/min
Muzzle velocity: 762m/sec (2,500ft/sec)
Effective range: 300m (330yd); max 5,484m (5,997yd)
Sights: Mounted on an upright bracket carried on the top of the carriage
Crew: 6 – commander, gunner lays the piece, loader and firer, two ammunition handlers, plus a driver of the towing vehicle.

BELOW 5cm Pak 38 in the Liri Valley. Italy. It has a split trail and solid rubber treads for the pressed-steel wheels. Note the field of fire, which allows the traverse to be used; also the low profile. *(Battlefield Historian)*

5cm *Panzerabwehrkanone* 38 (Pak 38)

The first German anti-tank gun that could be considered artillery, it was not available until late in 1940. It replaced the Pak 37, which had been rejected by the German authorities as it didn't meet the requirement for a higher muzzle velocity to counter improved tank armour (of the T-34/76 in particular). The Pak 38 employed a longer (L/60) gun with a barrel life of around 4,500 rounds and proved itself in combat using APCR tungsten-cored AP40 shells. It had an elevation of -8° to +27°, a traverse of 65°, a curved gunshield and was towed by a halftrack or lorry. Recoil was handled by the split leg carriage and a baffled muzzle brake.

Type: Anti-tank gun
Designed: Rheinmetall-Borsig 1938–39
Manufactured: Rheinmetall-Borsig 1940–43
In service: 1940–45
Number built: over 9,500
Length: 3.2m (10ft 6in)
Barrel length: 3m (10ft)
Height: 1.05m (3ft 5in)
Width: 1.85m (6ft 1in)
Weight: 1,000kg (2,205lb)
Feed: Semi-automatic breech mechanism with a horizontal sliding block
Rate of fire: 14 rounds/min
Muzzle velocity: 550m/sec (1,805ft/sec depending on round
Effective range: 2,700m (3,000yd); Penetration using standard AP round
250m 0° 88mm (3.46in)
250m 30° 67mm (2.46in)
1,000m 0° 61mm (2.40in)
1,000m 30° 50mm (1.97in)
Sights: ZF 3 × 8° (3× magnification; 8° field of view)
Crew: 5 minimum – spotter, gunner, loader and 2 × ammo; usually 8 – commander; gunner

(lays for direction and deflection); No 1 loads and fires; Nos 2, 3, 4, 5 ammo; No 6 driver of tractor.

7.5cm *Panzerabwehrkanone* 40 (Pak 40)

The main German anti-tank gun from late 1941 to the end of the war, the Pak 40 was a larger version of the Pak 38, using the same carriage. It was extremely successful with some 20,000 built primarily for use as towed artillery pieces although around 3,500 were used on such SP guns as the Marder, the Sturmgeschütz IIIs and IVs and in the Panzer IV. There was even a magazine-loaded version for ground-attack aircraft – the heaviest and most powerful forward-firing weapon fitted to a production military aircraft during the Second World War in the Hs129 B-3 with Bordkanone 7.5cm.

Forward-thinking planners realised during testing, even before it was issued, that the Pak 38 was not going to be powerful enough to penetrate the armour of the new and heavier generation of Soviet tanks. The conception of the Pak 40, therefore, started with heavyweight requirements, and a heavyweight it turned out to be. Its all-steel construction – unlike its predecessor that was predominantly light alloy – meant it could defeat most Allied armour throughout the war. However, its weight made it vulnerable to weather conditions; its height meant it was difficult to hide; and its expense and production complexities meant that it took around six months to manufacture a unit at a cost of RM12,000 – nearly RM2,000 more than a Pak 38. However, these figures compare favourably to the British 17pdr that weighed in at 3,034kg (6,689lb) and was 1.6m (5ft 3in) high.

The Pak 40 fired a range of ammunition which included the Pzgr 39 APCBC projectile; the Pzgr 40 APCR projectile until 1942 when scarcity of tungsten caused it to be banned from production; Pzgr 38 HL/B HEAT projectile; and the Sprgr-Patrone 34 HE shell.

The Pak 40 was towed by a range of vehicles: the halftrack artillery tractor Steyr Raupenschlepper Ost (RSO), 3-ton Opel Blitz and SdKfz 251 were among the best-known. Captured vehicles – the British Universal carriers, the French Renault UE and the Soviet Artillery Carrier 630 – were also used.

ABOVE Note the huge muzzle brake on this 7.5cm Pak 40 preserved at Le Dézert in Normandy – scene of a battle between the US First Army and a Kampfgruppe of Panzer Lehr. The muzzle brake deflects the propellant gasses to counter recoil – a feature common to most anti-tank guns.

Type: 7.5cm anti-tank gun
Designed: Rheinmetall-Borsig 1939–40
Manufactured: Various locations 1941–45
Number made: 20,000; some 3,500 others were modified for other uses
Weight: 1,425kg (3,142lb)
Length: 6.2m (20ft 4in)
Barrel length: 3.45m (11ft 4in)
Height: 1.2m (3ft 11in)
Width: 2.08m (6ft 1in)
Feed: Semi-automatic breech with a horizontal sliding block
Rate of fire: 14–15 rounds/min
Muzzle velocity: Pzgr 39 – 790 m/s (2,600ft/sec)
Effective range: 1,800m (5,906ft) direct fire; 7,678m (25,190ft) indirect HE.
Penetration using Pzgr 39:
500m 0° 132mm (5.83in)
500m 30° 104mm (4.09in)
1,000m 0° 116mm (4.57in)
1,000m 30° 89mm (3.50in)
1,500m 0° 102mm (4.02in)
1,500m 30° 76mm (2.99in)
Crew: 5–6
Sights: Upgraded ZF 3 × 8° (3× magnification; 8° field of view).

8.8cm *Panzerabwehrkanone* 43 (Pak 43)

Developed by Krupp to compete with the Rheinmetall 8.8cm Flak 41 AA gun, the Pak 43 proved to be the Wehrmacht's most powerful anti-tank gun and went on – in modified form – to arm the Tiger II tank.

Delayed during its development, Krupp produced a simpler version using what was designated the Pak 41 barrel. The weapon

ABOVE **The cruciform gun platform of the 8.8cm Pak 43 was transported by two single-axle bogies/limbers. When in position, the platform was winched down and released from the wheels, which were taken away from the gun. The outriggers were lowered forming the cruciform shape and then 'pegged'. This ensured a low-profile weapon with an angled, armoured shield. Note the barrel support for travel. This example was photographed at Troisvierges in the Ardennes.**

BELOW **This preserved 8.8cm Pak 43/41 at Clervaux is a mix-and-match weapon with suitably modified parts from stock components. The wheels on the weapon shown are not those on the gun when new. It was an effective weapon but not loved by the crews because it was heavy and awkward. They nicknamed it the 'barn door'.**

lacked the Pak 43's cruciform carriage, having a two-wheel split-trail from the 10.5cm leFH 18 field howitzer instead, and had a horizontal sliding block breech mechanism. While the barrel's performance was as good as that of the Pak 43, the Pak 43/41 wasn't popular in the field as its carriage was cumbersome.

When the Pak 43 finally appeared, there was approval for its new carriage, which allowed 56° traverse to left and right as well as elevation from -8° to +40°. The dedicated trailer, the *Sonderanhänger* 204, had two sections and was also used for moving the 5cm Flak 41. The Pak 43 was used on both fronts, most often at army level and proved to have exceptional penetration at long ranges. It performed best with new munitions, the Pzgr. 39/43 APCBC-HE projectile, but had to use the older Pzgr. 39-1 until the new rounds were ready.

Type: Towed 8.8cm anti-tank gun
In service: 1943–45
Designed: Krupp
Manufactured: Krupp, Rheinmetall-Borsig
Number built: 2,100
Weight: 3,650kg (8,047lb)
Height: 1.7m (5ft 7in)
Length: 9.2m (12ft 3in)
Barrel length: 6.35m (20ft 10in)
Feed: Semi-automatic sliding block breech, manual feed
Rate of fire: 6 to 10 rounds/min
Muzzle velocity: 1,000m/sec (3,300ft/sec)
Effective range: 4,000m (13,123ft) effective range; 15,300m (50,197ft) max range. Penetration of Pzgr 39/43 APCBC round was 165mm (6.5in) at 1,000m (3,280ft)
Sights: ZF
Crew: 6.

8.8cm *Raketenwerfer* 43 *Püppchen*

A small two-wheeled reusable anti-tank rocket launcher, heavier and more expensive to make than both the Panzerfaust and Panzerschreck, the Raketenwerfer 43 *Püppchen* (Dolly) fired the 8.8cm Raketen Panzer Granat 4312 HEAT round with a rimmed cartridge case from a closed breech. The carriage, which helped to absorb the recoil, was essentially a simple hollow tube with a percussion cap to ignite the rocket motor to launch the RPzgr 4312. Opening the breech cocked the hammer. The carriage allowed an elevation from -18° to +15° and also could be quickly disassembled into man-portable pieces. The rocket-propelled grenade was stabilised by fins contained within a drum on the tail section, and had a shaped-charge warhead. It had a slightly greater effective range and more stability than the Panzerschreck, but was decidedly heavier. It was mainly used by Fallschirmjäger.

The Tank Destruction Badge – awarded for destroying a tank single-handedly with a handheld weapon – was not awarded to anti-tank gun crews. As the 43 resembled an anti-tank gun, not a handheld weapon, the badge was not awarded for a Püppchen kill – although anyone who could hit a moving barn door at 700m (the max range on the sight) with a rocket travelling at 100m/sec deserved a medal!

Type: Anti-tank rocket launcher
In service: 1943–45
Designed: 1942–43
Number built: 3,000
Weight: 143kg (315lb)
Total length: 2.9m (9ft 6in)
Height: 89cm (2ft 11in)
Width: 1m (3ft 3in)
Barrel length: 1.6m (5ft 3in)
Feed: Hinged breech block with striker mechanism
Rate of fire: 10 rounds/min
Muzzle velocity: *c*100m/sec
Effective range: 230m (750ft) moving target; 500m (1,600ft) static target
Sights: Manual through barrel-mounted sights, grad 180m (195yd) to 700m (765yd)
Crew: 2.

8.8cm *Flugabwehrkanone* dual-purpose gun

Designed in 1934 as a semi-mobile AA gun, the famous 88 entered service as the Flak 18 seeing action with the Condor Legion in Spain where it proved to be accurate and versatile in both the AA and anti-tank role. An improved version followed, the Flak 36, which could fire while still on wheels in an emergency. A later model, the Flak 37, had updated instrumentation and communications. All 8.8cm guns in the family could be used in an anti-tank role. Other variations to both gun and ammo proved capable of dealing with the heaviest French tanks during the Battle of France in 1940.

The gun was mounted on a cruciform platform, which was carried on two-wheeled limbers – the almost identical and interchangeable Sonderanhänger 201 and 202 – towed by the 8-ton SdKfz 7 halftrack. The gun had a traverse of 360° and elevation of -3° to +85°. From 1940 the crew was protected by an armoured shield and, tactically, usually supported by smaller anti-tank guns in defensive positions around it.

It fired a round that weighed 32lb – light enough for one man to carry and load.

It was a devastatingly effective weapon – for example, two Flak battalions accounted for 264 British tanks in the northern desert in 1941 – most importantly for the range of its engagements, often five times that of the other anti-tank weapons.

Type: Dual-purpose AA/AT
In service: 1936–45
Designed: Krupp worked with Bofors in Sweden owing to the restrictions of the Versailles Treaty
Manufactured: Krupp and Rheinmetall 1933–45 in various forms
Number built: 21,000
Weight: Flak 36 – 7,047kg (15,536lb)
Height: Flak 36 – 2.1m (6ft 11in)
Width: Flak 36 – 2.3m (7ft 7in)
Length: Flak 36 – 5.78m (16ft 2in)

ABOVE The Raketenwerfer 43 was produced at the end of the war in small numbers. Using the same warhead and fusing as the Panzerschreck, its missiles were shorter (indeed, the ones held by the soldiers in this photograph are incorrect for the Püppchen and are Panzerschreck rounds). While it was more accurate and had a better range than the Panzerschreck, it was cumbersome and less easy to use.

ABOVE This 8.8cm Flak at Arromanches has recently been painted. Note the cruciform mount and barrel support.

Length of barrel: Flak 36 – 4.94m (16ft 2in)
Feed: Horizontal semi-automatic sliding block percussion fired, manually fed
Rate of fire: 15–20 per minute
Muzzle velocity: Flak 36 – 840m/sec (2,690ft/sec)
Effective range: Flak 36 – 8,000m (26,240ft) ceiling
14,860m (16,250yd) ground line of sight allowing penetration using Standard AP of:
500m 0° 207mm (8.15in)
500m 30° 182mm (7.17in)
2,000m 0° 159mm (6.26in)
2,000m 30° 139mm (5.47in)
Tungsten-cored:
500m 0° 274mm (10.79in)
500m 30° 226mm (8.9in)
2,000m 0° 184mm (7.24in)
2,000m 30° 136mm (5.35in)
Crew: 9–10 – gun commander, No 1 lays elevation, No 2 lays for line, No 3 loads and fires, Nos 4–7 ammo, No 8 sets range, No 9 sets lateral deflections
Sights: ZF20 telescopic.

Panzerfaust

Crew: 1 ... towards the end of the war, anyone!
Aimed: Through sight and top of projectile to target
Fired: Squeeze top-mounted trigger ... but beware of lethal backblast 2m behind
Numbers produced: Over 6 million of all models 1943–45.

By 1943 towed anti-tank guns were being replaced by man-portable systems. AT guns were heavy, slow to move, not very versatile, prone to get bogged down, expensive to make and to lose, and with the rapid development of thicker and sloping armour the heavier AT guns were

BELOW The instructions for use were duplicated on the warhead. As the end of the war drew closer, there wasn't time to train everyone on the weapon. This allowed non-combatants to use it – and they did! Note the sprung steel fins to give stability in flight.

1 Arming the warhead.
2 Pulling up sight.
3 Preparing to fire. When doing so, remember the backblast!

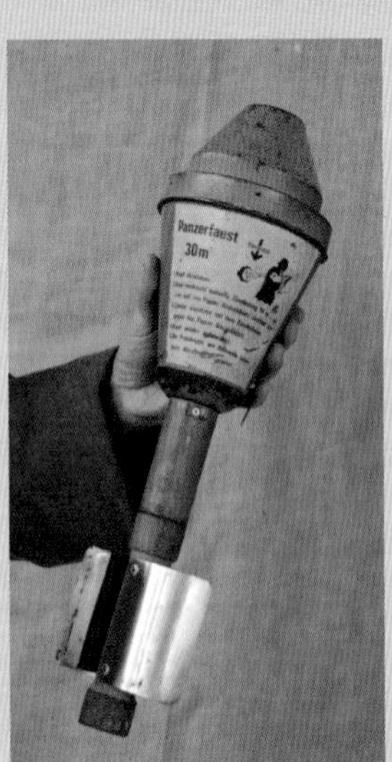

less likely to make a kill. The solution: the cheaply produced, man-portable lightweight rocket launcher firing pre-loaded or manually loaded missiles that could pierce armour at close range. A very popular weapon with the Americans – who considered the later version superior to their bazooka – the Panzerfaust (armoured fist or tank fist) was a recoilless system using forward thrust to counteract the recoil.

The arrival of the American M1 bazooka in Tunisia in 1942 made a significant impression on the Germans. This was a man-portable, inexpensive, simple to use, reloadable anti-tank weapon that was fired from the shoulder.

Development started in 1942 with the first model, the *Faustpatrone* 2 or Panzerfaust 30, a pre-loaded single-shot disposable launch tube firing a percussion propellant charge to project a hollow-charge grenade to its intended target.

Another model, the Panzerfaust Klein, a smaller version of the Faustpatrone 2, was called *Gretchen* (little Greta). Both had crude sights.

The concept of these weapons was a charge-propelled grenade fired via a recoilless system with a fin-stabilised missile.

Range: *c*30m for both
Penetration: Between 140mm (5.5in) and 200mm (7.9in)
Speed of projectile: 28–30m/sec.

The next model and the most common was the Panzerfaust 60 which reached full production in 1944 when 400,000 were produced each month. A higher velocity was achieved by increasing the diameter of the tube and adding more propellant. The sights were improved with apertures from 30m to 80m, as was the squeeze trigger.

Range: 60m
Penetration: 200mm (7.9in)
Speed of projectile: 45m/sec.

The Panzerfaust 100 was the last version produced in any quantity by the end of the war.

Range: 100m
Penetration: 200mm (7.9in)
Speed of projectile: 60m/sec.

ABOVE Panzerschreck missile showing circular tail-fin and nose fuse. *(Bundesarchiv, Bild 101I-710-0371-25/ Gronefeld, Gerhard/ CC-BY-SA 3.0)*

8.8cm *Raketenpanzerbüchse 43* (RPzB43) *Panzerschreck*

This child of war is best known as the *Panzerschreck* (tank terror) but was also called the *Ofenrohr* (stove pipe) because of the smoke generated when fired – whether that nickname was provided by the developers or by its operators is a matter of dispute.

Like the Panzerfaust, the Panzerschreck was modelled on the M1 bazooka but differed in a number of ways. A shoulder-launched reusable anti-tank weapon, heavier than the M1, it fired a fin-stabilised 8.8cm hollow-charge rocket-propelled warhead. This missile could penetrate thicker armour at a greater distance than the Panzerfaust.

The RPzB43 was percussion-fired. The operator had to wear a protective mask and clothing because on exit the rocket motor was still burning.

The RPzB54 was electrically fired via an impulse magneto and had a protective shield with an observation window clamped to the tube on the left-hand side. There was a protective bar around and below the muzzle to prevent dirt, mud, etc., from clogging the mechanism.

The RPzB54/1 had an improved rocket, a shorter tube and a greater range. A fierce smoky blast both forward and back produced a signature for retaliatory fire from armoured vehicle crews who were well aware of its destructive capabilities. Ideal for ambushes and close-quarters fighting, it wasn't suitable for firing in confined spaces because of the

ABOVE **Note the all-metal construction and the magnetised firing rod running under the tube within and through the shoulder brace. Once loaded, the No 2 would give the operator a tap on the helmet to indicate it was ready to fire. For obvious reasons the No 2 would then move to the side. '[It's] essential that the weapon is fired from a position which allowed the flame [backblast] sufficient area in which to escape. In the early days there were hundreds of cases of burning, many of them fatal, brought about by men unaware of this requirement and who had fired the rocket launcher in a confined place.' When firing from the prone position or from a trench there were dangers. 'The [Panzerschreck] round missed and the lumbering heavy vehicle moved to the firing point (a slit trench) and put a track over it. The machine spun slowly on this track, its engine roaring with the strain and effort. Above this we could hear screaming. . . .'**

BELOW **The 7.5cm recoilless LG40 looks like a post-war anti-tank weapon. The photograph doesn't do justice to the huge backblast or the noise.** *(Bundesarchiv, Bild 101I-567-1503E-34/Schneiders, Toni/CC-BY-SA 3.0)*

backblast. Towards the end of the war pre-prepared staggered trenches about 100m apart allowed fire on a target from many locations.

Type: Hollow charge rocket containing propellant in tail tube, with a nose fuse and stabilising fins
Designed and manufactured: HASAG – Hugo Schneider Aktiengesellschaft Metalwarenfabrik – by slave labour; other manufacturers also involved
In service: 1943–45
Number built: 289,000 of all variants
Weight: 11kg (24.2lb) empty; rocket weight: 3.18kg (7lb)
Length: 164cm (5ft 4.5in); rocket 64.77m (2ft 1.25in)
Feed: Manual, rear, making contact electrical leads restrained by a catch
Rate of fire: Subject to location and conditions
Muzzle velocity: 110m/sec (120yd) 240mph
Effective range: 120m (390ft); 180m (590ft) max; ideal range: 50–60m (55+yd) allowing penetration up to 16cm (6.5in)
Crew: 2 (operator and loader).

7.5cm *Leichtgeschütz* 40 (LG40)

Conventional guns recoil. Newton's third law of motion states that for every action there is an equal and opposite reaction: this is shown by a gun's recoil and the larger the projectile, the greater the recoil.

During the First World War some attempts were made to put guns back to back and eliminate recoil by firing both at the same time. Tried and dropped after 1918, the Davis aerial gun led the way. The idea was secretly revived in Germany in the 1930s to design and build a light gun for mountain and airborne troops. The results were seen first during the Battle of Crete in 1941.

To save time and research, shells for the 7.5cm *Gebirgsgeschütz* (mountain gun) 36 and 7.5cm *Feldkanone* 16 were modified to a recoilless system. Built in four pieces, each could be dropped by parachute: barrel, breech assembly, carriage and then wheel assembly. Ammunition – both modified HE and AP – made up the fifth element of the drop: a silk cloth bag containing the charge with a gunpowder igniter.

The LG40 used dispersal of gas via a funnel-shaped Venturi tube to dissipate the recoil. This caused a significant backblast danger area: 100m (109yd) in practice; 50m (55yd) in combat. The noise was also significant: the crew was advised to plug ears with whatever was available – even clay or mud. There was fouling of the mechanism and the frame was unable to hold together after multiple shots (about 300 rounds). The carriage allowed an elevation of -15° to +42° and a traverse of 36° below 20° elevation and 60° above 20° elevation.

The weapon was used by 2. Batterie Fallschirmjäger-Artillerie and Para units of Waffen-SS for remainder of the war. The Gebirgsjäger also made use of the lightweight weapon.

In service: 1940–45
Design: Krupp and Rheinmetall-Borsig with Rhein prototype accepted for production
Manufactured: 1941–44. Production ceased when it became too expensive to produce
Number built: *c*450
Weight: 145kg (319lb) reduced by using alloy parts when possible.
Length: 0.75m (2ft 6in)
Barrel length: 45.8cm (1ft 6in)
Feed: Manual separate-loading cased charge, sliding horizontal breech block percussion-fired
Rate of fire: 8 rounds/min estimate
Muzzle velocity: HE standard shell weighing 5.83kg (12.86lb), 350m/sec (1,148ft/sec)
Effective range: 6,800m (7,434yd)
Crew: 3.

Flamethrowers

Flammenwerfer 35 (FmW35)

A one-man flamethrower, the FmW35 backpack system had a carrying harness, a cylindrical metal pressure tank and a smaller bottle on the left-hand side. The main cylinder was filled with a mix of light and heavy tar oils (Flammöl 19). Benzol thickened with petrol or motor oil was also used. The propellant was in the smaller bottle, 5 litres (1.1 gallons) of compressed nitrogen. It was ignited at the mouth of the tube by a slow ignition system.

The Flammenwerfer 35 was redesigned in 1941 as the FmW41, a lighter and more easily carried version that was further modified in

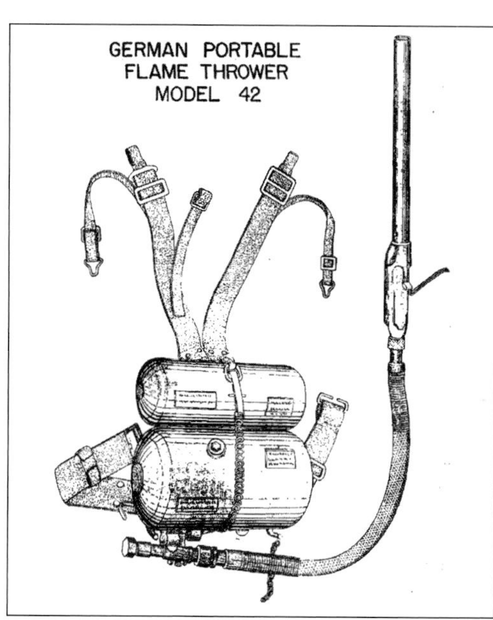

ABOVE, LEFT AND BELOW All nations made use of the flamethrower during the Second World War – as they had done in the First (the postcard dates from 1918). It's a horrifying weapon but proved effective in close combat, particularly in buildings, against pillboxes or entrenched positions.

1942 by the addition of a cartridge ignition system. Flamethrowers had been used by Germany in the First World War and were used extensively by all sides during the Second World War. The Wehrmacht used three types: man-portable; the two-man *mittlerer Flammenwerfer* 35 whose fuel tank was carried on a trolley – an engineer handcart with solid or pneumatic tyres which could carry up to 300kg (660lb); and the *Abwehrflammenwefer* 42 which was used as part of the Atlantic Wall and other fixed fortifications.

Type: One-man flamethrower
In service: 1935–45
Designed: Based on First World War equipment, developed at Weapon Proving ground 5/1
Manufactured: Hermann Göring awarded the first contracts in 1938 to Karlsruhe and Lübeck of DWM
Number built: 100,000 in a number of variations by the end of 1945 with the FmW41 being the most built of the Second World War
Weight: 35.8kg (79lb) empty – which was found to be too heavy; FmW41 – 21.3kg (47lb) with a 7.5-litre capacity
Range: With a filling pressure of 25 atmospheres, the range was 25–30m (up to 30yd).
Crew: 1
Sights: None.

Flak

2cm *Flakabwehrkanone* 30/38

An AA gun that could be used in the ground role, the Flak 30 – and the improved, but very similar, Flak 38, which had a higher rate of fire – was the principal German light AA gun throughout the war. It was easily manhandled but lacked punch and rate of fire as aircraft and armour developed. Rather than going for a heavier shell, Rheinmetall created the Flakvierling 38, combining four of the 20cm guns and therefore improving rate of fire in combat use to around 800 rounds/min – although as the magazines for each gun only held 20 rounds, that would require a magazine change every 5 or 6 seconds! The 20-round flat box magazine weighed 9.5kg (21lb).

The Flakvierling 38 proved to be a versatile weapon and was mounted – as was the Flak 30 – on trucks, ships and trains, as well as being trailer-mounted and towed. The single-axle Sonderanhänger 51 trailer could be pulled by truck or halftrack but was also easily split for difficult terrain and carriage by horses and men. Codenamed 'Erika', it was in common use by the end of the war and was adapted for use by Gebirgsjäger and Fallschirmjäger. The mounting allowed a 360° traverse and elevation from -12° to +90°.

Ammunition included HE; HE with self-destroying tracer (if the target was missed the round self-destroyed before hitting the ground,

RIGHT A four-barrelled Flakvierling 38 which had four 2cm Flak guns mounted together – here on an 8-ton SdKfz 7/1. Note the ten-round magazine storage above the standing man second from the right, and the ammunition trailer behind. *(via RCT)*

LEFT **Damaged postcard showing a single 2cm Flak 30 with crew. Note the elevation handwheel and loaders at the back. As ammunition expenditure was in clips, rounds/min were difficult to sustain without a good crew.** *(via RCT)*

thus preventing casualties); AP tracer; AP-HE-incendiary; and AP with a tungsten core.

The German Army was allowed two formations of AA Flak troops from 1941 and even went so far as to set up its own Flak school. The *Heeresflakbataillonen* (Army Flak battalions) were part of the infantry divisions and had, therefore, white Waffenfarben; the artillery Heeresflakabteilungen wore red.

Type: AA gun that could be used against ground targets
In service: 1934–45
Designed: Developed from the German Navy's Solothurn ST-5 by Rheinmetall
Manufacturer: Rheinmetall
Number built: 150,000 including the lightweight Gebirgsflak 38 and Flakvierling 38
Weight: 483kg (1,065lb) in action
Length: 2.3m (7ft 6in) without trailer
Barrel length: 1.3m (4ft 3in)
Width: 1.81m (5ft 11in)
Height: 1.6m (5ft 3in)
Rate of fire: 280 rounds/min cyclic; 180–220 rounds/min practical
Muzzle velocity: 900m/sec (2,953ft/sec)
Effective range: Effective ceiling of 2,900m (2,400yd) and a ground range of 2,695m (2,947yd) with an AP penetration of 45mm (1.77in) of armour at 92m (100yd)
Sight: Initially, the Flakvisier 35 reflecting mirror sight with an integral calculator; the Linealvisier 21, which replaced the complex and expensive Fkv35, had a simple stamped metal course and speed sight
Crew: 6/7 – gun leader (*Geschützführer*) chose where to place the gun and how to camouflage it as well as maintaining contact with other Flak units. In action he selected targets and estimated speed to the rest of the crew; driver: an extra loader when needed, otherwise in charge of limber, trailer and method of transport; *Kanonier* (gunner) 1: aimed with manual elevation and traverse wheels/mechanism, used the trigger mechanism – automatic or single-

BELOW **A 2cm Flak 38 at Chambois in the Falaise Pocket. The weapon is carried on a trailer that could be towed manually, by a horse or by a vehicle. Not shown is the netting designed to catch the ejected shell cases while in action.**

shot – from foot pedal; Kanonier 2: dialled the called target speed and distance on to the gunsight computer (if using the Fkv35); Kanonier 3: dialled the target's heading and altitude change on gunsight; Kanonier 4: loader; Kanonier 5: used the stereoscopic rangefinder calling out range in 200m (220yd) increments. The rangefinder was 1m (3ft 3in) in length and when in action was usually balanced/strapped to his shoulders. There was also a small tripod. Made by Carl Zeiss, magnification ×6 ranging from 800 to 26,000ft.

Infantry guns and howitzers

German infantry divisions had an organic artillery component that varied considerably throughout the war. As an example, at the start in 1939–40, the 1st Infantry Division had 20 × 7.5cm *leichtes Infanteriegeschütz 18* (leIG/light infantry gun), 6 × 15cm *schweres Infanteriegeschütz* 33 (sIG/heavy infantry gun), 36 × 10.5cm *leichte Feldhaubitze* 18 (leFH/light field howitzer) and 12 × 15cm *schwere Feldhaubitze* 18 (sFH/heavy field howitzer). Later, a more varied mix pertained, partly because the German conquests of 1939–41 afforded the use of weapons captured from other armies or manufactured in conquered territories (*Beutewaffen* = booty weapons), such as the 917 Russian M1910/30 field howitzers which became the 12.2cm sFH 388 (r) in German service or the more modern Russian M1938 (M-30) which became the 12.2cm sFH 396 (r).

7.5cm *leichtes Infanteriegeschütz* 18 (leIG 18)

Introduced in 1933–34 as an infantry close-support weapon, development had started in 1927 with wooden wheels for horse-drawing. Later the wheels were altered to steel with pneumatic tyres to facilitate towing by vehicles – as was true on most German artillery pieces of the period. There were two main versions: one for the infantry and one for the Gebirgsjäger. The infantry version was pulled by six horses or by a motor vehicle. That of the Gebirgsjäger could be split into six to ten loads each from around 75kg (165lb) for pack transport. It had a lighter shield. The gun took 1,200 man-hours to complete and at the start of the war nearly 3,000 were in service. Production continued until 1945, with nearly 2,300 built in 1944 alone.

In service: 1932–45
Designed: 1927 by Rheinmetall

BELOW Early war postcard showing a 7.5cm leIG 18 light infantry gun with its barrel at maximum elevation. Note the simple box trail with spade. German war artists were important proponents of propaganda. Ernst Eigener's work was used for postcards and posters.

BELOW RIGHT Preserved today, note the square-section casing to the barrel of this leIG 18; the spoked wheels indicate it was probably horse-drawn. *(Steinbesser/WikiCommons (CC0 1.0))*

HOW TO LOAD AND FIRE THE sIG 33

1. To open the breech, grasp the breech mechanism lever and press the catch inward. This raises the catch clear of the stop on the breech ring, so that the breech-mechanism lever can be rotated. Then rotate the breech-mechanism lever clockwise through 180°. The rotation of the breech mechanism lever forces the toe of the crank against the right side of the groove in the top face of the block, thrusting the block to the right into the open position.

2. Insert a round.

3. To close the breech, return the breech mechanism lever to its original position and release the handle, so that the catch is held behind the stop on the breech ring. The rotation of the breech mechanism lever forces the toe of the crank against the left side of the groove in the top face of the block, thrusting it to the left into the closed position.

As the breech closes, a projection on the toe of the crank comes into position behind the cam of the crank stop so that the block is locked in the closed position.

4. To fire the howitzer, pull the firing lanyard to the right rear. This rotates the firing lever on its axis pin so that the angle of the former bears against the head of the firing plunger, forcing it into the block against its spring. The recess in the plunger in which the upper projection of the trigger is engaged turns the latter in a clockwise direction. The toe of the trigger engages the toe of the tripping-piece, which is pivoted on the firing pin, so that both the firing pin and tripping piece are forced back against the firing pin spring. As the rotation of the trigger continues, its toe clears the toe of the tripping piece, and the spring of the firing pin asserts itself, driving the striker forward on to the primer of the cartridge. The firing lanyard is now released, and the firing plunger, under pressure of its spring, moves to the right. The upper projection of the trigger, being engaged in the recess of the plunger, turns the trigger in a counterclockwise direction. The toe of the trigger, riding on the inside of the tripping piece, forces it to the right so that the heel of the tripping piece forces the inner cover to the rear. At the same time the heel of the trigger, pressing against a projection on the striker body, forces it, too, to the rear. At the end of this movement, the toe of the trigger trips the toe of the tripping piece, which is returned by the firing pin spring to the normal position, with the firing pin half cocked and withdrawn from the firing hole bush.

Manufactured: Rheinmetall and others under licence
Number built: 12,000
Weight: 400kg (882lb); increased with steel wheels/rubber tyres to 570kg (1,257lb)
Barrel length: 88cm (3ft)
Width: 1.6m (5ft 3in)
Height: 1.2m (4ft)
Feed: Manual
Rate of fire: 8–12 rounds/min
Muzzle velocity: 210m/sec (690ft/sec)
Effective range: 3,550m (3,880yd); with extra charge 4,600m (5,030) max
Sights: Rundblickfernrohr 16 (RblF16) 4× magnification and 10° field of view
Crew: 5.

15cm *schweres Infanteriegeschütz* 33 (sIG 33)

This heavy infantry support weapon started life in the 1920s with wooden wheels for horse-drawing, but was soon modified for vehicle-towing. When found to be too heavy, its construction was modified to steel and light alloys, reducing the weight, but few of this type were manufactured. There were just over 400 sIG 33s in use when the war began. Production continued throughout the war – 1944 was the most productive year with around 1,500 built. It fired HE (38kg/84lb), smoke, a hollow-charge round (24.6kg/55lb) and the Stielgranate 42, which loaded on to a driving rod. This round was finned, weighed 90kg (200lb) and contained 27kg (60lb) of amatol.

In service: 1927–45
Designed: Rheinmetall
Manufactured: Rheinmetall and other factories
Number built: Over 4,500
Weight: 1,800kg (4,000lb)
Length: 4.42m (14ft 6in)
Barrel length: 1.65m (5ft 5in)
Width: 2.06m (6ft 9in)
Feed: Manual; horizontal sliding breech block with hydropneumatic recoil
Rate of fire: 2–3 rounds/min
Muzzle velocity: 240m/sec
Effective range: 4,700m (5,100yd)
Sights: RblF36
Crew: 9 – commander; gunner who operates the sights; No 1 operates the breech; No 2 rams the round home; No 3 operates the elevating mechanism; Nos 4, 5, 6 and 7 handle the ammunition.

ABOVE AND BELOW 15cm sIG 33 in action: a shell is being rammed in. It will be followed the cased charge. Note the attempt at camouflage. The preserved example is at Belgrade Museum in Serbia. *(Dungodung/WikiCommons)*

10.5cm *leichte Feldhaubitze* 18 (lFH 18)

The Krupp leFH 16 was the standard 10.5cm weapon of the First World War and was superseded by the lFH 18 in 1935. It had a split-trail carriage and was one of the best weapons available to any army in 1939, at which time there were around 4,800 in service. This was a fine quality gun whose barrel had a life of around 11,000 shots. It took about six months to make and cost around RM16,400. A further 7,000 were built during the war, some of which were converted into the newer version (lFH 18M) which had a muzzle brake and recoil system adjustments to allow it to fire a longer-range shell propelled by a stronger charge. This increased the barrel length to 3.3m and the combat weight to 2,040kg (4,500lb). The maximum range increased to 12,325m (13,480yd) at 540m/second (1,772ft/sec) muzzle velocity. Another variant was the lighter leFH 18/40 which combined the barrel of the leFH 18 with the carriage of the Pak 40. It needed larger wheels but weight was reduced to 1,900kg (4,188lb). The design proved to lack the staying power of the original.

In service: 1935–45
Designed: 1927–30, Rheinmetall
Manufactured: Rheinmetall, Krupp
Number built: Around 12,000
Weight: 1,985kg (4,376lb in combat)
Length: 6.1m (20ft 2in)
Barrel length: 2.94m (9ft 8in)
Width: 1.98m (6ft 5.8in)
Height: 1.9m (6ft 2in)
Feed: Manual; horizontal sliding breech block with hydropneumatic recoil
Rate of fire: 6–8 rounds/min
Muzzle velocity: 470m/sec (1,500ft/sec)
Effective range: 10,676m (11,674yd)
Sights: RblF36
Crew: 6.

LEFT AND BELOW **The 10.5cm leichte Feldhaubitze 18 (lFH 18) was one of the best guns of the early war period. An 'improved' version, the sFH 40 (photo below) proved too heavy.** *(Wisnia6522/ WikiCommons; Balcer/ WikiCommons)*

15cm *schwere Feldhaubitze* 18 (sFH 18)

The sFH 18 was nicknamed 'Evergreen' (*Immergrün*) for good reason: its antecedents dated back to the sFH 13 of the First World War. The first artillery piece to fire rocket-assisted ammunition, it saw service throughout the war and was used to equip the Hummel SP gun. Its production history exemplifies many of Germany's problems in the Second World War. Krupp and Rheinmetall touted for the business. The army liked the Krupp carriage but preferred the Rheinmetall gun, so the two were combined. There were 1,350 in service in 1939; a further 2,700 were built between 1939 and 1943. Then, in 1944, production increased to 2,295 as other factories – Spreewerk Berlin-Spandau, M.A.N. Augsburg, Dörris-Füllner Bad Warmbrunn and Skoda in Dubnica – got involved. Each unit cost RM40,000 and took nine months to build.

During the war there were a number of attempts to improve the weapon, initially because it proved difficult to ensure the sFH 18 could keep up with the other fast-moving Blitzkrieg forces. Later, similar Russian weapons had more range and that's why the rocket-assisted RGr19 round was developed. This had a range of 18,200m (19,900yd), closer to its Russian counterparts.

Other attempts at improvement were the 18M with a muzzle brake; the sFH 36 with significant

RIGHT **The 15cm sFH 18 weighed just over 5 tons and was tractor-pulled. The pressed-steel wheel was the same as used on the 8.8cm Pak 43/41. This one is at Chérain in the Ardennes.** *(Richard Wood)*

weight reductions thanks to use of lighter alloys (but this had to be shelved when it became too expensive to use them); the sFH 40 had a longer barrel and a better carriage – but proved too heavy; other ideas didn't proceed to trial.

In service: 1934–45
Designed: Initially Krupp
Manufactured: Krupp, Rheinmetall and others
Number built: 5,400
Weight: 5,512kg (12,152lb) combat
Length: 7.85m (25ft 9in)
Barrel length: 4.44m (14ft 6.8in)
Feed: Manual; horizontal sliding breech block with hydropneumatic recoil
Rate of fire: 4 rounds/min
Muzzle velocity: 520m/sec (1,700ft/sec)
Effective range: 13,325m (14,572yd)
Sights: Model 34
Crew: 10 with additional help from battery personnel.

RIGHT Ammunition box for 15cm sFH 18 special or supercharge ammunition. The cartridge was of the separate-loading QF type, consisting of a brass case containing a charge in six sections. The special charge – sections 7 and 8 – was packed separately and was only inserted into the cartridge case in place of the normal six-section contents when required.

RIGHT *Zündmittel für je 9 S.Mi.35* – this box held S-mine 35 accessories. Typical contents were: 9 Z35 igniters, 10 ZZ42 or ZZ35 igniters, 30 Sprengk. Nr. 8 A1 detonators (2 boxes of 15) and various other bits and pieces. *(both Ken Davies collection)*

Ammunition

Space is too restricted to spend much time discussing ammunition – particularly as the Germans had so many different types. Thanks to the Beutewaffen – weapons captured in the first half of the war or made subsequently by the industry of conquered territories – the German ammunition requirements were hard to fulfil.

What can be said is that most artillery pieces used cased cartridges, with separate loading used above 10.5cm. Usually the cases were brass but lack of raw materials saw many substitute materials used. As unidentified ammunition could be dangerous to the user, considerable information was included on the packaging and labelling. Cartridge cases and bullets were also marked with colours.

As an example, take the small-arms

Some small-arms packaging abbreviations/colours:

B-Patronen = *Beobachtungsgeschoß Patronen* = observation (explosive) bullets
Br. = Brand = incendiary
für MG printed in red = for MGs
für Gew or *nur für Gewehr* printed in red = (only) for rifles
i.L in large black or red lettering = *in Ladenstreifen* = on stripper clips
L'spur = *Leuchtspur* = tracer bullet
Patr = *Patrone* = cartridge
Patr. 318 = *Patrone* 318 = anti-tank rifle cartridges
Patr. s.S = *Patronen schweres Spitzgeschoß* = heavy pointed bullet
Pist. Patr 08 = *Pistolenpatronen* 08 = 9mm pistol or SMG bullets
P.m.K = *Phosphorgeschoß mit Kern* = armour-piercing incendiary
S.m.k printed in red = *Spitzgeschoß mit Stahlkern* = pointed bullet with a steel core (armour-piercing)
A green diagonal band with *l.S* = *leichtes Spitzgeschoß* = light, pointed ball ammunition
A wide vertical blue band = steel cartridge cases rather than brass

classifications. The labels were in white with black printing, with special colours for identification:

- Yellow – tracer
- Pale blue – pistol
- Brick red – blank (training).

Labels also had to display the following information:

- Number and type of cartridge
- Lot number and year of loading
- Type of powder for which weapon
- Place and year of manufacture
- Specifications.

Base markings for small arms

All small-arms rounds had markings showing:

- Manufacturer's mark – **P** for Polte of Magdeburg, **P154** Polte OHG, Werk Grüneberg (Nordbahn)
- Type of case – brass or steel: **S*** means brass cartridge case
- Delivery number – **2**
- Year of manufacture – **38** = 1938.

Belted ammunition for MGs

Machine-gun ammunition came boxed and loose. The non-disintegrating metallic-link belt wasn't expendable and was reused many times. The cartridges were belted by the unit that drew the issue. They came in a wooden case holding 1,500 rounds in five cartons, each holding 300 rounds packed in 20 cardboard packages and each holding 15 rounds.

Larger-calibre shells

Shells had basic body colours that indicated their use:

- Olive green, olive drab or field grey: high-explosive (only non anti-aircraft), anti-concrete, smoke, chemical or hollow charge shells, and case shots
- Black: armour-piercing shot or shell
- Yellow: anti-aircraft high-explosive shell
- Red and blue: anti-aircraft incendiary shrapnel shell
- Pale green: star shell.

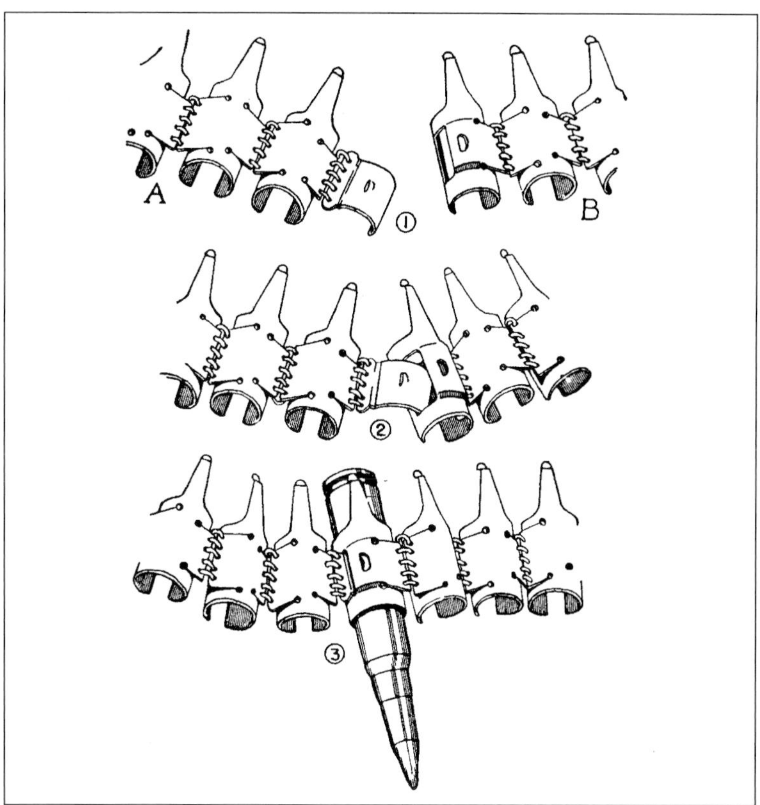

ABOVE Belted ammo for the MG34/42 came loose and had to be inserted manually into the non-disintegrating link belt. The belts could be linked together as required.

BELOW Another of Kurt Kranz's *Winteralltag im Urwald Lapplands* (Winter Life in the Lapland Forest) sketches. This shows links being cleaned prior to use. *(via RCT)*

Chapter Six

Transportation, bridging and communications

The Wehrmacht brought the world Blitzkrieg: fast, incisive, combined arms' attacks that mixed radio-equipped Panzers, air support and – if possible – mechanised infantry. In reality, the infantry component of Blitzkrieg usually used horses and shank's pony rather than mechanised transportation. It worked brilliantly in 1939 and 1940, but in 1941 the size of Russia and its weather showed that Germany should probably have spent more time and money on trucks and armoured personnel vehicles than on heavy tanks.

OPPOSITE The German Army was mainly horse-drawn: over a million horses were in use by the army in 1945. *(Tanis)*

ABOVE The German Army made great use of trains – in particular on the Eastern Front where they converted over 35,000km (22,000 miles) of Soviet track to German standard gauge. In 1944 the Deutsche Reichsbahn ran 37,810 steam locos, over 985,000 freight wagons and 70,000 carriages. *(via RCT)*

Transportation

No coverage of the transport abilities of the Third Reich can start anywhere other than its railway system. Important during the First World War, it was even more crucial in the Second World War as German troops and armaments were transported to the fronts, the wounded returned to hospitals and the railways sorted out the complicated logistics of total war.

On 10 February 1937 the Deutsche Reichsbahn Gesellschaft became the Deutsche Reichsbahn. It would play a huge role in the coming years both in the distribution of war materiel for industry and in carrying men and munitions. Added to that, it had to accommodate the increase in its territory as the Third Reich expanded into conquered countries and was required to cope with different stock, gauges and systems. It also played a significant role in the transport of people to concentration camps, in the deportation of citizens of conquered territories and in the furtherance of the worst excesses of Nazism.

The ability of the Reichsbahn to carry men and fighting equipment the length of breadth of Europe, in spite of Allied air attacks, continued until late in the war: one thinks of the movement of reinforcements to the front during Operation Market Garden and, more remarkable, preparatory to the Battle of the Bulge.

Although the German military machine is often thought of as being highly mechanised, this was actually far from the truth. When Hitler came to power in 1933, the vast majority of the native population had no experience whatsoever of motorised transportation. As a comparison, the ratio of cars to people in the USA was 1:5, whereas in Germany it was 1:89. Consequently, as the build-up to war progressed, a lot more training was required to produce the necessary number of drivers. Likewise, the German manufacturing base just didn't exist to make the requisite number of vehicles, and despite strenuous efforts to ramp up production, the output never got close to meeting demand. It hit a peak in 1943 when 109,000 trucks were made; however, battlefield losses were so high that more than this were lost in the first seven months of that year. As a result, the mainstay of the Wehrmacht transportation system was the horse. Even by late 1944, only 16% of the army divisions were fully motorised, and in February 1945 the Wehrmacht still had nearly 1.2 million horses.

One of the biggest problems with horses when compared with vehicles is that they are easily put out of action. Whereas the latter can sometimes be repaired after being shot up, even a lightly injured animal takes time and care to return to duty. The disablement of horses usually results in the loss of the carriage or gun

LEFT The US *Handbook on German Military Forces* identifies *Infanteriezüge* (infantry trains) of 55 cars carrying 350 soldiers, 20 vehicles and 70 horses. *(via RCT)*

LEFT The German Army was always dependent on horses. They hauled guns, ammunition, supplies, medical and bridging equipment and had more horse-drawn than motorised vehicles. They needed significant veterinary services to care for them. *(via RCT)*

RIGHT 'Comrade Horse: As the muddy roads begin to be covered by snow, our faithful horses drag food to our grenadiers.'

they were towing, which can make a massive difference on the battlefield. This was especially so when the Allies broke thorough in Normandy after D-Day when vast amounts of equipment had to be abandoned by the retreating German forces due to losses of horses.

Special efforts were made on the motorisation front for big campaigns, however, such as Operation Barbarossa, the invasion of Russia, when transportation was considered vital and large numbers of extra vehicles were made available. On this occasion around 600,000 accompanied 3 million men and 600,000–750,000 horses. Enemy vehicles were also taken whenever the opportunity arose, but although extra mobility was always welcome, having vast numbers to service and provide fuel for added all manner of complexities to the logistical situation. Huge quantities of motorcycles, cars and trucks were captured in both the 1940 campaign in Belgium and France (mostly French, British and American makes) as well as in Russia a year later. As an example, when the British evacuated at Dunkirk, they left

RIGHT The infamous *rasputitsa* caused travel chaos. Thousands of horses died in the awful weather and arduous conditions. *(via Tanis)*

behind some 65,000 vehicles. More were lost when the British were driven out of Greece. These included Bedford and Morris-Commercial trucks in the 8cwt to 3-ton range as well as the much heavier Scammell Pioneers and AEC Matadors which were used for hauling tanks and recovery purposes.

Although some captured vehicles performed well, others proved unreliable when used under military conditions. The Russian trucks were very basic indeed, but kept going even when put through very severe conditions. Many of the French makes, however, were considered temperamental unless they were constantly nursed by skilled mechanics.

Luxury cars – either requisitioned from civilians or captured from the enemy – were usually put into service as staff vehicles, while lesser examples would be used for more mundane tasks such as ferrying troops or were modified for special purposes. These included such things as ambulances, signals vehicles, towing guns and for general maintenance work.

Since motorcycles could often get through roads and tracks that were impassable to other vehicles, they were in high demand when the war began. Many entered military service as the result of requisition as the factories could not produce enough of them. Since it also took a lot to train a rider to the necessary standard, the owners of such seized machines often found themselves in uniform too. They called themselves *Kradmelder*, and generally ended up as couriers, as scouts, in specialist tank hunting teams or attached to rifle troop units. While some were lucky enough to have special heating systems installed on their bikes, most had to endure unbelievably hard conditions, especially on the Eastern Front.

Cars

Einheits-PKW

When rearmament began in 1935, it was envisaged that the Wehrmacht would be supplied with militarised versions of civilian vehicles that could cope with severe cross-country conditions. These would be of three types, which were referred to as *Leichter Einheits-PKW* (lightweight cars), *Mittlerer Einheits-PKW* (medium-weight cars) and *Schwerer Einheits-PKW* (heavyweight cars). All would conform to standardised designs to optimise spares supply, training and maintenance, and would come with advanced features like four-wheel drive. Unfortunately, this proved to be a completely unachievable ideal as the large number of factories involved had so many different component suppliers that they were simply unable to make them in the desired

RIGHT Gebirgsjäger stand in front of a Horch Type 901, Kfz 15, as used famously by Rommel in the desert. Nearly 15,000 of these vehicles were delivered up until 1943. *(via RCT)*

manner. For pragmatic reasons, each factory therefore manufactured its own version, mostly using non-standardised parts including engines. In spite of this, they could not achieve anywhere near the required number of vehicles, and so around 60% of all the Wehrmacht's cars were actually converted civilian models, including some which had been captured. Examples included those made by Auto Union (Horch and Wanderer), BMW (Werk Eisenach), Ford Germany, Hanomag, Opel (Werk Brandenburg) and Stoewer.

Kübelwagen

The Kübelwagen was a light military vehicle that was initially built by Volkswagen to Dr Ferdinand Porsche's design. Derived directly from the VW Beetle, it was later also made by Mercedes, Opel and Tatra. The prototypes were designated Type 62, but when it came into production in February 1940, the designation became Type 82. Among the many modifications this version had were better off-road performance and the ability to travel more slowly in order to keep pace with soldiers on foot. Few changes were made during the war, but it did receive a bigger engine, and by the time hostilities ended, 50,435 had been built.

Schwimmwagen

Schwimmwagen – which translates as swimming car – was the name given to the VW Type 128 and 166 amphibious four-wheel drive off-road vehicles used throughout the Second World War. Like the Kübelwagen, it was derived from the VW Beetle, and with 15,584 Type 166 Schwimmwagen cars produced between 1941 and 1944, it was a relatively common sight on the battlefield.

ABOVE Some 500,000 CMP (Canadian Military Pattern) trucks were built by Chevrolet and Ford: many captured vehicles saw use by the Germans. Note the swastika flag on the bonnet for aerial recognition – especially important if you were using captured transport equipment *(Beutefahrzeuge).*

CENTRE The Type 82 Kübelwagen was the Wehrmacht's most successful run-around produced from 1940, although the US and British assessment of captured examples was less than complimentary.

RIGHT The Germans built around 15,000 Schwimmwagen but fewer than 200 survive today. It was powered in the water by a propeller lowered at the rear and steered by use of the wheels. *(Alf van Beem/WikiCommons (CC0 1.0))*

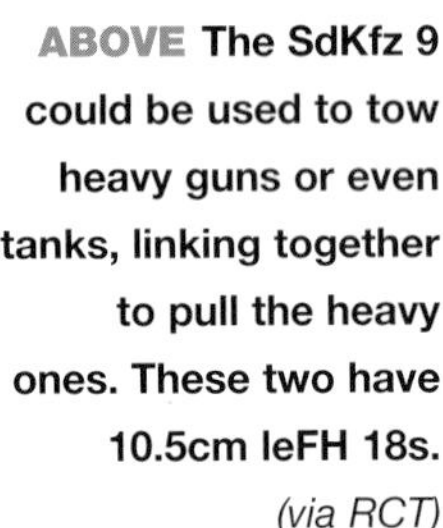

ABOVE The SdKfz 9 could be used to tow heavy guns or even tanks, linking together to pull the heavy ones. These two have 10.5cm leFH 18s. *(via RCT)*

BELOW This SdKfz 9 in North Africa is towing a 15.5cm sFH 18. Note the two-wheel carriage attached to facilitate towing. The SdKfz 9 was designed to pull 24cm heavy guns or 35.5cm mortars.

ABOVE There were 23 different versions of the SdKfz 251 including command, ambulance and engineer vehicles, as well as being one of the most important of all Panzergrenadier APCs.

Halftracks and armoured cars

Although the Wehrmacht had a significant number of wheeled vehicles when the war started, it was soon discovered that they were severely compromised when they encountered thick mud. This was particularly true on the Russian steppe, where decent roads were few and far between, and supplying the troops across such terrain became a massive problem. As a result, halftracks like the SdKfz 11, a 3-ton light version, which was able to cope with such conditions, were needed in large numbers. The problem was that there simply weren't enough of them to fulfil the requirements, and it would take too long to build them from scratch. In order to deal with the issue, standard trucks made by the likes of Opel (especially the Blitz model S), Daimler-Benz, Alfa Romeo and Ford were modified to take redundant Panzer I track assemblies to speed the process along. Referred to as Maultier or SdKfz 3, they didn't perform as well as the purpose-built versions; but they were certainly an indispensable part of the German military effort.

SdKfz – short for *Sonderkraftfahrzeug* (special purpose vehicle) – numbers were assigned to all German tracked and halftracked military vehicles. Those issued to halftracks ranged from the 1-ton SdKfz 10 to the heavyweight SdKfz 9, which was an 18-ton

crane platform. In between these extremes were a wide variety of other versions, which were used as everything from Flak gun carriers (SdKfz 7, SdKfz 10/4 and SdKfz 10/5), to Nebelwerfer rocket launcher mounts (SdKfz 4), artillery gun tractors (SdKfz 6/1), smoke generators (SdKfz 11/1 and SdKfz 11/4) and so on. The SdKfz 2 was an interesting variant – it was effectively a halftracked motorcycle, and was designated as a cable-layer.

Armoured versions included the various models of the SdKfz 250 (lightweight) and SdKfz 251 and 252 (medium-weight) halftracks. These were used for many different purposes, including reconnaissance and observation, carrying cables, transporting machine guns and mortars, as searchlight mounts and as flamethrowers.

LEFT Classic Wolfgang Willrich 1940 sketch of a motorcycle messenger. Willrich (1897–1948) was a war artist, much of whose work appeared on postcards – such as this. As well as senior officers and officials, he produced many studies of ordinary fighting men. *(via RCT)*

Motorcycles

Although the German military machine had visions of an idealised situation where everything was standardised in order to simplify logistics, nowhere was the reality more different than with the supply of motorcycles. Essential for all manner of duties, from carrying dispatches to fast-moving patrol work, they could not be supplied by any single source. Consequently, they came from several different manufacturers in a plethora of varying models. The main providers included BMW, Zundapp, DKW, NSU and Victoria, but there were also over 12,000 250cc Triumphs made under licence.

A large number of these machines had sidecars which were manufactured by Zundapp, BMW, Stoye, Royal and Steib. The shaft-driven Zundapp KS750 and BMW R75 were unusual in having their third wheels powered, which made them far better than most of the competition when crossing rough terrain – such as in thick mud or on loose sand – when lesser-equipped machines would invariably get stuck.

LEFT One of the reasons that motorcycles fell out of favour was that they bogged down all too easily when the roads weren't good – although, to be fair, few vehicles would have found mud this deep any more passable than the bogged BMW R12 combo.

RIGHT The BMW R75 motorcycle and sidecar proved sturdy and manoeuvrable but heavy; even before its crew, weapons, etc., were loaded it weighed 800lb! *(via RCT)*

BICYCLES

RIGHT The German military put bicycles to good use throughout the war. Each Volksgrenadier division had a battalion of bicycle troops. *(via RCT)*

FAR RIGHT This re-enactor has attached a variety of kit to his original wartime bicycle, including a Panzerfaust 30 anti-tank rocket launcher.

KETTENKRAD

ABOVE The SdKfz 2 – the *Kleines Kettenkraftrad HK 101* – was a maid of all work in the German Army, mainly used in Russia as a light artillery tractor. It was also used for casualty evacuation, cable laying and many other duties.

LEFT The driver's seat in a Kettenkrad. While the handlebars could be used to steer and make small course corrections, wider turns were accommodated by using a Cletrac tractor drive. *(Zandcee/WikiCommons (CC BY-SA 3.0))*

Although prototypes of the BMW R75 had 750cc side valve engines, it was soon found that overhead valve versions gave far superior performance in the field, and so this is what the production versions were supplied with. The Zundapp KS750 was, however, considered by the OKH to be superior to the BMW offering as it was more rugged. The latter company refused to make their rival's machine under licence, though, and stuck with their own version. A degree of standardisation was later achieved when the two companies began working together to streamline production, and about 70% of their motorcycles ended up using the same components

Manufacture of the R75 continued throughout the war until Allied bombing finally destroyed BMW's Eisenach factory in 1944, and Zundapp stopped production in early 1945.

ABOVE The range of vehicles used by the German Army was considerable: Mercedes, Renaults, Opels ... but there were never enough to replace the horse. *(via RCT)*

Lorries

The Wehrmacht used a wide variety of lorries to transport various equipment and/or stores. The mainstays were 3-ton category vehicles like the Opel Blitz (of which 82,356 were produced during the war) and the Mercedes-Benz L3000 (27,700 produced), both seeing action on all fronts and in the harshest of terrains. Others of similar size included the likes of the German-made Fords, the Borgward B 3000, as well as captured examples like the Swiss Berna and the Czech Skoda. Most of these were available in different variants to suit particular requirements – the Opel Blitz, for instance, had seven basic formats – some of which were four-wheel drive. These included the following:

- Kfz31 – heavy ambulance
- Kfz68 – radio or telephone communication van
- Kfz305 – standard truck used mainly by Luftwaffe in 127 subvariants
- TLF 15 – fire truck/2500l tanker
- Fliegerkraftfahrspitze – airbase rescue/emergency vehicle
- Kfz385 – airbase fuel tanker
- Kessel-kraftwagen 2100L – 2100l fuel tanker.

In the smaller categories were light off-road trucks known as *leichter geländegängiger Lastkraftwagen* – abbreviated to lglLkw. The Steyr 1500 series – made by Steyr, Audi and Auto Union – is an example, and like the other lorries was produced in many forms, from basic cargo trucks to soft-skinned infantry carriers. Slightly heavier medium off-road vehicles were also produced – these were

BELOW Opel was the largest truck producer in Germany – but it was the largest of many. Unlike the US or Russians who standardised, the Germans used many different vehicles and, as a consequence, getting spare parts was a nightmare. The Opel Blitz lightning logo is noticeable on this pretty restoration. *(WikiCommons)*

ABOVE **One of the key components of Blitzkrieg was speed of advance. Europe is criss-crossed by rivers, so rapid bridging was essential, particularly in the face of bridges destroyed during the fighting (an Ernst Eigener sketch).** *(via RCT)*

referred to as *Mittelschwerer geländegängiger Lastkraftwagen*.

Another widely used vehicle was the Krupp-Protze, of which about 7,000 were manufactured in total. These were six-wheeled trucks which saw action on more or less all fronts. Although they were mainly intended for towing Flak guns and light artillery pieces (like the Pak 36), as well as transporting infantry, they also came in several other variants. These included the following:

- Kfz19 – telephone truck
- Kfz21 – staff car
- Kfz68 – radio mast carrier
- Kfz69 – standard configuration for towing the 3.7cm Pak 36
- Kfz70 – standard configuration for carrying personnel
- Kfz81 – ammo carrier conversion for 2cm Flak gun, usually towed
- Kfz83 – generator carrier for anti-aircraft spotlight, usually towed
- SdKfz 247 Ausf A – armoured personnel carrier, six-wheeled version.

BELOW **Horse-drawn artillery crosses a pontoon bridge. This is from one of Ernst Eigener's wartime sketchbooks. The war artist died on 20 November 1942 in the Ukraine.** *(via RCT)*

Quite often – especially on the Russian front – the mud and/or snow were bad enough to defeat both wheeled and halftracked vehicles. In order to deal with this, a fully tracked lightweight truck was developed called the Raupenschlepper Ost or RSO, which translates as caterpillar tractor east. It came in two basic formats – one was as a cargo carrier, the other a self-contained anti-tank vehicle, and as such was armed with a Pak 40 gun.

Bridging

Bridging is a fundamental requirement for any European military advance. Europe abounds with rivers of every conceivable size, and it's impossible that every bridge can be taken intact – or will carry an army. The trials and tribulations of XXX Corps advancing on Arnhem or Leibstandarte trying to reach the Meuse through the Ardennes emphasise this point.

The larger rivers required an assault river crossing, using Sturm boats or assault craft. After creating a bridgehead, engineers then started on the bridge itself. Engineer battalions usually had a bridging column, but these were sometimes grouped together and assigned from the Army GHQ engineer pool – particularly if the division was operating in terrain where bridging was unnecessary. In 1942 this ad hoc arrangement became fact and the bridging columns became independent of the divisions.

There were a number of different bridge types, perhaps the most important in the early war years being the Type B medium combat bridge. Others included light recce bridges (Type D), light combat bridges (Type C), mountain bridges (Type G) and the medium combat Type T bridges of Czech design, which

BRÜCKEKOLONNE B (*BRÜKO* B)

Suitable for loads of 4–16 tons, Brüko Bs could carry lorries and light armoured vehicles. The maximum dimensions of the bridges were:

- Length: 130m (426ft) for 4 tons; 83m (272ft) for 8 tons; and 54m (177ft) for 16 tons
- Width: 3.14m (10ft 4in)

The Brüko B could also build ferries – motor ferries, rowed ferries and trail or cable ferries: 8 ferries of 4 tons; 4 ferries of 8 tons; 2 ferries of 16 tons; and one ferry of 20 tons

Brüko B personnel: 2 officers, 13 NCOs and 87 men. Equipment comprised:

- 1st pontoon train: 8 half-pontoons, 1 M-boat
- 2nd pontoon train: 8 half-pontoons, 6 assault boats
- Supplementary train: ramp parts, ferry ropes, 20 small and 24 large dinghies
- Food and luggage with field kitchen and fuel-LKW.

were attached to many infantry divisions in both motorised and horse-drawn forms.

Communications

We all know about ULTRA and the breaking of the Enigma codes. The Heer, along with the rest of the Wehrmacht, had its codes broken for long periods of the war. The Allies could decode Heer radio communications erratically during 1941 and reliably from 1942. Just how useful this was tactically, because of the length of time it took to break and interpret the information, has been debated,

ABOVE AND BELOW Combat engineers hurry to build a bridge; behind them *Schlauchbooten* – inflatable boats – ferry troops across a defended river. The Pionier battalion of an infantry division would have had 58 small and 60 large inflatable boats.

RIGHT If the invasion of Britain had gone ahead, the infantry might have hit the beaches in these. This photograph was taken in Belgium in 1940. *(via RCT)*

LEFT **This well-known photograph – one of a sequence – shows 'Schnell Heinz' (General der Panzertruppen Heinz Guderian) in his Sdkfz 251/6 command vehicle. Cut off from the bottom of the photo is an Enigma machine. The radio station is an FuG (Funkgerät) 8, comprised of a medium-wave 0.84–3MHz receiver and a 1.0–3.0MHz, 30W output transmitter.**

although it proved hugely important on certain occasions – such as the attack on the HQ of Leo Geyr von Schweppenburg's Panzer Group West. However, ULTRA didn't give notice of the Ardennes Offensive because the Germans maintained excellent radio security and because much of their communications were by landlines rather than radio.

Communications are crucial in warfare: air support, artillery information and contact with mobile forces all demand a high flow of communications. The German system was to lay wire, with each junior unit laying wires to its senior. Wire, however, can easily be broken – by bombardment, guerilla or resistance action or simple bad weather – and needed to be supplemented by radio communications. Radios were also vital for mobile and ground-to-air communications.

The Germans knew how easily compromised radio communications could be. Much of Rommel's success in North Africa resulted from the information derived from decrypting US military attaché Frank Fellers' messages – Rommel called him *die gute Quelle* (the good source). Possibly as important was the excellence of Rommel's radio interception unit

BELOW **Much of German battlefield communications depended on wire. These drawings from Ernst Eigener's sketchbook capture infantrymen laying wire.** *(via RCT)*

THE GERMAN PHONETIC ALPHABET

(Heer and Luftwaffe – Kriegsmarine was different)

Anton	Otto
Ärger	Ödipus
Berta	Paula
Cäser	Quelle
Charlotte	Richard
Dora	Schule
Emil	Siegfried
Friedrich	Theodor
Gustav	Übel
Heinrich	Ulrich
Ida	Viktor
Julius	Wilhelm
Konrad	Xanthippe
Ludwig	Ypsilon
Martha	Zeppelin
Nordpol	

Source: Various including http://www.gyges.dk/reporting_grids.htm

BELOW This Czech TP25 crank field phone is very similar to the German FF-33. It has a Bakelite case roughly 26 × 17 × 9cm (10.25 × 6.75 × 3.5in) in size. The Czech writing – *POZOR, NEPRITEL NASLOUCHA!* – translates as 'Attention, the enemy's listening!'

... and the laxity of British radio procedure. After capturing the intercept unit (Captain Alfred Seebohm's Nachrichten Fern Aufklärungs Kompanie 621), British radio communication improved immensely. German radio operators were taught to strive for the utmost security and to limit radio messages to subjects which contained no secret information – but there were always mistakes and operators who were less secure than others.

The German infantry signals units were based around wire with, for example, a battalion's signals platoon having two light telephone teams in 1939 (with 10km of wire, six handsets and a switchboard); this increased to three in 1944 with a corresponding increase in wire and handsets. Beside the field telephones, the signallers used *Feldfunksprecher* (FeldFu) radios, which were also used in mobile warfare – although only after the enemy had been engaged. German radio operators were taught not to use radios in the advance and in defensive positions so as not to give locations away. Once an attack was launched or a defensive battle started, short-range communications with other troops – especially mortars or artillery – was by FeldFu.

The FeldFu range was produced for the lowest levels of command, typically battalion or company level. The B and C series covered a frequency range of 90–160MHz, while the F and later H series covered 27.2–33.3MHz, enabling communication with tanks at operational level on the move. Individual groups of frequencies were used by infantry, engineers, Panzergrenadiers and artillery batteries between their own units. The range was 0.8 to 1.5km. The equipment itself weighed around 2kg (4.5lb).

TOP AND BELOW Usually multiple telephones ran to a switchboard, but when one wasn't available multiple connections could be fed back to the same command post. The Feldfernsprecher 33 (FF-33) was the standard field telephone of the Wehrmacht. Introduced in 1933, it replaced the FF-26 of 1926. It could be connected to the TornFu D2, BI, and F series radio sets as a remote handset. *(via RCT)*

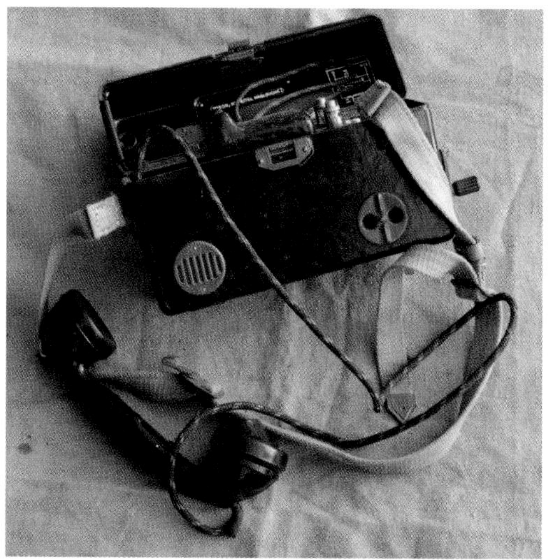

ABOVE Pre-war or training image of a signals unit – probably from an artillery battery.

For medium-range coverage, the bigger brother of the FeldFu, the *Tornisterfunkgerät* (TornFu) was also portable, weighed at least 20kg (45lb) and could be carried by one man, although two was more common. The TornFu was produced in four versions, the B1, C, F and K. The K was a later version of the B1. The C version covered 1.5–2.3MHz when transmitting; on receive 1.45–2.6MHz. The B1 (and later K) and F versions were the same, the difference being in the transmitter frequency coverage. On transmit the B1 and K covered 3–5MHz, while the F version covered 4.5–6.67MHz. Both receivers covered 3–6.6MHz. The transmitter power output was 0.65W on Morse using continuous wave; 0.325W on voice. The power supply consisted of a 2.4V battery for the valve heaters (low tension), and a 130V battery for high tension which was tapped at 4.5V for the grid bias supply. All versions were to be found throughout the German Army to provide low-level communications.

Messenger dogs, carrier pigeons and rockets (visual or sound) were used to supplement the two basic methods of radio and wire.

RIGHT AND BELOW DDR R-105d backpack radio, very similar in size to the Tornister FeldFu B/C/F radios used by the German Army (as shown in the wartime photograph). There are two points at the top for straps and the field kit fastens to the outside (note the D rings on top of the radio in wartime photograph). *(Bundesarchiv, Bild 101I-198-1395-08A/ Henisch/CC-BY-SA 3.0)*

BELOW The TornFu B1 was introduced in 1936 and could be carried by two men: one for the transceiver (seen here) and one for the battery pack which also contained the microphone, key, headsets, antennae etc. Note the words *Feind hört mit!* ('The enemy can hear too!'). As with the Czech telephone, operators were warned about insecure use of all communications equipment, on both sides. The Germans proved particularly adept at intercept intelligence.

ABOVE A divisional radio station. The centre unit is a *Hellschreiber* fax machine with its power supply unit (PSU) to the left of the picture and the 15W SE B *Sender/Empfänger* – transmitter/receiver) to the right. The Hellschreiber was used for sending fax messages over line and radio, and is of a similar type to the one Rommel is reputed to have used to communicate with Berlin. Used by the German Army from 1935, it could send up to 150 signals (characters) a minute using 12V, derived in this case from its power supply working from AC mains. The 15W SE B worked from a 2.4V battery power supply to receive, and a pedal generator or rotary convertor to transmit. The 15W SE B was a portable radio – a man-pack with a struggle – which was used throughout the German Army for higher-level communications, although primarily designed for artillery communications. Operating from 3.0–7.5MHz in two bands using Morse or voice, it proved its worth right up to Rommel's level.

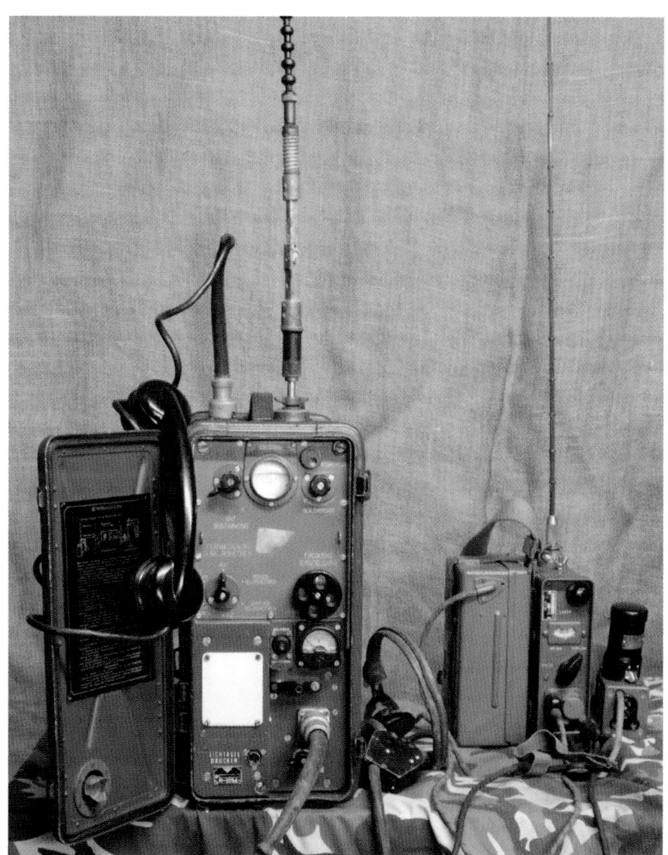

LEFT On the left, a DDR post-war R-105d, similar to the Tornister Feldfu B/C/F. On the right, a Czech post-war version of the Kleinfunksprecher D (Dorette). The German walkie-talkie equivalent had a range of about 2–4km (these instructions on the side of the transceiver):

Operating Instructions!

1. For operation on the move: Fasten the transceiver tightly onto the left side of your chest using the strap and buckle. Fasten the battery onto your belt with the leather strap. For operation when stationary: Attach battery pack and transceiver together.

2. Connect the power cable, antenna, microphone and headphones.

3. Transmit: Set the spring to a horizontal position, then press and set the desired frequency.
   Receive: Same process as with transmitting. Listen for a receiving station within range.

Do not change any settings while communicating.

Also refer to D 1037/5.

Soldatenheim

Chapter Seven

Medical services

The 20th century saw the destructive power of infantry weapons grow substantially. The German losses in the Second World War reflect this: over 3.5 million dead and over 5 million wounded or sick. However, significant advances in medical care and surgical techniques ensured that many wounded were able to return to battle. As well as surgeons and doctors, some 400,000 German Red Cross nurses, nursing assistants, and nursing aids worked for the German armed forces during the Second World War.

OPPOSITE The German Red Cross was the main provider of nurses for the Wehrmacht. They worked in hospitals at home and in war zones, and in soldiers' homes (Soldatenheime), as here.

ABOVE A casualty is evacuated from the battlefield to a battalion aid post. Note the lack of armbands or red cross identifying marks.

RIGHT In practice, regular medical staff identified themselves mainly with armbands – although this was more likely to be honoured in the West than on the Eastern Front. There is debate as to whether or not white helmets/red crosses were used outside those medics working in captivity.

LEFT Every morning the medical sergeant does his rounds and deals with light wounds on the spot. *(via RCT)*

The infantryman

Medical training starts with the private soldier. In the Heer each soldier carried two first-aid packets – one large and one small – and was trained in the application of these dressings. Additionally, inside the tunic there was a small, thin interior pocket that was designed to hold two first-aid dressings. Other items that were often carried in tunic pockets included extra first-aid bandages, salves and creams – often in commercial containers and tins – to treat such things as frostbite and cold weather sores. Another common item was foot powder, which was supplied in a small tin.The medical personnel of the combat units included *Krankenträger* (stretcher-bearers) with special training in first aid and moving the wounded. In addition, a trained medical NCO or private was assigned to each unit. All the medical personnel, including the stretcher-bearers, carried a medical kit on their belt. The stretcher came in two equal-sized collapsible halves, easily carried and assembled. If conditions permitted, casualties could be transported on two-wheeled carriers.

In addition to the dedicated stretcher-bearers who were part of the *Sanitätsdienst* (Medical Service), a number of others in each unit were appointed as *Hilfskrankenträger* (auxiliary stretcher-bearers). They were either regular soldiers or, later in the war, Hiwi (volunteers). Note that bandsmen were used as Hilfskrankenträger.

Krankenträger were specifically trained for their mission. They were also trained as medical orderlies and as such carried out duties in medical installations. The regular soldiers who became Hilfskrankenträger had only rudimentary first-aid training, and remained with their units.

Battalion

There was a *Bataillonsarzt* (battalion doctor) with an assistant (*Assistenzarzt* or *Hilfsarzt*). Additionally, there was a medical NCO (*Sanitätsunteroffizier*) – specially trained in a medical school (training lasted about six months and there were also supplementary courses) – and a stretcher-bearer at each rifle company HQ, plus a stretcher-bearer at each platoon HQ. The battalion medical equipment was sufficient for major operations and included water purification gear. It was carried in a special medical car and provided all that was needed for the battalion aid station. Provision was made for support by medical companies that went into action when casualties were heavy and mainly served the purpose of collecting the wounded in the zone of action.

ABOVE **Our medical re-enactor sports a suitable armband and two medical pouches at his waist. (Note that he's also wearing an HBT jacket and gaiters. In addition he carries an extra, larger water flask. The pouches came in different versions with stamps (such as T = Träger = Krankenträger = stretcher-bearer or S = Sani = Sanitäter = medic). The pouches were about 16.5 × 14 × 9cm (6.5 × 5.5 × 3.5in) and contained bandages, tourniquets and field dressings, as well as tweezers, scissors, pins, etc.**

Division

A senior MO (*Divisionsarzt*) was responsible for supervising the employment of the battalion medical services and the evacuation of sick and wounded.

The medical units within an infantry division comprised the following.

Divisional field hospital

Located some way back from the front this was primarily intended for reception and retention of casualties requiring urgent operations, or those whose condition would not allow further evacuation without a period of rest and recuperation. Completely mechanised and fully equipped, it could be set up in three hours and could cater for around 200 casualties. Mobile units often had the field hospital replaced by a third motor ambulance train, to meet the constant need for casualty evacuation – particularly during the early weeks of Operation Barbarossa when the German divisions advanced so quickly and deeply into enemy territory.

Sanitäts Kompanie(n) – medical company(ies)

There were usually two medical companies in a division, one mechanised and the other horse-drawn, although in some divisions both were mechanised. On the march it set up casualty clearing posts; in locations where the stay was for more than three to four nights, temporary hospitals were set up as far as possible in conjunction with local civilian hospitals.

In action, each company's three platoons had definite responsibilities. One was responsible for establishing a field dressing station and a lightly wounded collecting post; it included at least one surgeon-specialist. The second was the stretcher-bearer platoon; the third was held in reserve. Usually an ambulance car post was also formed.

The equipment of a medical company included canvas for the erection of the division aid station (where buildings were not available) and modern surgical equipment. Like the battalion medical equipment, the equipment of the medical company was suitably packed in individual chests. Four horse-drawn or motor ambulances were assigned to the company.

At the beginning of the war in Europe, all divisions had two medical companies. At the end, only the armoured and mountain divisions had two each, but the corps surgeon had under his control one Sanitäts Kompanie for use where needed. When two medical companies were available, two *Hauptverbandplatzen* (field dressing stations) were often established. At the beginning of an offensive, one horse-drawn medical company was placed only 3–4km behind the battle line to receive casualties. The other company, which was motorised, was held in reserve to be used after substantial gains

MEDICAL UNITS OF THE 268TH INFANTRY DIVISION

1. Sanitäts Kompanie 268
2. Sanitäts Kompanie 268
1. Krankenkraftwagenzug 268
2. Krankenkraftwagenzug 268
Feldlazarett 268

A medical company was organised as follows in 1939:

Gruppe Führer (HQ Staff)
Medical officer (company commander), pharmacist, Oberfeldwebel, paramedic, sergeant of the vehicles squad, writers, 2 couriers, 1 driver and 1 horse holder.
Total: 1 officer, 1 official, 2 sergeants, 5 men, 3 horses, 1 car, 1 sidecar, 1 motorcycle.

Communications group
Telephone squad with a sergeant and three operators.
Total: 1 sergeant and 3 soldiers.

1. Zug – *Krankenträgerzug* (Ambulance Section)
Medical officer as a *Zug* leader, 3 stretcher-bearer group leaders, 41 stretcher-bearers and 5 coachmen.
Total: 1 officer, 3 NCOs and 46 men, 10 cart horses, 1 horse, 5 horse-drawn vehicles.

2. Zug – *Hauptverbandplatzzug* (Main Aid Station Section)
Medical officer as a Zug leader, 1 assistant surgeon as surgeon, 2 auxiliary doctors, 6 sergeant paramedics (1 orthopedic surgery, 1 instrumentalist, 2 aids of operations, 1 facilities, 1 of disinfection), 8 soldier paramedics, 20 stretcher-bearers.
Total: 4 officers, 6 NCOs, 40 men, 4 cart horses (heavy), 12 cart horses (light), 4 horses (ride), 7 horse-drawn vehicles.

3. Zug – *Ergänzung* (Replacement Section)
Sanitätsunteroffizier (medical NCO) as platoon leader; 3 groups of stretcher-bearers; 3 group leaders, 24 stretcher-bearers; group aid station; a paramedic as group commander, 4 soldier paramedics, 10 stretcher-bearers, 2 coachmen.
Total: 5 NCOs, 40 men, 2 cart horses (heavy), 2 cart horses (light), 2 horse-drawn vehicles.

Logistic train
Personnel of quartermaster corps, sergeant of transport, supply sergeant, 3 coachmen, 2 cooks.
Total: 1 official, 2 sergeants, 7 soldiers, 2 cart horses (heavy), 4 cart horses (light), 3 horse-drawn vehicles, 1 motorcycle.

Source: http://www.lexikon-der-wehrmacht.de/Gliederungen/SanEinheiten/Sankp-R.htm

had been made. Then, if further gains were made and the Hauptverbandplatz was required further forward, the motorised company moved, leaving its patients to be taken over by the horse-drawn company. The patients of the previous horse-drawn company were left to be taken over by a *Feldlazarett* (field hospital). Thus there were often two divisional units performing surgery ahead of the most forward Feldlazarett. With a large-scale offensive, division, army, and army group hospitals might all perform primary surgery only on the less seriously wounded, putting aside more critical wounds in favour of those who were more likely to live and return to full duty.

Motorised ambulance trains

Two of these were attached to field hospitals in infantry and mountain divisions. In motorised and armoured divisions there were three. They were employed in evacuating casualties from the Hauptverbandplatz to the Feldlazarett or from either of these and the lightly wounded collecting post to the casualty collecting post established by army ambulance units. These each comprised 15–18 vehicles and around 42 all ranks.

German motor ambulances were designated Kfz31 *Krankenkraftwagen* (Krkw) but also nicknamed 'Sankas' or 'Sankras' (from *Sanitätskraftwagen*). Common models (accommodating around four lying, or two lying and four sitting, or eight sitting patients) were the Opel Blitz Typ S, Phänomen-Granit 25H and Steyr 640; smaller vehicles included the Phänomen-Granit 1500A and Mercedes-Benz LE1100. Some buses could also be fitted with stretcher racks to carry wounded and emergency medical teams. As always, the Germans made use of captured equipment such as the British Bedford ML ambulances that could carry four stretchers or ten seated patients.

Both in Russia and North Africa the weather and terrain often militated against use of ambulances and meant that air evacuation was best. The Fieseler Storch (Fi-156) was exceptionally good at front-line operations but could only carry one or two severely wounded patients. Further from the front, Tante-Jus (Junkers

ABOVE Chevrolet ambulance at an aid station in Normandy. Even with red cross markings it's carefully concealed under trees to reduce the possibility of air attack. *(Battlefield Historian)*

ABOVE Aid station set up under a bridge to provide air cover. The KStN of a 1944 medical company included three platoons: 1 × stretcher-bearer Pl (*Krankenträgerzug*); 2 × field dressing station Pls (*Hauptverbandplatzzüge*; 1 × sterilisation Pl (*Truppenentgiftungszug* – 1 section for bodies, 1 for objects). Total manpower was 222 with 50 horses and very few vehicles. *(Battlefield Historian)*

BELOW Adam Opel AG was bought up by General Motors in 1929 – and was taken over by the Nazis in 1940. Its main asset was the Opel Blitz, of which some 100,000 would be built as general-purpose lorries, radio vehicles and ambulances. They were well-liked in the desert.

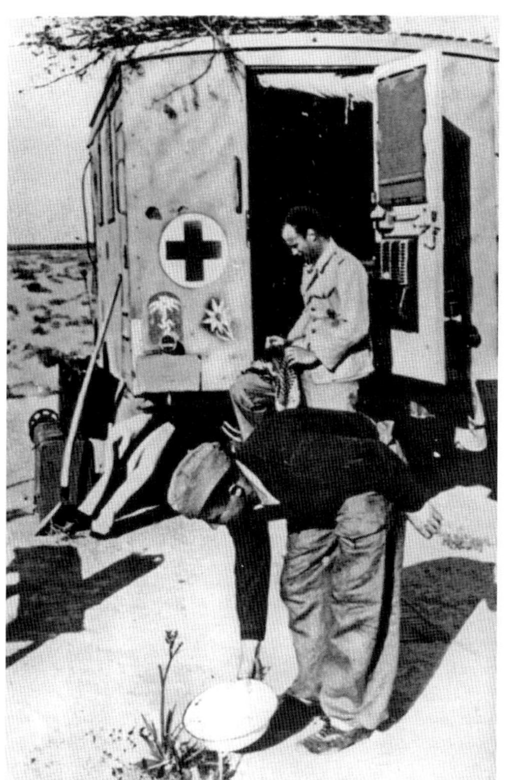

BELOW Diagram showing the casualty evacuation process from battlefield to convalescence in Germany and elsewhere.

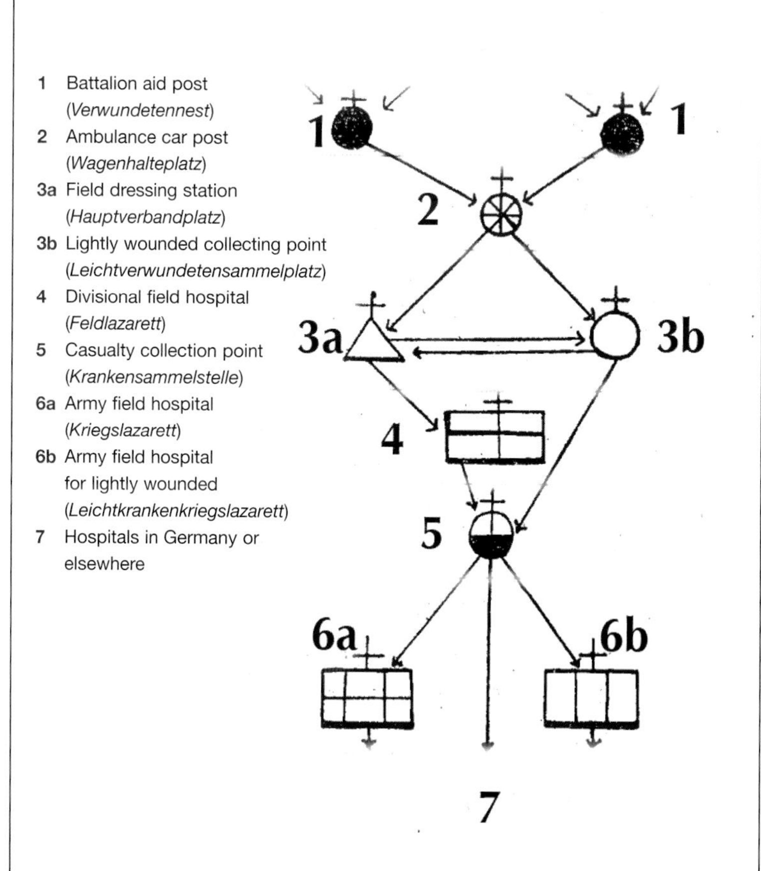

ABOVE Convalescing soldiers pose for a group photograph. *(via RCT)*

BELOW There were various nursing bodies in wartime Germany – such as the German Red Cross (*Deutsches Rotes Kreuz*), freelance nurses (*freie Schwestern*) and auxiliary nurses (*Schwesternhelferinnen*) – as well as an increasing number of male nurses. In spring 1944 over 1,000 members of the RAD/wJ were also transferred to Wehrmacht hospitals as nurses. The closest nurses were supposed to get to the front was in a Kriegslazarett, 50–70km (30–45 miles) away. *(via Tanis)*

Ju52m transport aircraft) were modified to take stretchers – but in the absence of such an aircraft, injured and wounded were taken in any cargo or transport aircraft. This had to be handled carefully because air pressure can affect wounds, forcing unpressurised aircraft to fly at lower altitudes.

Corps

No medical units are allotted at corps level, although various medical units were at the corps medical officer's disposal. This officer supervised directives from the army medical service, the progress of the division medical service and took corrective action as necessary. He moved the medical elements within the division to balance their strength. He could also call upon the army chief medical officer for additional medical units if required.

Army

The army medical unit comprised medical companies, field hospital detachments and ambulance sections.

The medical companies reinforced or relieved those of divisions as required. The field hospital detachments carried out functions similar to those of the division. The ambulance sections were normally employed to evacuate the sick and wounded to casualty collection points set up at railheads, ports and other traffic centres in which the casualties were accommodated while awaiting evacuation to hospitals in the rear.

System of aid to/ evacuation of casualties

Platoon/company aid station (*Verwundetennest*)

First aid to the wounded was rendered initially in a Verwundetennest by a Sanitätsunteroffizier, in an extreme forward position. Here the first dressing, improvised splinting for transportation ease, traction splinting, pressure bandages and tourniquets were applied.

Battalion aid post (*Truppenverbandplatz*)

The wounded were evacuated from the Verwundetennest to the Truppenverbandplatz, where the first medical officer practised. Treatment given at this station included: checking dressings (unless there was some indication the dressing was not to be disturbed); tracheotomy; application of dressings to open chest wounds; pain relief; preparation for further evacuation to the rear; shock therapy; prevention of infection, pressure bandage, and arrest of hemorrhage by application of tourniquet; and catheterisation.

Ambulance car post (*Wagenhalteplatz*)

From the Truppenverbandplatz all the wounded were evacuated by ambulance to either a Hauptverbandplatz or a Leichtverwundetensammelplatz.

Field clearing station (*Hauptverbandplatz*)

Established about 4 miles to the rear of the combat line by the division's Sanitäts Kompanie, this unit was staffed to perform the functions of both clearing and hospitalisation. It had two operating surgeons, but in times of stress six or eight more might be added. The unit was designed to hospitalise 200 patients, but often expanded to 300–400. When the flow of casualties was not heavy, all those patients with abdominal wounds and other non-transportable cases were given primary surgery at this installation. In addition, primary surgery was performed on minor wound cases here. All cases with major compound fractures, brain wounds and chest wounds were evacuated to the Feldlazarett or to a Kriegslazarett, where they were treated with more definitive care. In the German medical field manuals the functions of a Hauptverbandplatz are listed as: tracheotomy; closure of open chest wounds; emergency amputations; final arrest of haemorrhage; administration of blood and blood substitutes; and surgery on the non-transportables.

Lightly wounded collecting station (*Leichtverwundetensammelplatz*)

Each German division had an Ersatz company which served as a replacement depot and reconditioning unit for lightly wounded

LEFT With so much winter warfare – in Norway, Finland and Russia – the German Army produced many suitable manuals. This drawing shows the fireman's carry for casualty evacuation on skis from the German Ski Training and Tactics manual.

BELOW More casualty evacuation techniques for snow: (1) using an akja (a boat-shaped sledge); (2) a skier dragging a casualty; (3) using an akja while under fire; (4) two-man extraction in difficult terrain.

who had received primary surgery at the Hauptverbandplatz. The wounded sent to this Ersatz company were given light exercise under the direction of a doctor, and were ordinarily returned to duty after one week. There were usually between 50 and 100 lightly wounded in the Ersatz company, in addition to the replacements sent from Germany, who only stayed long enough to be equipped before being sent into combat. The officers and the doctor of the Ersatz company were limited service personnel by nature of previous wounds or illness.

Divisional field hospital (*Feldlazarett*)

The next unit in the chain of evacuation, the Feldlazarett, was an army unit designed to care for 200 patients. Ordinarily those with head wounds and transportable patients with chest wounds, severe muscle wounds, buttock wounds, and major compound fractures received primary surgery in the Feldlazarett. While performing intra-abdominal surgery was attempted as far forward as possible, such cases were often evacuated to the Feldlazarett for surgery whenever the Hauptverbandplatz was too busy. The Feldlazarett was staffed with only two surgeons, but in periods of pressure it was often augmented by surgeons from other units.

Casualty collecting station (*Krankensammelstelle*)

Established by an army ambulance unit at a railhead or other traffic centre, normally this was for the retention of casualties awaiting evacuation. Only minor treatment was possible here. From the Krankensammelstelle the patient was taken either to the Kriegslazarett or the Leichtkrankenkriegslazarett.

Army field hospital (*Kriegslazarett*)

The Kriegslazarett was usually assigned to an army group. It was their function to hospitalise all patients who were not returned to duty from the more forward units. In addition, certain groups of the wounded received primary surgery at the Kriegslazarett, such as penetrating head wounds complicated by involvement of the eye or ear, and maxillofacial wounds. In very busy periods, all patients with major wounds might be evacuated to the Kriegslazarett for surgery while the more forward units confined their surgery to men with wounds of such a nature that they would be able to return to their units and full duty within a reasonably short period of time after surgery. Also, as frequently occurred during heavy attack periods, abdominal and head wound cases were given no surgical care.

Army field hospitals for lightly wounded (*Leichtkrankenkriegslazarett*)

In the army areas and in the general hospital centres, hospitals for the lightly sick and wounded were established by elements of transport units (*Krankentransportabteilungen*). They received their patients from Feldlazaretten in the army area and from Kriegslazaretten in the army group area or hospital centres. Most patients sent to these particular hospitals stayed for two or three weeks. One such hospital was located at Bolzano. On 6 May 1945 there were 1,600 patients. The commanding officer reported that 500 would be able to return to duty in two weeks, 600 in one month, 300 in two months, 100 in three months and the remaining 100 in six months.

German war graves

Today, the German War Graves Commission (*Volksbund Deutsche Kriegsgräberfürsorge*) is responsible for the maintenance and upkeep of German war graves in Europe and North Africa. Founded as a private charity on 16 December 1919, during the Second World War the Volksbund's work was mostly carried out by the Wehrmacht's own graves service.

Shortly before the Second World War the National Information Office was opened in Berlin and took up its duties on 26 August 1939 as an Office of the Wehrmacht High Command with the title *Wehrmachtsauskunftstelle* (WASt): the Wehrmacht Information Office for War Losses and POWs. It provided information about foreign POWs, but its main tasks were the registration of German Wehrmacht casualties (wounds, illnesses, deaths, missing in action), the processing of these cases including personal status control and official grave service.

In August 1943 the Wehrmacht Information Office was moved to Thuringia, part of it to Saalfeld and part to Meiningen. From 12 April 1945 onwards, the WASt worked under the supervision of the American Military Commission.

After the war the Volksbund established more than 400 war cemeteries in Germany. Today it looks after 833 war cemeteries and graves in 46 countries – the final resting places of over 2.7 million war casualties.

The cemeteries outside Germany include El Alamein German war cemetery; La Cambe, Andilly and Champigny-Saint-André in France; Sandweiler in Luxembourg and Ysselstyn in the Netherlands; Rossoschka and Sologubovka in Russia; and a number of Allied countries including Cannock Chase in the UK.

ABOVE A field burial in Russia. There were, obviously, a lot of them and many of the graves were lost. Note the specialist badge above the 'Piston Rings' on the sleeve of the Spieß. Most of these badges were worn on the right arm, a few on the upper left (mainly signallers/radio mechanics) and gunners' badges on the lower left. *(via RCT)*

BELOW Crete 1941: a Fallschirmjäger (note Luftwaffe eagle and Fallschirmjäger helmets) and a Gebirgsjäger (note Edelweiß badge) pause for a moment in memoriam.

BELOW The main German Second World War cemetery in Belgium is at Lommel where there are over 39,000 burials. There's a smaller one (shown here) at Recogne near Bastogne with 6,807 burials.

Chapter Eight

Tactics

The Germans excelled at battlefield tactics. While the Allies sat back in the interwar period the Germans trained their NCOs and junior officers to solve battlefield problems themselves. It was just as well they did. After the early war successes, the increasing professionalism of the Allies and Hitler's adoption of total control of military strategy condemned the Wehrmacht to fighting retreats on many fronts. Few armies would have survived as long as they did.

OPPOSITE Truppenführung: the essence of German military command was to tell people what to do but not micromanage and tell them how to do it. Flexibility allied to strong motivation ensured an active approach by all levels of command.

Introduction

In 1933 the Berlin-based *Kriegsakademie* (War Academy) – closed by the Treaty of Versailles – reopened, and between 1935 and 1939 the United States was allowed to send four officers to take part in the courses. These reports led to the publication in 1942 of *German Tactical Doctrine* by the Military Intelligence Service and much of the information in this chapter comes from that publication and *The German Squad in Combat*, published in 1943.

BELOW *Keil und Kessel* (wedge and cauldron) Classic German offensive action. (1) The wedge: with air assistance Panzers and Panzergrenadiers make the breakthrough. (2) The speed of the armoured offensive encircles the enemy. (3) The infantry follows up encircling the enemy. The critical battle ensues with the *attackers* (the Germans) actually *defending* against relief attacks from outside the Kessel and attempts by those trapped inside to break out. (4) Pressure on the Kessel kills or captures the enemy forces.

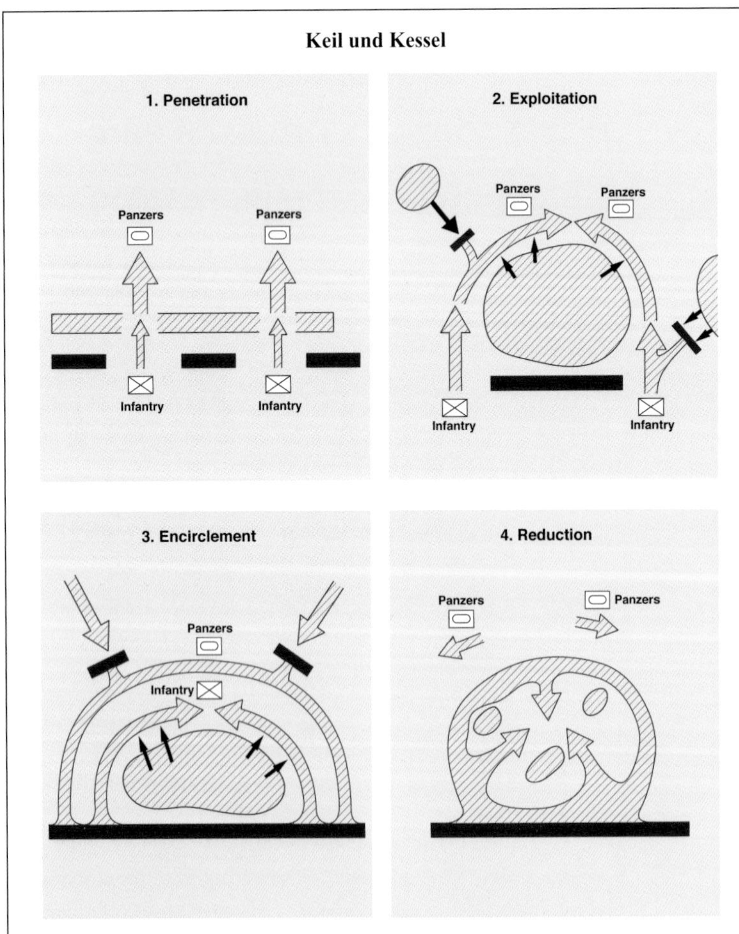

The cornerstone of German military doctrine was the *Truppenführung*, mentioned earlier, which was issued to all officers and senior NCOs. It highlighted an intense education that glorified the military spirit, a highly trained officer corps capable of bold decision making and learning from their opponents. It emphasised the need for subordinates to be self-starters, capable of taking on responsibilities and showing their initiative. Above all, it promoted the aggressive handling of all military operations and the combination of surprise and offensive action to achieve success.

In the attack

The emphasis was always on the attack and counter-attack. Four forms were identified: traditionally the most frequently adopted, the *frontal* attack, needed superiority in strength and modern mechanised/motorised combat provided other options.

As was shown during Operation Barbarossa, the *enveloping* attack was an effective manoeuvre. It had to be employed aggressively but envelopment on both flanks often annihilated the enemy. It was speed of manoeuvre that allowed the German armies to envelop huge swathes of Russia, creating *Kessel* (cauldron) battles – where the German forces had to fight to stop the encircled adversaries fighting out of the pocket at the same time as forces outside sought to penetrate in.

> *As to surprise, the enemy must not be given the time necessary to take countermeasures. As to mass, strength must be concentrated on the flank of the envelopment so that hostile extension of the line can be overrun or circumvented, and hostile defensive moves quickly and effectively frustrated. As to fixing the enemy, the hostile forces in the front must be contained simultaneously with the enveloping attack.*
>
> *German tactical doctrine*

The other two other key forms of attack are *penetration* – an attack to split or separate the hostile line of resistance – and the *limited objective* attack which is intended to win important terrain features, to contain the enemy frontally, or to stop the hostile advance.

Certain general considerations for an attack were reinforced:

a) Obtain unity of command and action; avoid piecemeal attacks.
b) Establish a main effort.
c) Assign narrow zones of action.
d) Reinforce fire by additional artillery and heavy infantry weapons.
e) Coordinate and intensify the fire of all weapons.
f) Make timely employment of tanks and reserves.
g) Exploit successes quickly and fully even though the location of the main effort may have to be changed.
h) Recognise the crisis in a battle and react appropriately. Be alert to every advantage, to each success no matter how small, to any mistakes made by the enemy – and exploit these to the fullest degree. If the attack appears definitely stopped by strong hostile resistance at a certain point, further success may be better accomplished by injecting fresh troops, by concentrating fires on a different area, or by changing the disposition of troops.

While the width of a zone of action depended upon terrain and mission, it was suggested that a battalion of *infantry* with both flanks protected was assigned an area 400–1,000m (roughly 440–1,100yd) wide. The zone for an infantry *division* in a meeting engagement where terrain was favourable for employment of supporting weapons was put at 4,000–5,000m (4,400–5,500yd) wide, although this was reduced to 3,000m (3,281yd) against a strong, hostile position.

Commanders were urged not to include too much detail in an attack order and thus restrict initiative. Specifically, the mission must be clear – what to do – but not how to do it.

All weapons were tasked to enable the infantry to close with the enemy and to drive deep into the enemy position in order to crush all resistance or to annihilate him. This end could be accomplished only if the hostile automatic weapons and artillery were neutralised or destroyed. Coordination between infantry and artillery must at all times and in all situations have been carefully arranged.

The last 100m of an assault was thoroughly indoctrinated into training, as was the desire to destroy the enemy. At short range, close

ABOVE With grenades and machine gun at the ready, an attacking force prepares to go in.

LEFT Firing from the hip in the attack. Ideally the sling would be around the neck and attached to the pistol grip for extra stability and control. Note the AA sight.

PATROLLING

ABOVE LEFT All ready for a patrol, probably in Greece or North Africa, this unit is well armed with hand grenades and rifles. The second man carries a Czech ZB-26 LMG. In German service it was named the MG26(t). It's famous for being the progenitor of the Bren gun. *(via RCT)*

ABOVE A Gebirgsjäger mountain patrol heads up through the snow. Note the Bergmütze field caps, rucksacks, Alpenstocks and climbing ropes. *(via RCT)*

CENTRE A long-distance patrol in Finland from Kurt Kranz's ***Winteralltag im Urwald Lapplands*** (Winter Life in the Lapland Forest). Note the akja – the perfect method of transporting equipment, munitions or food across the snow. *(via RCT)*

LEFT The German Army adopted the akja for use in Russia and identified its use and manufacture in Winter War pamphlets. *(via RCT)*

support was given by 50mm mortars and smoke grenades with flanking bursts from LMGs. Noise, shock, fear and ferocity: all were exploited. Attack combined speed and momentum on a narrow front.

Note that German machine-gun terminology differed to that of the Western Allies being based on usage not calibre. Thus light machine guns used a bipod; heavy a tripod. Indeed, MG34 gunners were trained that, 'If a firing position is not attainable, the LMG should be used during the assault and fired from the hip.' Firing the LMG during movement required the use of the drum magazine, the carrying strap around the neck and shoulders and attached to the pistol grip. This shortened the overall length of the gun as the butt went under the right arm. The left hand held the bipod for better control.

Fire was to be opened at the shortest distance; before beginning to fire, the safety should be released.

Gefechtsaufklärung (battle reconnaissance)

When an opposing force began to deploy, combat patrols were tasked to gather information to provide the basis for the conduct of the battle. For example, a combat patrol using *Gefechtsspähtruppen* or *Stoßtruppen* (assault detachments) commanded by an NCO – usually a sergeant – with some 15 to 20 men divided into two sections, each commanded by a junior NCO. These were raiding patrols and their mission often included snatching a prisoner – an increasingly valuable source of information as the war progressed. The patrol would probably probe an enemy position/outpost and if weakly held would attack and hold the position until relieved by follow-up troops.

The patrol would be armed with MP40s and a number of LMGs to cover an approach or withdrawal with flanking fire, or to cover engineers if attached to clear minefields or clear wire.

There would be artillery support – including mortars – providing harassing fire prior to an assault or as a diversion to mislead the enemy as to where the recce area was.

A *Flammenwerfer* (flamethrower) team might also be attached as could a smoke detail to provide smoke cover.

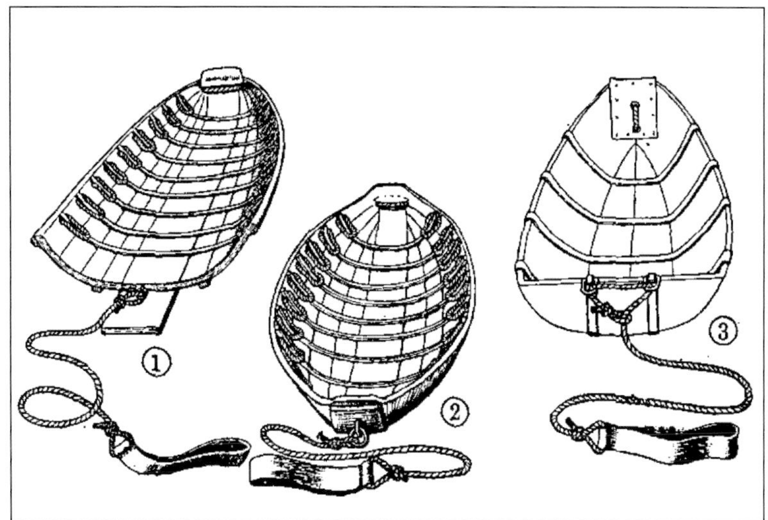

ABOVE Three different types of akja: (1) for weapons; (2) a boat; (3) a light akja.

WHAT A COMBAT PATROL NEEDS TO KNOW

a) Start line: where they have to go to start the mission.
b) Information: what adjacent patrols (if any) are doing.
c) Sector boundaries: direction of operation.
d) Objectives: what is the purpose of the patrol?
e) Phase lines: how far to go at each stage of the mission; gets shorter nearer the objective.
f) Instructions for transmission of reports: how to get information back. Radios were usually too bulky to take patrolling; runners were used or, if sufficient numbers, via the escort of prisoners back to the lines.
g) Location of immediate objectives: to be reported once secured.
h) Instructions regarding air–ground liaison: smoke, ground markers – flags – or as agreed during planning. Less important because there was little German air cover as the war progressed!
i) Timings and route: time of mission and objectives of the main force. Possible route for the main advance.

Squad weapons										
Weapons carried	**Leader**	**MG**	**No 2**	**Ammo**	**R**	**R**	**R**	**R**	**R**	**2I/C**
K98k	✓		✓	✓	✓	✓	✓	✓	✓	✓
MP40 after 1941	✓									
6 × 32-rd mags										
= 192 rd										
MG34 then MG42		✓								
Pistol		✓	✓							
50-rd MG drum		✓								
4 × 50-rd drum			✓							
1 × 300-rd ammo box			✓							
2 × ammo boxes				✓						
9 × clips of 5 rd				✓	✓	✓	✓	✓	✓	✓
= 45 rd										
Extra as needed			✓	✓	✓	✓	✓	✓	✓	✓
2 × grenades				✓	✓	✓	✓	✓	✓	✓

The squad in combat

Note: as the war progressed the principles remained but there were no hard and fast rules.

Role and responsibilities of each member

Squad leader: commanded unit and designated targets for the LMG and rifle fire. Ensured that there was sufficient ammo for the task and that the team's equipment was in good order.

2I/C: took command if squad leader elsewhere or a casualty. Responsible for communication with adjacent squads; vital for coordination.

Machine gunner: responsible for the workings of his gun and – with the help of his No 2 – setting up the gun as commanded.

MG No 2: ensured supply of ammo. To the left of the LMG, he fed the gun, helped clear stoppages and changed the barrel with the spares he carried. He would take control of the LMG if gunner became a casualty or was not available.

Ammo carrier: responsible for the condition of the ammo and refilling the non-disintegrating belts. Stayed to the rear but used his rifle when necessary.

Rest of squad: as commanded with rifle, bayonet or grenade; also acted as ammo carriers for the LMG subject to task.

Formation of squad in a non-hostile environment

The drawings opposite show: (1) close order squad in line (*Reihe*); (2) close order squad in column (*Kette*); (3) march order. Note the MG and No 2 always at the front – the MG was the key member of the squad. Most of the photos of German infantrymen on the march show large numbers of them carrying ammo boxes for the machine gun.

Close order was abandoned if the situation changed – either the terrain or hostile activity.

Formation of squad in a hostile environment

The squad would go into extended order (EO). Spacing was important and there needed to be 3.5m (12ft 6in) between squad individuals. This was a very flexible system and these are only guidelines. During offensive action the squad generally would not act alone, being one of four squads in a platoon.

EO squad column (*Schutzenkette*)

The squad column used the lie of the land to advance, making use of available cover. The 2I/C at the rear ensured that the squad stayed together. When necessary this formation could be easily echeloned to right or left.

SQUAD

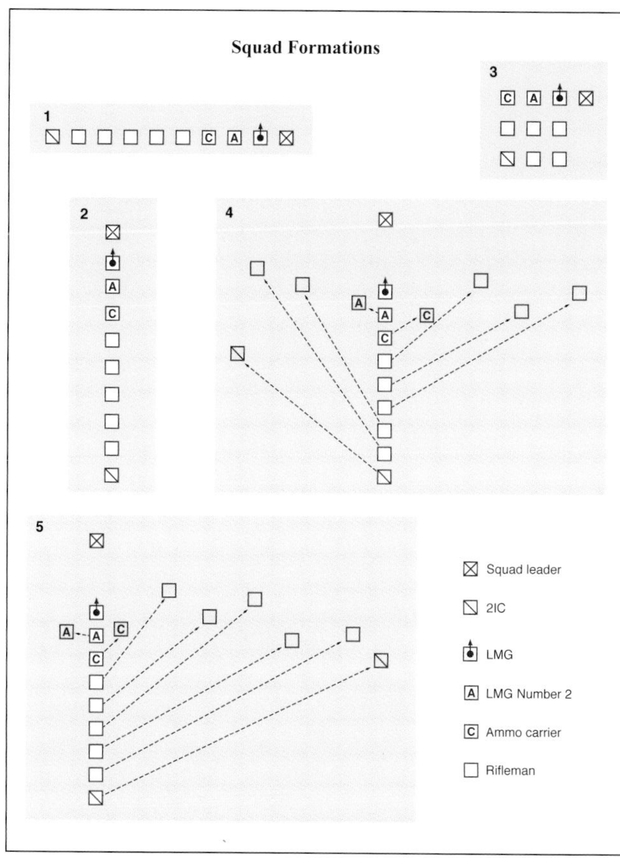

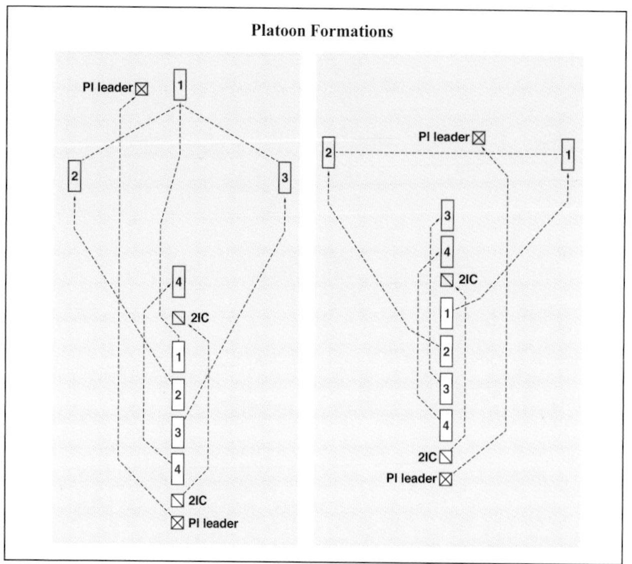

LEFT Various squad formations: (1) in line; (2) in column; (3) in march order; (4) moving from column to skirmish line; (5) moving from column to skirmish line echeloned right.

ABOVE The four-squad platoon moves from column to wedge (left) or broad wedge (right).

RIGHT The key component of the squad was the machine-gun crew – gunner and No 2 who acted as loader, spotter and main ammunition carrier.

BELOW The importance of the machine gun to the squad is emphasised in this well-known photo showing troops in Russia from *Signal* magazine. In the middle is the MG34 gunner carrying his weapon, his right hand grasping the bipod. The three men at left all carry ammunition boxes with a length of wood allowing them to transfer its weight to their backs. The man in front of the machine gunner also carries an ammo box by the same method, along with a spare barrel tube. *(Battlefield Historian)*

Extended order skirmish line (*Schutzenreihe*)

The skirmish line in EO was used if maximum firepower was necessary. From column the MG + No 2 + ammo move forward while the riflemen move to the right × 3 and to the left × 3 (including 2I/C). This formation was dependent on the terrain, which might force a deployment.

The key stages of an attack

Development: First stage in attack – command decides what the company is tasked to do. Each platoon breaks down into four squads of ten men each.

Deployment: Organising troops into combat formation, squad leader receives orders.

Advancing: Squad designated to lead advances knowing that, as they do so, MG fire or other weapons will cover either flank. If/when the squad comes under effective fire (*ie* when the squad starts to take casualties) it needs to use its own firepower. Fire and movement (manoeuvre) are used to get to a position to start suppressing the hostile fire to allow the rest of the squad to move forward. Areas covered by enemy fire (artillery etc) needed to be crossed in quick rushes if this cannot be avoided. Rush, fire, rush to the attack line.

Attack: Advancing and firing on the enemy was a continuation of the advance, although firing took place only when necessary. It was supported by artillery, heavy MGs and infantry support artillery. These weapons concentrated on the destruction or neutralisation of strongpoints. It was not the task of the rifleman to engage in a firefight of long duration in order to gain fire superiority (supporting arms are tasked to do this). It was the shock power of the rifleman with bayonet which would overcome the enemy.

BELOW **An MG34 in the defensive role behind a wooden revetment.** *(via RCT)*

Penetration: Final stage, initiated about 100m from the objective, where the whole group rushed and fired as a unit. Ideally the platoon leader directed his squads to attack from various directions to cause the enemy fire to be scattered. This was now a platoon attack. In German training, particular emphasis was placed on infiltration tactics round flanks and between individual defensive positions to encircle and squeeze out those positions singly.

It was vital that maximum fire was used in an assault. The LMGs should find a position to directly engage the enemy to allow the attack to succeed. If not able to, then they should be part of the assault by firing from the hip and if possible support the attack from another direction, assisted by neighbouring units. Once suppressive fire had achieved its aim, the infantry follow up using grenades. Under command of their squad leader they cleared the objective.

Squad leaders would then prepare for counter-attacks. The Germans were known for counter-attacking and always expected their enemies to do so. Their defensive plan was to identify when the counter-attack was coming, delay it through the deployment first of advanced positions and then an outpost line, and destroy the oncoming enemy by an increasing weight of fire before launching their own, immediate, counter-attack.

Infantry in the defence

One section of *The German Squad in Combat* concentrated on the defence, emphasising organisation in depth, security of flanks and the use of suitable ground so that inferior forces could stop superior numbers. It was a lesson that the German Army put to great effect in Normandy and on the Eastern Front.

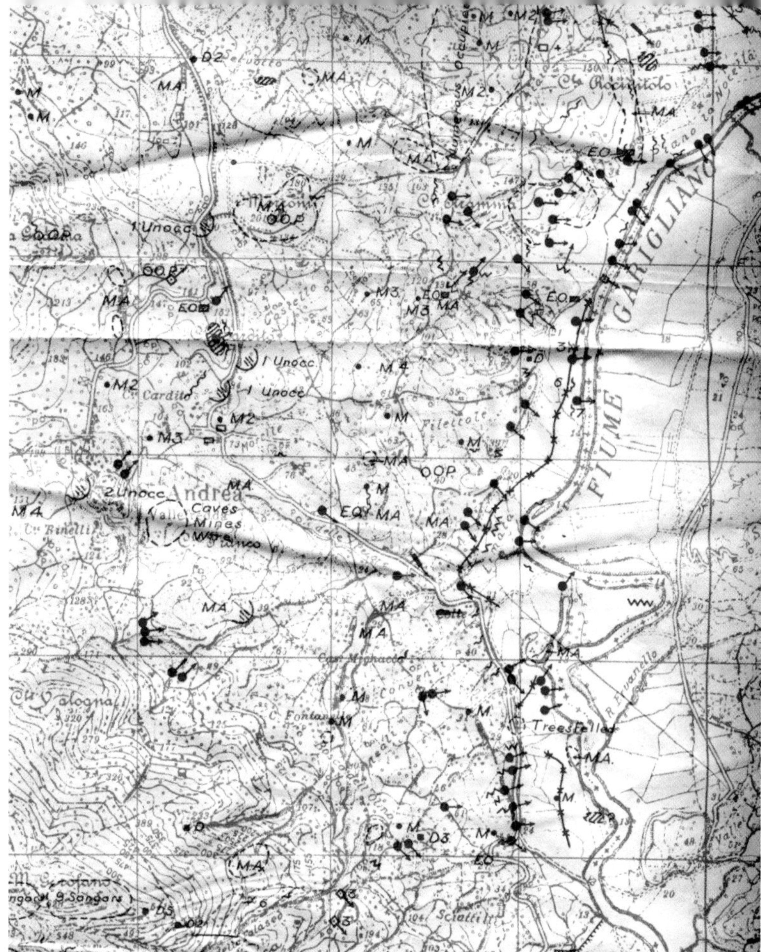

RIGHT **A US Fifth Army map of the German defences on the River Garigliano, near Monte Cassino, with a British overlay dated 2 May 1944. Part of the Gustav Line, the Garigliano was assaulted and crossed as part of Operation Diadem, the fourth battle of Cassino. M = mortars; MA = military activity.** *(via RCT)*

Anti-tank gun defences

The German infantry became adept at siting its anti-tank weapons in the optimum positions during the long months of retreat on the Eastern Front. They had learnt from painful experience that distributing these weapons piecemeal in small packets didn't work. Neither did their preferred option of an immediate counter-attack. What did work in the face of Soviet dominance was defence in depth – a tactic that also performed well against the British and Canadian assaults south of Caen.

The key thing was to group anti-tank guns to cover specific killing zones, which could ambush an enemy that had been channelled into their field of fire. The first line of defence was an advanced position some 4,570m (5,000–7,000yd) in front of the main line of defence, within range of medium artillery. This line was intended to damage recce detachments and thus delay an attack.

The second line was a line of outpost positions some 1,820m (2,000–5,000yd) in front of the main line of defence. It was to this line that the advanced forces retreated. Heavily camouflaged, the anti-tank weapons here were ideally in enfilade.

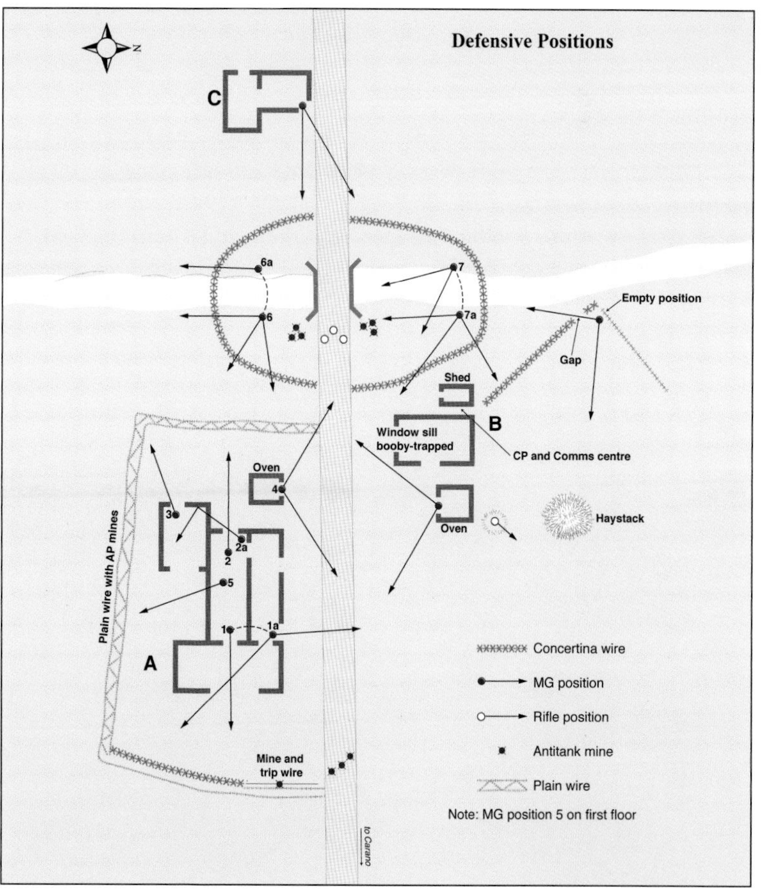

RIGHT **A German position in the Anzio area showing how destroyed buildings were used in the defence. Two platoons – 50–80 men – covered a bridge over a stream. The defenders were grouped into three locations: *House A* had three machine guns inside the house hidden from sight so that muzzle flash was concealed. MG at position 4 was inside an external oven and protected against small-arms fire. Position 5 on the first floor was taken by a soldier armed with an MP40. *House B*: with the command and communications posts, there was an MG34 in the external oven and a rifleman dug in to protect its back. The bridge was defended by two machine guns behind wire, one on each side of the river.**

DEFENSIVE POSITIONS

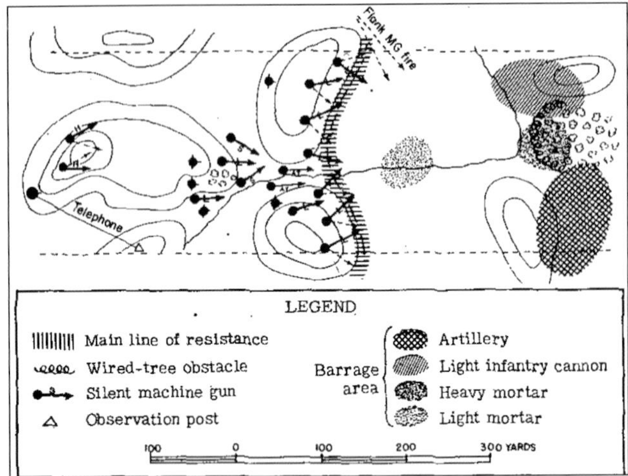

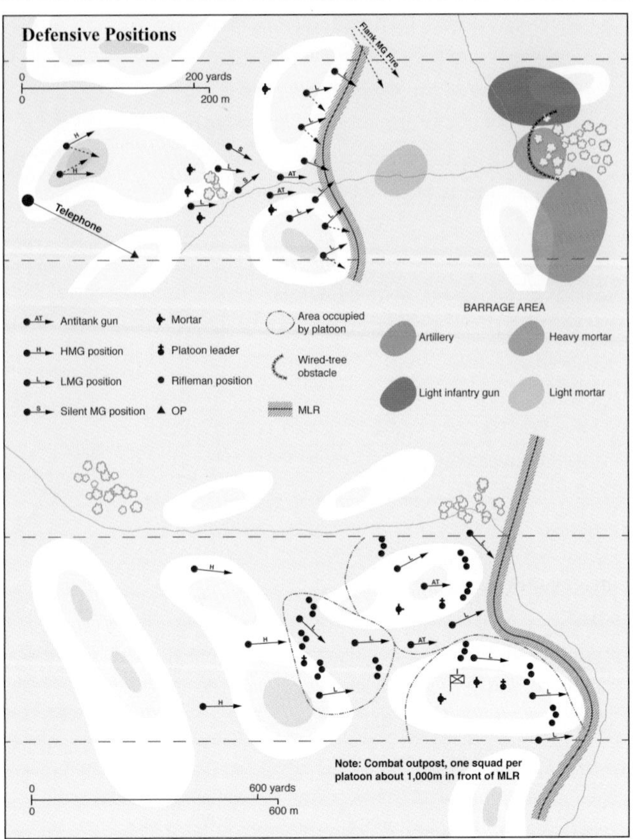

ABOVE The importance of coordination of fire in the defence – emphasising good communications, interlocking fields of fire, the use of mortars and artillery and the importance of isolated silent machine guns that only participate with surprise fire if the enemy look as if they will overrun the position.

RIGHT The organisation of a rifle company in the defence: individual strongpoints whose combined fire breaks up enemy attacks. If any section of the line is taken, counter-attacks must retake them. In the defence, the position must be held to the last man. There must be no withdrawal.

ANTI-TANK

BELOW A typical end-of-war scene: youngsters – barely teenagers – move off to defend the Reich armed with Panzerfaust anti-tank weapons. The era of the mass-produced one-time weapon had arrived and it could be fired, literally, by anyone.

ANTI-TANK EMPLACEMENT

BELOW A more traditional anti-tank gun emplacement with crew and ammunition dugouts and overhead camouflage to lessen air attack or observation. The only drawback to the 8.8cm Flak/anti-tank gun was its height. Digging in reduced this.

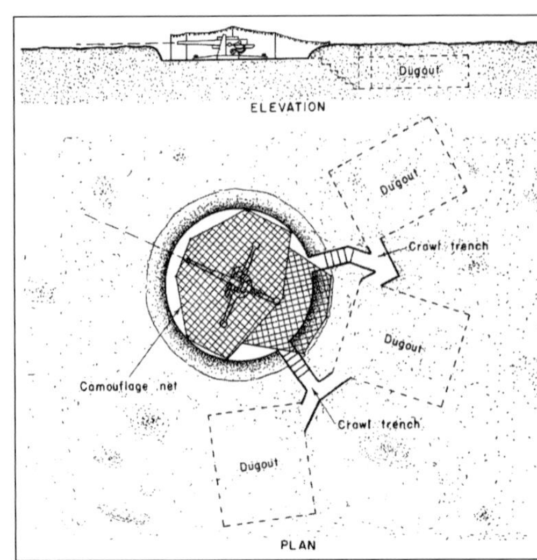

STREET DEFENCE

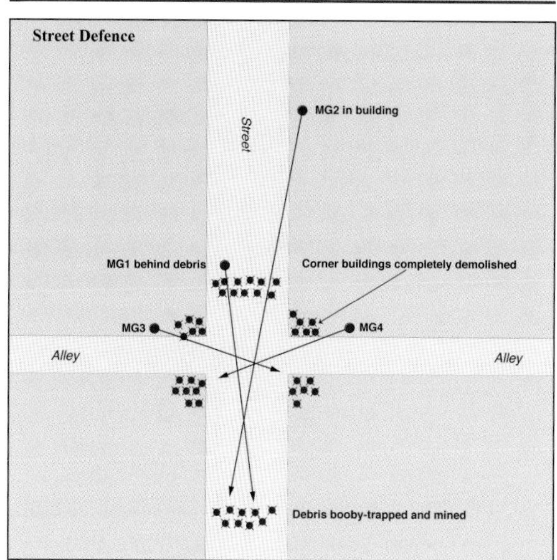

ABOVE Typical defensive position at an intersection of street and alley as taken from the defence of Ortona. Demolished buildings created debris obstacles – all mined with S-mines and Tellermines – and anti-tank guns reduced tank support. These channelled the Canadian troops into a killing ground where machine guns had been carefully sited. As the Canadians advanced, they had to take each building: often when they did, pre-positioned demolition charges were fired. 'It was only by attacking with the greatest determination that we were able to win these areas from the enemy and, by so doing, eventually complete the occupation of Ortona.'

ABOVE The siege of Budapest lasted for seven weeks, 24 December 1944–13 February 1945. The death toll was huge with over 39,000 German and Hungarian soldiers and 38,000 civilians killed. Huge swathes of the city were destroyed in the fighting.

The main line of defence was a line of strongly fortified positions with all-round defence, deploying mines, barbed wire, heavy weapons, MGs, mortars and infantry. Wherever possible, maximum use was made of reverse slopes.

If small groups of the enemy broke through, they had to be destroyed immediately. Box barrages placed in their rear precluded their withdrawal, allowing rear defences to stop them. If, however, a larger breakthrough took place, the commander of the defensive force had a difficult decision: whether to shift position or counter-attack. If the latter, all weapons needed to be carefully coordinated, a limited objective was assigned, and air and tank support provided.

SQUAD DEFENSIVE POSITION

Two layouts for a squad defensive position.

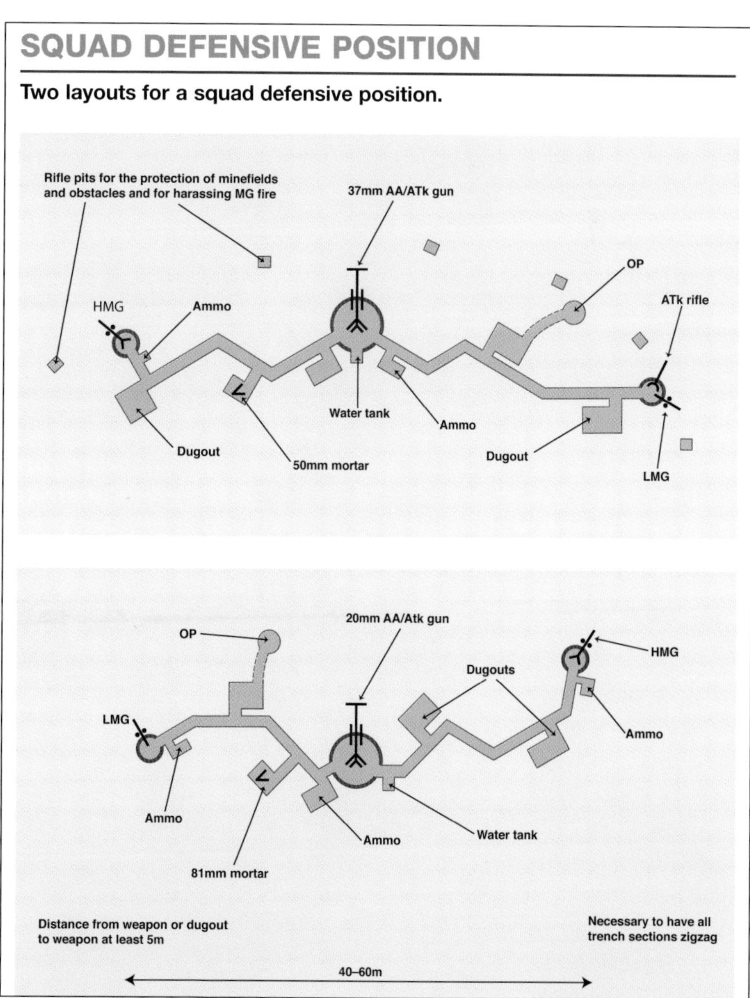

Sniping

The main German sniping weapon issued in the Second World War was the K98k bolt-action rifle, which was well known for its accuracy and long-range shooting capabilities. They were issued in tens of thousands, and were used with good effect in every theatre of war that German snipers fought in.

Some G43 semi-automatic rifles were also issued for sniping but in much smaller numbers than the K98k. The gas-operated G43 had its receiver machined to accept a telescope sight mount, in addition to the standard adjustable open sights. Feed was from ten-round detachable box magazines. The G43 had good mid-range accuracy, but as a sniping rifle it wasn't ideal for targets at more than 400yd or so. Where it did score well was in fairly close engagements against multiple targets, because its speed of fire – combined with the sniper's skill – could prove devastating in breaking up enemy attacks.

RIGHT A Fallschirmjäger patrol in Crete, with a sniper in the lead. The scope on his Mauser K98k looks like a ZF39. Note the distinctive K98 ammo bandolier he carries and the Fallschirmjäger helmets.

Many different scope-and-mount combinations were used with the K98k, including a variety of commercial (sporting) scopes from Ajak, Hensoldt, Kahles, Zeiss and other manufacturers. These were usually of excellent optical quality and were probably some of the best in the world at the time. Magnification was usually 4× but some 6× models were also made. Model designations were ZF (*Zielfernrohr*) followed by the year of introduction – ZF39 and so on – except the ZF4 (in this case the 4 standing for 4×), which was originally designed for the G43 semi-automatic rifle.

The ZF41 extended eye relief scope had a magnification of only 1.5×, and was used almost like a point sight aiming aid rather than a true sniping scope. It was mounted to standard K98k rifles and was issued to what we might call today designated marksmen; in other words the recipients were good shots, but not usually trained snipers, although combat experience would soon educate them, if they survived. The ZF41 was mounted well forward of the action; the user would acquire the target by direct sight (not using the scope) and would then draw a quick bead with the scope. It worked well at close to medium range as a personal and support weapon, and was also no doubt used in a sniping role by ordinary soldiers, as were iron-sighted standard-issue K98k rifles for that matter.

The most common scope mounts were quick-release, side-mounting models – early pre-war versions were short and fitted to a dovetail machined into the left-hand side of the K98k receiver, while post-1943 models were longer and fitted to a dovetail base screwed on to a flat surface machined on to the receiver. In addition, single claw, double claw and turret mounts were also used.

The ZF4 was an attempt to standardise and mass-produce a telescopic sight, originally being made for the G43, but later being issued for K98ks and other rifles. Although it was a reasonably good design, by the time production was under way the quality was dropping because of the extensive damage being caused by Allied air raids to manufacturing plant, skilled workmen and raw material supplies.

Unlike most other scopes of the period, the ZF4 had the elevation turret on the right, with windage on the top. The three-post reticle was not optically centred; therefore, like the Russian PU, it would actually move across (or up/down) the sight picture when adjusted for zero.

Zielfernrohr K98k

Specially selected K98ks were fitted with an optical sight.

Type: Zf41 telescopic sight
Magnification: 1.5×
Number manufactured: 100,000 by Zeiss among others
Introduced: 1941
Production: Up to 1945.

As far as the Western Allies were concerned, German sharpshooters came to the fore in Normandy, where battle-hardened veterans made use of every advantage of cover that the bocage countryside afforded them. They went after the officers first; without identification by badge of rank they'd pick off the men with field glasses, a pistol rather than a rifle or SMG, or with a map – even a moustache because the man with one was more likely to be an officer or senior NCO. Other priorities were vehicle commanders, signallers, gun crew, observers and so on.

In Normandy they targeted crossroads, bridges and the narrow lanes. They dug in well under hedges, in deserted buildings, church steeples, towers – anywhere that gave them a good shooting position.

Patrick Fahey quotes Josef 'Sepp' Allerberger, the second most prolific German sniper:

> *I would bide my time until the next four waves were on their way towards our lines, then open up rapid fire into the two rear waves, aiming for the stomach. The unexpected casualties at the rear, and the terrible cries of the most seriously wounded, tended to collapse the rear lines and so disconcert the two leading ranks that the whole attack would begin to falter.*

In fact the Russian snipers outclassed the Germans and so the latter set up training schools. Allerberger had 257 confirmed kills; Matthias Hetzenauer, 345.

In an interview for the Austrian *Truppendienst* magazine in 1967, Hetzenauer, Allerberger and Helmut Wirnsberger (another German sniper who had served on the Eastern Front) answered questions on their weapons and methods. All had used scoped K98k rifles and all claimed accuracy of 400m (437yd) for a head shot, the same for a chest shot and 600m (656yd) or more in one case for a standing man – but overall success rates were approximately 65–80% at 400m and 20–30% at 600m, and most successful shots were taken closer than 400m. Hetzenauer and Wirnsberger had also used the semi-auto G43 rifle with a four-power scope, but found that it was not as accurate or reliable as the K98k.

When asked about successful use of snipers, Hetzenauer answered that the best success for snipers did not reside in the number of hits, but in the damage caused to the enemy by shooting commanders or other important men. This sound judgement was proven time and again by German snipers, who found that removing officers and NCOs – thereby depriving the Soviet advance of their leadership – could be extremely effective when many of the Russians were raw recruits, in some cases being 'driven' by political commissars. All three interviewees agreed that defence was the sniper's best strategic use. When asked what qualities (other than marksmanship) made the best snipers, they all answered in different ways, but it basically boiled down to patience, perseverance, observation and good tactical judgement.

GERMAN 'SNIPERS CODE', 1944

1 Fight fanatically.
2 Shoot calm and contemplated; fast shots lead nowhere; concentrate on the hit.
3 Your greatest opponent is the enemy sniper; outsmart him.
4 Always only fire one shot from your position; if not you will be discovered.
5 The trench tool prolongs your life.
6 Practice in distance judging.
7 Become a master in camouflage and terrain usage.
8 Practise constantly, behind the front and in the homeland, your shooting skills.
9 Never let go of your sniper rifle.
10 Survival is ten times camouflage and one time firing.

Appendix 1

Abbreviations, German words and designations

German words are used in preference to translations. Please note the following German spellings of locations: Braunschweig (Brunswick, Hannover (Hanover, Köln (Cologne, München (Munich and Nürnburg (Nuremburg. In German nouns are always capitalised and I have followed that example.

The use of the *Eszett* symbol – ß – in German writing has changed since the Second World War. Today, since the orthographic changes of 1996, it isn't used after short vowels (*eg Küss* = kiss even if it ends a word. In the past, it was always used for double ss at the end of the word.

Transliteration – especially of Russian names – is different in English and German. For example, we'd call it Demyansk; the Germans Demjansk. Vladimir is Wladimir in German.

German terms will be italicised on first mention in the book, and set in roman thereafter.

Abbreviation	German	English
Abt	*Abteilung*	detachment or battalion
Ausb	*Ausbildungs*	training
Bde	*Brigade*	brigade
bo	*bodenständige*	static as in static division or unit
Btl	*Bataillon*	battalion
d	*der*	the or of
Div	*Division*	division
DivNr	*Division Nummer*	replacement and training division
DivStb	*Divisionstab*	division administrative staff
DivStb zbV	*Divisionstab zbV*	division special administrative staff
Ers	*Ersatz*	replacement
ErsH	*Ersatzheer*	Replacement (or Home Army
Fld	*Feld*	field
Fld-Ers	*Feldersatz*	field replacement
Fu	*Funkgerät*	radio equipment
Geb	*Gebirgs*	mountain
Gren	*Grenadier*	grenadier
HGrp	*Heeresgruppe*	army group
HIG	*Hohlladungs-Granate*	hollow charge grenade
Igr	*Infanteriegranate*	shell fired by an infantry gun
Inf	*Infanterie*	infantry
Jag	*Jäger*	hunter/rifleman
Kdr	*Kommandeur*	commander
Kdr d ErsTrpn	*Kommandeur der Ersatztruppen*	Commander of Replacement Troops
Kdr d PzTrpn	*Kommandeur der Panzertruppen*	Commander of Armoured Troops

Abbreviation	German	English
Kdr d SchnTrpn	*Kommandeur der Schnellen Truppen*	Commander of Fast (mobile) Troops
KGrp	*Kampfgruppe*	battle group
KStN	*Kriegsstärkenachweisungen*	war establishment or TO&E
Ldschtz	*Landesschützen*	local militia
le IG	*leichte Infanterie-Geschütz*	light infantry gun
Luft	*Luftwaffe*	German Air Force
(mot	*Motorisiert*	motorised
Pz	*Panzer*	armoured
PzGr	*Panzergrenadier*	armoured infantry
RAD	*Reichsarbeitsdienst*	Reich Labour Service
	Reiter	rider, cavalryman, mounted
Regt	*Regiment*	regiment
ResDiv	*Reserve Division*	reserve (training) division
RM	*Reichsmark*	German currency
Schn	*Schnellen*	fast
sFH	*schwere Feld Haubitze*	heavy field howitzer
Stb	*Stab*	staff
Trpn	*Truppen*	troops
u	*und*	and
VG	*Volksgrenadier*	'People's' infantry
WehrBef	*Wehrmachtsbefehlshaber*	Armed Forces Commander
Wkr	*Wehrkreis*	military district
zbV	*zur besonderen Verwendung*	for special purposes

Weapons: abbreviations and notes	
Weapons with a calibre under 20mm were classed as small arms and measured in mm. Higher than 20mm, the calibre was measured in cm – so, 8.8cm rather than 88mm.	
AP	armour-piercing
APCBC	armour-piercing, capped, ballistic cap
APCR	armour-piercing, composite rigid
G/Gew	*Gewehr* (rifle
HE	high explosive
HEAT	high-explosive anti-tank
Pak	*Panzerabwehrkanone* (anti-tank gun
Patr	*Patrone* (cartridge
Pzgr	*Panzergranate* (armour-piercing – *Gewehr Panzergranate* (GPzgr = rifle grenade
Schr	*Schrapnell* (shrapnel
Sprgr	*Sprenggranate* (HE round – *Gewehrsprenggranate* (GSprgr = rifle grenade
Üb	Übung (exercise, practice inert
Zerl	*Zerlegung* (self-destructing
German Panzergranate (anti-tank shells used the following designations:	
Pzgr	early AP shell, probably Pzgr 18
Pzgr 39	AP shell
Pzgr 39-1	improved AP shell
Pzgr 40/41/42	APCR shell variants
Pzgr 43	AP shell replacing APCR after tungsten supplies ran out
Pzgr 44/45	APDS shell

Appendix 2

Comparative ranks

German Army	Waffen-SS	US Army	British
	Reichsführer-SS		
Generalfeldmarschall		General of the Army	Field Marshal
Generaloberst	SS-Oberstgruppenführer	General	General
General der Artillerie, Infanterie,	SS-Obergruppenführer	Lieutenant General	Lieutenant General
Kavallerie, Panzertruppen			
Generalleutnant	SS-Gruppenführer	Major General	Major General
Generalmajor	SS-Brigadeführer	Brigadier General	Brigadier
	SS-Oberführer		
Oberst	SS-Standartenführer	Colonel	Colonel
Oberstleutnant	SS-Obersturmbannführer	Lieutenant Colonel	Lieutenant Colonel
Major	SS-Sturmbannführer	Major	Major
Hauptmann	SS-Hauptsturmführer	Captain	Captain
Rittmeister		Captain (Cavalry)	
Oberleutnant	SS-Obersturmführer	1st Lieutenant	1st Lieutenant
Leutnant	SS-Untersturmführer	2nd Lieutenant	2nd Lieutenant
Stabsfeldwebel	SS-Sturmscharführer	Warrant Officer	Regimental Sergeant Major
Oberfeldwebel	SS-Hauptscharführer	Master Sergeant	Sergeant Major
Feldwebel	SS-Oberscharführer	Staff Sergeant	Company Sergeant Major
Unterfeldwebel	SS-Scharführer		Sergeant
Unteroffizier	SS-Unterscharführer	Sergeant	Sergeant
Stabsgefreiter			
Obergefreiter		Corporal	Corporal
Gefreiter	SS-Rottenführer	Lance Corporal	Lance Corporal
	SS-Sturmmann		
Obergrenadier	SS-Oberschütze		
Oberschütze		Private First Class (Pfc)	
Schütze, Grenadier, Jäger, etc.	SS-Schütze	Private	Private

Bibliography and sources

Articles

Hartleben, Lt Col. H. 'The Organization of the Medical Service of the German Army and its Employment in the Campaign against Poland', *Military Review*, September 1940 (www.feldgrau.com).

Johannes, Jeff and Nash, Doug (ed. and additional info). 'German Rations at the Front: A Snapshot of What the German Soldier Consumed during the Battle of the Bulge' (www.dererstezug.com).

Nash, Doug. 'German "Iron" Rations (*eiserne Portionen*)' (via www.dererstezug.com).

Reid, Andy. 'German Anti-Tank Weapons, Shell Types and Armour Penetration Capabilities' (www.miniatures.de/anti-tank-weapons-german.html).

Salt, John D. *WW2 Penetration Figures* via http://mr-home.staff.shef.ac.uk/hobbies/ww2pen3.pdf.

Tobey, Eric and Bocek, Jonathan. 'The German Army "K-Ration"' (www.dererstezug.com).

Publications

Beiersdorf, Horst. *Bridgebuilding Equipment of the Wehrmacht 1939–1945* (Schiffer, 1998).

Bull, Dr. Stephen. *World War II Infantry Tactics*: *Company and Battalion* (Osprey, 2005).

Bull, Dr. Stephen. *World War II Infantry Tactics: Squad and Platoon* (Osprey, 2004).

Davies, W.J.K. *German Army Handbook* (Ian Allan, 1973).

Davis, Brian L. *Badges & Insignia of the Third Reich 1933–1945* (Arms & Armour Press, 1992).

Davis, Brian L. *German Army Uniforms and Insignia 1933–1945* (Brockhampton Press, 1971).

Ellis, John. *The World War II Databook* (BCA, 1993).

Forty, George. *German Infantryman at War 1939–1945* (Ian Allan Ltd, 2002).

Handbook of the German Army, 1940 (IWM and The Battery Press Inc., 1996).

Handbook on German Army Identification (Washington, 1943).

Hogg, Ian and Weeks, John. *Military Smallarms of the Twentieth Century* (BCE, 1974).

Hogg, Ian V. *German Artillery of World War II* (Greenhill Books, 2002).

Intelligence Bulletin, Vol. II No. 11 (Washington, 1944).

Intelligence Bulletin, Vol. II No. 12 (Washington, 1944).

Kershaw, Robert. *War without Garlands: Operation Barbarossa 1941/42* (Ian Allan, 2000).

Koch, Fred. *Flamethrowers of the German Army 1914–1945* (Schiffer, 1997).

Lucas, James. *German Army Handbook: 1939–1945* (Chancellor Press, 1998).

Lucas, James. *War on the Eastern Front: The German Soldier in Russia 1941–1945* (Jane's Publishing, 1979).

Lumsden, Robin. *A Collector's Guide to Third Reich Militaria* (Ian Allan Ltd, 1987).

Medawar, Jean and Pyke, David. *Hitler's Gift. Scientists Who Fled Nazi Germany* (Piatkus, 2001).

Military Intelligence Special Series. *4 German Motorized Infantry Regiment* (Washington, 1942).

Military Intelligence Special Series. *9 The German Squad in Combat* (Washington, 1943).

Military Intelligence Special Series. *14 German Infantry Weapons* (Washington, 1943).

Military Intelligence Special Series. *20 German Ski Training and Tactics* (Washington, 1944).

Military Intelligence Special Series. *21 German Mountain Warfare* (Washington, 1944).

Milsom, John and Chamberlain, Peter. *German Armoured Cars of World War Two* (Arms & Armour Press, 1974).

Milsom, John. *German Military Transport of World War Two* (BCE, 1975).

Nafziger, George F. *The German Order of Battle: Infantry in World War II* (Greenhill Books, 2000).

Norris, John. *Infantry Mortars of World War II* (Osprey, 2002).

Oliver, Tony. *German Motorcycles of World War II* (Almark, 1978).

Oswald, Werner. *Kraftfahrzeuge und Panzer der Reichswehr, Wehrmacht und Bundeswehr* (Motorbuch Verlag, 1975).

Pocket Book of the German Army 1943 (War Office, 1943).

Sáiz, Agustín. *Deutsche Soldaten* (Casemate, 2008).

Technical Manual TM-E 11-227. German Radio Communication Equipment (War Department, June 1945).

Technical Manual TM-E 30-451. Handbook on German Military Forces (War Department, 15 March 1945).

Thomas, Nigel and Caballero Jurado, Carlos. *Wehrmacht Auxiliary Forces* (Osprey, 1992).

Williamson, Gordon. *Afrikakorps 1941–43* (Osprey, 1991).

Williamson, Gordon. *Gebirgsjäger* (Osprey, 2003).

Windrow, Martin. *The Waffen-SS* (Osprey, 1982).

Wray, Maj. Timothy A. *Standing Fast: German Defensive Doctrine on the Russian Front during the Second World War* (Fort Leavenworth, 1983).

Websites

There are a number of excellent websites looking at the German armed forces of the Second World War. I can recommend:

https://forum.axishistory.com
http://www.lexikon-der-wehrmacht.de
http://www.dererstezug.com.

This site has various books and pamphlets online:
http://www.lonesentry.com.

Index

Afrika Korps 35, 86-87
Ardennes Offensive 18, 38, 81, 146
Arnhem landings and bridge 10, 23, 35
Austro-Hungarian Empire break-up 29

Battle of the Bulge 54, 136
Beer Hall Putsch 28, 44
Belgrade Museum 130
Berlin Treaty 1926 27
Blitzkrieg 8, 27, 144
Brown Shirts (Sturmabteilung) (SA) 44
  flag consecration ceremony 44
  SA Military Training Defence Group 44

Camouflage 36, 83-84
  patterns 84
  smocks 84
  winter 85
Casualties (losses) 9
  civilians 9
  convalescing soldiers 156
  evacuation 142, 152, 154-158
  field burials 159
  German 7, 9-10, 29, 31-32, 40-41, 45
Cemeteries and graves 158-159
Chemical weapons 82
Communications 145
  Enigma codes and machines 145-146
  field telephones (FeldFu and TomFu) 147-148
  phonetic alphabets 146
  radio 146-149

D-Day 9-10
Defences
  Atlantic Wall 22
  Ostwall 22
  Westwall 21

Education and schooling 13-23, 33
  expulsion of teaching staff 14-15
  Göttingen University 14
  Hitler Youth (Hitlerjugend) (HJ) 15, 19, 21, 43
    drum and bugle corps 15
    SS-Panzer Division 16
    war duties 16
  Minister of Science, Education and National Culture 15
  National Political Institution of Teaching (Napola) 17
  National Socialist Teachers League (NSLB) 15
  Nazi curriculum 15
  NS-Ordensburgen 17-18
  Reichs Leadership Schools 17
  Special schools 16-18
    Adolf Hitler Schools 17-18
  Women's education and role 18-19
    AA guncrew 19
    Bund Deutscher Mädel (BDM) 18-19
    Jungmädel (Young Girls) section 19
    number attending universities 18
    Work, Faith and Beauty Society 19
Executions for desertion 10

Fascist organisation in Northern Europe 19
First World War 7, 27, 29, 49, 82, 125
French Army 31

German Army organisation 11, 32-41
  divisions 11, 36-41
  engineers 22
  Fallschirmjäger (paratroop divisions) 37, 40-41, 47, 62, 64-65, 89, 91, 159
    battle drops 40
  Field Army (Feldheer) 32, 35-36, 47
  Gebirgsjäger mountain infantry 39-40, 89=91, 164
  infantry divisions 37-38
  Kriegsmarine land units 41
  Luftwaffefelddivisionen 41, 62
  Panzergenadier divisions 38-39, 52, 71, 77, 81
  regiments 11
  Replacement Training Army (Ersatzheer) 32-35, 38, 45, 47
  shadow divisions 35
  unit nomenclature 36

German Army soldiers
  conscription 23, 28, 33, 43-45
    drafting (Aushebung) 44
  construction troops (Bautruppen) 22-23
  discharged 52
  enlisted 61
  facial hair 49
  generals 62
  goosestep marching 47
  Hauptfeldwebel 61
  hygiene 70, 77
  inducted (Einstellung) 44
  Landser nickname 11
  life in the field 52-55
    bodily functions 55
    Feldpost system 55
    food and rations 52-54
    mess kit 54
  men serving 7, 45
  mobilisation waves 45-46
  NCOs 10, 28, 33, 47-49, 59, 61, 71
  officers 10, 33, 48-49, 62
  personal documentation 50-52
    Erkennungsmarke identity disc (dogtag) 51-52
    Soldbuch 51-52
    Wehrpaß 50, 52
  recruitment 28
  registration (Musterung) 44
  retreating 10
  training 28, 33, 37, 43, 47-49
    drill 47
    in Russia 27
    weapons 47-48, 70
German High Command 27
German invasions and occupations 30-31
  Austria 29
  Belgium 37
  Bohemia 30
  Channel Islands 41
  Crete 31, 37, 41, 64, 83-84, 89, 159
  Czechoslovakia 21, 30, 33
  Denmark 31
  Finland 32

France 8, 31, 37
Free City of Danzig 30
Greece 32, 37, 41
Holland 37, 41
Hungary 30
Low Countries 8, 31
Moravia 30
Norway 8, 31, 37
Poland 8, 23, 27, 30-31, 33, 38, 99
Russia 7-9, 11, 32, 37, 164
Sudentenland 21, 29, 33
Yugoslavia 31, 37
German Labour Service (DAP) 17, 43
German population growth 30
German Trades Union (AGDB) 17
Great Depression 19

Hyperinflation 19

Imperial German Army 27
Truppenamt 27
Italian attack of the Balkans 31

Jews 14-15, 21, 44

Kriegsmarine (German Navy) 41
personnel 65

League of Nations 30
Luftwaffe 23, 31, 37, 41, 62, 64, 89, 143
Luftwaffe-Flakhelfe 23

Maginot Line 31
Medals and badges 16, 27 59, 64-69, 159
Army proficiency badges 67-68
campaign shields 67
decorations 66
Knights Cross 9, 62
marksmanship lanyard 65, 68
Pour le Mérite 62
trades and specialist badges 66-67
Medical services 151-159
aid stations and field hospitals 155-158
armbands 152-153
battalion doctors 152-153
divisional field hospitals 153
equipment 153
examination 44
medical companies 153-154, 156
officers 62
pouches 153
training 152
268th Infantry Division medical units 154
Military districts of Germany (Wehrkreise) 33-34
Molotov-Ribbentrop Pact 1939 27
Munich Agreement 30

National Socialism 14-16
National Socialist Labour Service (NSAD) 21
Nazi Party (NSDAP) 10, 15, 17
eagle and swastika 58
rise to power 15, 26
Night of the Long Knives 28, 44

OBW 32
OKH 7-8, 32
Operation Barbarossa 32, 137, 162
Operation Market Garden 35, 136
Operation Marita (Greece) 41
Operation Merkur (Mercury) (Crete) 41, 83
Operation Sea Lion 41
Organisation Todt 22

Prisoners of war (POWs)
British 91
German 29, 32, 35, 71-72
Soviet troops 9
Propaganda 10, 19, 26, 47, 55, 86

RAD Abteilungen 23, 29
RAD Act 21
construction troops 22
districts and working groups 20
divisions 23
training Wehrmacht 23
transfer of units to Heer 22
workforce 21-22
Rapallo Treaty 1923 27
Red Cross 19, 152, 155-156

Soviet army 8
Spanish Civil War 30-31, 38
Spectator, The 29
SS-Einsatzgruppen mobile death squads 9
Steel Helmet-League of Front Soldiers 27

Tactics 161-173
battle reconnaissance 165
infantry in defence 168-169
key stages of an attack 168
offensive action 162-163
patrolling 164-165
sniping 170-171
sniper's code 173
squads 166-171
defensive position 170
in combat 166-168
street defence 171
Theatres of conflict
Arctic Circle 11, 31
Eastern (Russian) Front 9-10, 23, 37, 41, 136, 152, 154
France 9
Italy 9
Low Countries 9
Normandy 41
North Africa 9, 31, 35, 87, 140, 146, 154
Norway 9
Sicily 9
Western Desert 11
Transportation and bridging 38-40, 135-145
aircraft 87, 154
akja 164-165
bicycles 40, 142
bridging 144-145
Brüko Bs 145
cars 138-139
Einheits-PkW 138
Kübelwagen 139
Schwimmwagen 139
Deutsche Reichsbahn 136
halftracks and armoured cars 38, 140-141
horses and mules 9, 39-40, 90, 128, 136-137, 143-144, 154
inflatable boats 145
Kettenkrad 142
motor ambulances 154-156
motorcycles and sidecars 91, 141, 143
trains 130, 136
trucks and lorries 136-138, 143-144
Treaty of Locarno 29
Treaty of Versailles 1919 7-8, 26-28, 33, 162
Black Reichswehr 28
repudiation 28, 33
restrictions on German Army 26-27, 48
violation 29

Unemployment 19, 21

Uniforms and equipment 57-91
ammunition pouches (patronentaschen) 80-81, 84
binoculars (doppelfernrohr) 80
blankets 74
boots 71-72
Marschstiefel (jackboots) 47, 70, 72
bread bag (brotbeutel) 79
clothing 58
desert 86-88
winter 84-86
entrenching tool (kleines schanzzeug) 79-80
gasmask 82
Gebirgsjäger 89-91
gloves 89
headgear 72, 74-77, 87, 91, 164
Fallschirmjäger helmet 89, 159
forage caps 76-77
peaked caps 87-88
pith helmets 87
steel helmets 64, 75, 87
knapsack (Tornister) 78-79
map case (meldekartentasche) 80
motorcycle troops (Kradfahrer) 91
goggles 91
overcoats 91
rank and insignia 58-65
cap 64
cuff titles 68-69
Litzen 59
shoulder straps 60-62
rucksacks 78, 88, 90, 164
snipers (scharfschützen) 88-89
uniforms 69-77
belts 70
desert 68
field tunic 70-72
greatcoat 73
standard combat 69-74
tropical 88
working 72
Skijäger (ski-mounted troops) 85-86, 157
Waffenfarbe 62-63
Luftwaffe 64
water bottles (feldflasche) 79

Voluntary Labour Service 21

Waffen-SS 7, 17, 29, 47, 84, 89, 91
leadership schools 18
War Academy 162
War artists 86, 141

Weapons 10, 90, 93-133 , 163
ammunition 132-133, 167
anti-tank guns and rocket launchers 115-125, 142, 169-170, 172-173
armour penetration 116
defensive positions 170
emplacements 172-173
built in Russia 27
First World War 49
flamethrowers 125-126
flak guns 126-128, 144
hand grenades 108-111, 163-164
operating procedure 109
infantry guns and howitzers 128-132
loading and firing the SIG33 129
machine guns 7, 36, 47, 49, 105-108, 163, 165
changing barrels 105
MG34 accessories 106
mines 114-115
mortars 111-114
pistols 94-95
rifles 47-48, 95-101, 164
bayonets 97-98
cleaning 100
stripping 100
squad 166
sub-machine guns 102-104
operating the MP40 102
Wehrmacht 17, 21, 28-29, 136, 140, 143
growth 28-32
strength 29
Winter Relief Organisation 85
Winter War 1939-40 8

People

Axmann, Artur 16
Bormann, Martin 16
Born, Max 14
Buckholz, Bernhard 29
Buchrucker, Maj Bruno 28
Chamberlain, PM Neville 30
Courant, Richard 14
Dönitz, Großadmiral Karl 41
Eigener, Ernst 128, 144, 146
Einstein, Albert 14
Fellers, Frank 146
Franck, James 14
Frederick the Great 7, 11
Fromm, Gen Fritz 33
Gessler, Otto 28
Goebbels, Joseph 19
Grubba, Erwin 47
Guderian, Heinz 146
Halder, Gen Fritz 8
Hatynagel, Ob 87
Hierl, Konstantin 21
Hilbert, David 14
Himmler, Reichsführer SS Heinrich 33, 38
Hitler, Adolf 7, 9
assassination plot 33
gains power 28
meets von Seeckt 27
Mein Kampf 14
takes control of OKH 7, 32
views on education 14, 16-17
Keynes, John Maynard 26
Kranz, Kurt 8, 86
Kuntze, Gen de Pionere Walter 34
Lutze, Viktor 44
Mulholland, John 45
Mussolini 44
Napoleon 9, 11
Niehorster, Dr Leo 45
Oppenheimer, Robert 14
Ott, Eugen 28
Overmans, Rüdiger 32
Ramcke, Ob Bernhard-Hermann 64
Röhm, Ernst 44
Rommel, FM Erwin 31, 40, 62, 87, 138, 146
Rust, Bernhard 15, 17
Sattler, Gen Robert 73
Schick, Johan Georg Otto 84
Seebohm, Cap. Alfred 147
Seldte, Franz 27
Sluyterman, Georg 77
Stalin, Josef 9
Streicher, Julius 17
Student, Genmaj Kurt 40
von Bock, Ob Fedor 28
von Hammerstein-Equord, Reichswehr Kurt 28
von Langewyde, Georg Sluyterman 10
von Mackensen, FM August 27
von Manstein 7
von Niedermayer, Oskar 28
von Rundstedt, OBW 37
von Schirach, Baldur 15-16
von Schleicher, Kurt 28
von Seeckt, Gen Hans 27-28
Wessel, Wilhelm 87
Mit Rommel in der Wüste book 87
Willrich, Wolfgang 141
Witzig, Rudolf 62